THE ANXIETY AND OCD WORKBOOK

A CBT And Acceptance-Based Guide To Managing Intrusive Thoughts And Compulsive Behaviours

JOHN CRAWFORD

Copyright © 2023 by John Crawford

All rights reserved.

First Published: November 2023

ISBN: 9798867223809

www.youcanfixyouranxiety.com

This book is written in British English. Some spellings vary from US English.

Disclaimer

I am a fully-qualified experienced hypno/psychotherapist. I am not a medically trained Doctor, Psychologist, or Psychiatrist. I have taken every care to ensure that the information presented in this book is both ethical and responsible and the information and techniques within this book have been safely used with my clients during my career.

However, if you have been diagnosed with or believe you may be suffering from any form of psychiatric condition, you should seek professional help and you should not use this book without the consent and blessing of your qualified formal medical healthcare provider. It is offered as complementary information. To all readers, please ensure that you read, understand and agree to the following disclaimer before proceeding: -

This book is provided on an "as is" basis. I cannot assess nor guarantee that this book is suitable for your needs or for use by you. You use this book at your own risk. The information offered in this book is offered as complementary therapeutic information. Information and content offered throughout this book are not offered as medical treatment or diagnosis of a medical condition and no such suggestion may be implied by you or me. If you are suffering from any medical condition or believe that you may need medical or psychiatric treatment, you are advised to see your Doctor or formal healthcare provider. By your use of this book, no medical, advisory, therapeutic or professional relationship is implied or established between you and myself. Any information provided in this book is for information purposes only and does not replace or amend your Doctor's advice. Any action you may take arising from your use of this book or any of the exercises contained within, including the use of hypnotherapy/relaxation recording/s, is undertaken entirely at your own risk and discretion. If any of the exercises contained within this book make you feel uncomfortable or distressed in any way, you agree to discontinue using them immediately. Use of this book does not guarantee a cure of any mental, emotional or medical condition and no such suggestion may be implied. This book and the information contained within it have not been audited by any official bodies, either, professional, regulatory or governmental.

Free Book Offer

As a valued reader, I'd like to invite you to join me by becoming a member of my free reader's group and download my third book *Dear Anxiety: This Is My Life* plus two professionally recorded relaxation recordings delivering authentic hypnosis experiences for beating stress! – All free of charge. No strings. Just sign up with your email address and I'll add you to the group. You can unsubscribe at any time!

When John's frantic search for spiritual accomplishment delivered way more than he expected, things suddenly got extremely weird! A reality-shattering event propelled John, an ordinary twenty two year old Londoner, into a terrifying world where the very fabric of reality itself could not be trusted. This sounds like fiction.

It is not.

Get John's FREE full ebook today and find out what it took to get home...

Download your free copy instantly below!

Here's the link: -

http://www.youcanfixyouranxiety.com

How This Book Can Help You 1

Preface 4

Introduction 6

Chapter One – Our Beautiful Flawed Brains 9

Our Perilous World 11

Invisible Dangers 14

Chapter Two – The Zealous Guard 16

Avoidance 20

Chapter Three – Why Do I Have Intrusive Negative Thoughts? 24

Generalised Anxiety Disorder (GAD) 24

Trauma & PTSD 25

Obsessive-Compulsive Disorder (OCD) 27

Brain Plasticity 33

Poor Mental Hygiene 35

Medical Conditions 38

Chapter Four – Shock And The Suggestible Mind 41

Chapter Five – Weird Worries 49

Chapter Six - Am I A Bad Person? 51

Chapter Seven - Dying To Live. Risk And Reward 59

Chapter Eight – Rock Solid Defiance 64

Chapter Nine - The Hydra 72

Chapter Ten – The Superstitious Human 76

Correlation And Causation 79

Chapter Eleven – Certainty, Truth, Lies, And Doubt 83

Beliefs 83

True Doubts 86

Chapter Twelve - OCD Or Anxiety? What's The Difference? 90

Chapter Thirteen – Anxiety Relief 99

Relaxation 100

How's Life? 102

Mental Hygiene 103

Changing Your Thoughts 105

Tolerance 107

Mindfulness/Meditation/Hypnotherapy 107

Control 111

Food, Drink, Drugs, & Exercise 113

Chapter Fourteen – Stiff Upper Lips 116

Chapter Fifteen – Do We Do It To Ourselves? 120

Chapter Sixteen – The Heart Bears Witness 135

Stilling The Mind 142

Sitting With Difficult Feelings 144

Self-Soothing & Reassurance 146

Summary 156

Chapter Seventeen- Reassurance Is A Conversation For Never 159

What To Do Instead 167

Chapter Eighteen – Morality - Don't Get Snagged! 170

Chapter Nineteen – Preparations 178

Chapter Twenty - The Great Pushback 188

Behavioural Experiments 192

Positive Re-Focusing Activities 197

Chapter Twenty-One - The Next Ten Yards 210

Chapter Twenty-Two - The Road To Victory 215

Chapter Twenty-Three - What Does Recovery Look Like? 222

Chapter Twenty-Four - Pep Talks For The Road 227

The Limbic System 227

Experiment Design 229

Tips for "Pure O" 232

Thought Exposure 234

Asking For Help 235

Friends And Family Support 237

Digging In 239

I've Heard It All Before 240

What's The Worst That Could Happen? 241

Do Your Worst 242

Naming The Voices 243

Balloons, Leaves, And Rubber Stamps 245

Gratitude 247

New Science 248

No. I Can't Do It! 249

Chapter Twenty-Five – Common Concerns 252

Pure O 252

False Memories 254

Dwelling On The Past 256

Contamination And Cleaning 258

Health Anxiety 260

V(omit) 265

Sex On The Brain 268

Sleep 276

Chapter Twenty-Six - Family And Carers 278

What's The Plan? 281

What Can You Do To Help? 284

Chapter Twenty-Seven – A Bright Future 288

One Last Thing 291

Other Works By This Author 292

About John Crawford 293

Full Copyright Notice 295

How This Book Can Help You

This book is for you if: -

* You have thoughts that regularly frighten, upset or disturb you.

* You suffer from anxiety that causes repetitive worries.

* You worry that you may harm yourself or somebody else, accidentally or otherwise.

* You worry that you might be criminal, evil, perverted, blasphemous, or any other kind of unacceptable.

* You feel anxious if you don't take time-consuming steps to minimise or eliminate imagined threats.

* You compulsively check your environment for safety and/or hygiene.

* You've been diagnosed with Obsessive-Compulsive Disorder (OCD) and you want to deepen your understanding of the condition and how to treat it effectively.

* You suffer from any other kind of intrusive, repetitive negative thinking or behaviours.

* You are already in exposure and response prevention treatment for OCD.

If any of the above apply to you, you have my sincere empathy. These are joy-sucking difficulties and I recognise that these are sometimes very serious illnesses.

I have fifteen years of professional one-to-one experience as a qualified hypno/psychotherapist helping people recover from anxiety-related difficulties, including OCD. I have used the questions that so many of my clients have asked me over the years to inform the content of this book.

If you are already in treatment for anxiety or OCD or have read other books on the subject, then I'm confident that you will find this book a highly useful companion. While it is written as a complete and standalone workbook for recovery from intrusive thoughts and compulsions, its true power lies in the fact that it is at heart also a gentle but authoritative coaching book.

The instructions for dealing with negative intrusive thoughts and behavioural compulsions are not secret, exclusive, or difficult to find but we need to understand the condition before we can outsmart it. Instructions without a fuller explanation are often insufficient. This book aims to change that for you.

A cursory web search will furnish you with the following clinically approved method for overcoming OCD and anxiety-driven intrusive thoughts. It is a therapy that is usually discussed and prepared for in the therapy session and then actioned in daily life by the client: -

Exposure (and) Response Prevention (ERP) - This is the model that most mainstream treatments follow for relief from intrusive thoughts and anxiety-driven behaviours. This is as it sounds: -

Exposure – Whatever your thoughts and/or feelings tell you to fear, you deliberately expose yourself to those situations through graded challenges.

Response Prevention – Through (managed) exposure to the things that we fear, and a refusal to action compulsions or avoidances, we desensitise the brain's anxiety responses as we prove that nothing awful happens when we refuse to "do" a compulsive safety behaviour, or we deliberately do something that anxiety insists we should avoid. In time, the brain will adjust.

* Recognise that your intrusive thoughts and urges are an OCD or anxiety-related symptom, not a fact, and label them as unhelpful.

* Refuse to give those thoughts and feelings your "buy-in" and cease any avoidance behaviours or safety compulsions (because you have rejected their reality in step one.)

* Repeatedly hold this position until your brain accepts the message that there is nothing to fear. Natural desensitisation will occur and the anxiety response will adjust downwards.

Those are the basic instructions. I know from experience though, that when you present an anxious intrusive-thought or OCD sufferer with this information and ask them to go away and make it so, you are met with blank looks. Understandably. Without further elaboration, the instructions appear unactionable. For a start, there are feelings! Like fear. And then, there are questions about feelings. And thoughts.

A large part of this book is dedicated to answering the questions you have about these finer details and helping you to become watertight in your understanding of how these intrusive-thought difficulties operate: that is, **without doubt.** That's a very important position to step into when remedying anxious thoughts because doubt is anxiety's fuel.

When you have a clear awareness of the machinery of obsessional thoughts, then you can no longer be hoodwinked by them.

These are doubting diseases. To beat them, we must learn how to be clear in our intention, un-swayed by doubt, and certain in our refusal to bow to anxiety's demands.

You may have argued with your intrusive thoughts ten thousand times. Now, you're going to stop arguing with them and walk out on them instead.

It's their turn to do the doubting.

Big words! Indeed. But we have a secret weapon here - compassionate acceptance – a proven method for self-support that connects us with the deepest safety available – that already within ourselves. Once you truly have your own back, things can be different. We'll learn exactly what that means and how to make it happen here.

This book is more than a workbook. It is also a friend, an educator, a coach, a comfort, and a cheerleader. Welcome.

Preface

Thank you for choosing this book. A few words about my experience to speak here.

I began my anxiety journey in 1993. It was pure hell for several years and a slow-burn misery for a few more still. I know anxiety-related suffering and the road to recovery personally.

In 2003, after much personal therapy and subsequent professional training and qualification, I opened my hypnotherapy/psychotherapy practice and assisted others with anxiety-related suffering. I knew the territory. I helped a lot of people. It was nice. Fifteen years later, in 2018, I hung up my therapist's hat. Now, I write. I can help many more people this way.

In 2016, I published my first book, *Anxiety Relief.* Seven years on, it continues to sell and enjoy an enthusiastic readership. I have noted all of your wonderful reviews. Thanks to all who have shared your successes and supported my work.

This is a book written for ordinary people, including anxiety beginners. You'll need no previous therapeutic knowledge to use it. I've strived to use clear language here that everybody can easily understand and relate to, and the book is structured so that you'll receive a gradual building of understanding; not huge data dumps.

You will note that some key points are reiterated throughout the book in different contexts. Please know that this book has been thoroughly considered and extensively edited. This is not hurried or lazy work. The reiterations are deliberate. Few people can retain everything written on the first pass. Reiteration of the most important points ensures that the key takeaways will remain with you, as felt understanding, long after you read the last page. Yes. We need to drum those salient points home. These are doubting diseases. Clarity and certainty are everything here.

Taking notes as you read also improves information retention when compared with passive reading. There is content here that may ring bells for you, specifically. You'll want to remember those "Aha!" moments.

Many people find that summarizing in writing what they just understood helps to consolidate that understanding within the brain, especially when those writings are reviewed later. Since these difficulties thrive on doubts, note-taking, while reading this book, is recommended. If you re-write your learning in your own words, it will solidify your understanding and help to make this knowledge your own.

Thanks for being here. I hope this book is everything for you that I tried to make it. I put a lot of love into this project. Now, let's recover your peace!

John Crawford – Bristol UK - November 2023

INTRODUCTION

As my friends and I approached the picturesque coastal bridge, I felt a rare sense of wonder. Wildflowers swept in waves along the edges of the sunlit path; a July explosion of colour and form, vibrant against the cloudless blue backdrop. It was summer perfection.

A few steps later, I was at the centre of the bridge, looking down into a boulder-strewn ravine, a long drop below. I saw a vivid image of my body smashing into the rocks below. My mind presented numerous versions of the fall. I even heard and felt the crunching sound below. I cringed. All in seconds.

Would it hurt? What if I survived it? Does this mean that I'm suicidal?

I became aware of a deep unease gathering where my joy had been sitting moments before and remembered to shake this nonsense from my head. I walked on and noticed the flowers again...

Most people have experienced this when at height. We all wonder about falling when we peer over a ravine. This is the brain's idea of security. It's logical. The survival instruction is that the brain must identify any actual or potential threats in the environment and neutralise them. Humans are born with a natural fear of heights. My brain is running mental simulations of what could go wrong if I fall and then generating fear and discomfort in my guts to let me know that I need to be on guard. There is danger here.

When it comes to falling from a great height, the danger is obvious, so most brains will run the "falling" simulation immediately. We may not only visualise the images of this messy demise but we might also feel the churning dread in our guts that would accompany it. That's because the brain responds to imagined threats and real-world threats similarly.

If you're reading this book, there's a chance that you have plenty of your own horror visions to share because that's what anxious brains do. They simulate horrors so that we can avoid them happening in real life. It works. Few of us wander mindlessly off cliff edges.

With high anxiety levels or OCD though, the security system can become much more of a problem than a solution...

Part One – Knowledge

Chapter One – Our Beautiful Flawed Brains

Picture this...

It's been a tough month. I had some recent bad news. Work has been stressful.

I'm driving my kids to their weekly football practice. We've got their friend Tim with us. We're on the motorway, in the middle lane, passing a slow truck.

Suddenly, I am seized by terrible feelings. My guts are tense. I feel sick, hot, shaky, dizzy, and breathless. Raw fear courses through my nervous system. My mind is racing. I feel a thin film of sweat form on my forehead.

What's happening!? Am I having a stroke? A heart attack? The thoughts scream alarm.

The energy that is unleashed is a literal physical jolt, like a hard gear change. I feel disembodied; more a witness to this moment than a participant. The detachment is alarming. The hands at the end of my spaghetti-jelly arms suddenly feel far away, alien and untrustworthy.

Am I even in control of this car right now? What if I pass out?

It takes but a microsecond for this unpleasant shift into discomfort to deliver the next horrifying message.

Or worse, what if I'm not in control and my arm suddenly yanks the steering wheel?

Sheer panic grips my insides. My knuckles are white on the wheel. I'm concentrating hard. I'm appalled by the thought but it's there now and I see the outcome of my unwanted fantasy unfold in graphic mental images. Our car flips and tumbles. The truck veers across the road and jack-knifes. I see Tim's fragile body crumple as our container folds like a concertina and I cringe. It's nothing more than a flash but I'm shaking now. My arms and legs are thick and heavy with adrenaline. The steering wheel is slippery in my sweating hands. I'm hot and cold all at once. I wonder whether my heart will give out. It's beating so fast and hard that I can't even feel the space between the beats any more. It's like one huge thud. Where is my breath?

Has my heart stopped? This can't be right. Something is seriously wrong here.

We are past the truck now. I cross into the slow lane and take a necessary deep breath, exhale slowly, and calm begins to return. I wipe the thin layer of perspiration from my forehead with my sleeve. Then, another thought.

*How can I be sure that I **won't** do that?*

I breathe deeply and am determined to steady myself. My white-knuckle grip on the wheel relaxes a touch.

*Why **would** I do that, then?*

My thoughts argue.

Well, I don't know. I mean, can you trust yourself? What if you suddenly just lost control of yourself?

Another wave of alarm follows these thoughts. I grip the wheel with resolve, breathe deeply and focus on the road. I cannot afford to have this conversation with myself right now. I am driving. I have responsibilities here. I force a moment of clarity but new thoughts appear.

What would that be like for Tim's parents though? Imagine the shame. Even if nobody knew how it had happened... I'd know.

I tell myself to stop it. It continues anyway.

Even if I died. Well... yes... we would all be dead. Imagine that? It's awful. It would be on the news... our loved ones would never know why... or how... imagine their anguish...

Then, a recognition...

Why *the heck am I thinking about this!?*

I try, unsuccessfully, to think about kittens and spring blossoms instead. My heart is still thumping like a jackhammer.

Fifteen minutes later, we're at football practice. The kids know nothing of my ordeal but I'm haunted by terrible images of what might have been, and still trembling inside. My confidence is shot. I feel like I'm betraying Tim's parents by even being a guardian to their son right now. I know it's irrational but I feel soiled, unsafe, and fraudulent. I don't want to drive home.

Our Perilous World

We are fragile beings in an uncertain and perilous world. We can drown in two inches of water. Large objects do occasionally fall on unsuspecting passers-by. If we are in the wrong place at the wrong time... well, it doesn't bear thinking about. In a world of perfect comfort, we wouldn't think about it but comfort isn't the priority - survival is. Fear, as unpleasant as it is, moves us to defend against a threat or escape from a dangerous situation. Without fear, we would do something outrageous and die quickly.

Our human fragility demands that we respond to threats to our safety, and our brains have evolved a powerful set of automatic defences to ensure that we do just that, including a "look ahead" function.

If we can forecast a disaster, then we may be able to avoid it.

When your brain knows what to eliminate or avoid, then you'll be more likely to live to see another day. So...

Brains collect things to be afraid of.

As we move through life, we accrue a brain-stored catalogue of perceived harms and threats - some inherited, some experienced, and some only imagined. If we encounter a similar danger in real life or have reason to believe that one is imminent, then the alarm is automatically sounded. We experience an overwhelming sense of discomfort and peril that moves us to either disable the threat or make our escape. We call this feeling fear. Fear in regular residence within us, we call anxiety.

Once activated, anxiety and fear can feel all-consuming. One cannot reasonably pay attention to much else, and that is how it is meant to be.

Fear is designed to not be ignored.

It should be some comfort for you to know that approximately eighty per cent of the world's population report being troubled by unwanted, intrusive negative thoughts. Anxiety affects approximately ten per cent of people at any given time. Both are common.

In a 2015 study undertaken by Concordia University, Professor Adam Radomsky published results showing that 94% of his research group experienced unwanted thoughts or impulses. This burden seems to be spread equally across cultures. It doesn't matter where you're born or what you believe in, the incidence of mental "noise" (sometimes shrieking!) is fairly uniform. Nearly all brains are susceptible to worry and torment. It's just the themes and triggers that change.

The human brain has evolved to be highly attuned to the presence of threats. When a threat is detected in the environment, the brain **automatically** shifts into a protective/evasive mode known as "fight or flight". The body is swiftly flooded with powerful chemical hormones that prime the human-animal for battle or escape. Muscles become tense, breathing is shallow, the heart pounds, palms are sweaty and fear grips our insides. These are all part of the process of the body readying itself to take powerful action, either running away or standing to defend. It's generally uncomfortable.

Alongside this physical response to threat, the mind itself enters a trance-like state. The purpose of this state is to screen out all unnecessary information so that our complete attention is focused on dealing with the perceived imminent emergency.

Logic and calm are temporarily suspended.

That means that the rational brain goes offline temporarily. During a crisis, we are running on fear and adrenaline, and our thoughts and actions are driven not by logic and reason but by the primitive "instinctive" brain that controls our emotional responses.

You could liken the anxious state to the "safe mode" on a Windows computer. Only the most basic software is running; just enough to run and rescue the machine. The usual complex processing required for complex problem-solving is temporarily bypassed. That means not thinking critically.

Anxiety temporarily blocks access to our logical and solution-creating faculties.

It's only later, when I'm back at home, feet up, with a cup of tea and with Tim delivered safely home to his parents, with my thinking brain back online, that I reflect on my crazy day and wonder just what was that all about? *Why all the fuss when nothing happened?*

Well, the rule is, that as far as the protective human brain is concerned, threatening scenarios either real or imagined are treated as imminent. In this example, the panic ramped up when the disturbing imaginative imagery and thoughts arrived.

The brain's security system will respond to real threats and imagined threats with a similar intensity.

In short, we don't have to be facing a **real** threat to experience anxiety.

We only need to "believe" that we face a threat. Either now, or in the future.

Invisible Dangers

Unfortunately for anxiety sufferers, the human brain will err on the side of caution, making sure not to miss any possible "invisible" dangers. There's a logic to this. Our hunter-gatherer ancestors needed to remain aware of being ambushed in the wild. The brain learned that just because a danger is not obvious, it doesn't mean that there isn't a **hidden** danger in the long grass. Our senses have learned to pay keen attention to fine details - a spider, a snake, a scorpion, a fish, a mosquito, poisoned water, dangerous plants, or lions in wait. Hidden dangers are potentially everywhere. This leads to a state that is known as "hypervigilance."

Our genetic programming, learned through this experience of thousands of generations, continues to alert us to the possibility of hidden dangers. The negative emotional arousal (anxiety) that follows when a threat is detected often includes "worrying" that something damaging will happen. Worry stops us from forgetting where the lions might be.

Worrying can also extend to running numerous mental simulations of possible scenarios, usually negative, sometimes horrific, in an attempt to forecast the future. The brain's logic is that if we can foresee what is to come, then we may be able to avoid or mitigate the damage.

Worrying promises relief but it delivers the opposite.

Worrying is often accompanied by that churning gut feeling that something terrible is imminent. If there's nothing in sight, it will make something up because there **has** to be a reason for this anxiety.

The brain can frighten itself with imagined horrors that will never come to pass.

Allowing "What if?" to become the dominant theme in our day-to-day thinking can open the way to a potentially endless world of mental torture. If I make "What if?" questions a part of my daily inner dialogue, then anxiety can thrive.

So goes the saying: -

He who worries dies a thousand deaths.

The worry is worse than the disease. You live the disasters over and over in your imagination – the disasters that almost certainly won't happen. Your mind doesn't know that though. It lives it as if it were real. It becomes quickly convinced that you live in a chaotic environment filled with active threats. It's treating imagined threats with a similar intensity to real-world threats. This is a problem.

Chapter Two – The Zealous Guard

You might conclude, logically, that if something creates anxiety within you, then the best course of action would be to avoid it.

You'd be wrong.

Firstly, you'd miss out on all the exciting stuff in life. Most of that is on the other side of at least a small barrier of courage. Secondly, you'd be inviting more anxiety into your life. There is a wonderful psychological maxim that sums this counter-intuitive fact up beautifully: -

What you resist... persists.

If I had known this in 1993, I might have spared myself years of mental agony. Instead, I did what most people do and fought ardently against the presence of nightmarish thoughts and feelings. It never crossed my mind that the correct course of action might be to go **into** the fear, into the pain. Well, it wouldn't, would it? That's just a ridiculous idea. Except, strangely, surprisingly, as it turns out, it is the way to go. I'll explain why.

Inside your brain, there are two brains.

At the front of our brain, just behind and above the eyes, we have the "Frontal Lobes." These lobes contain the brain's "Pre-Frontal Cortex (PFC)". The pre-frontal cortex does most of our logic, problem-solving, and complex thinking, best remembered as **logic, reason, planning, and control**. It's referred to therefore as the **executive** brain. It's the boss.

Our capacity for complex thought is believed to be a relatively recent development, in evolutionary terms. Science/biology proposes that it's maybe only a hundred thousand years old. Under normal conditions, the frontal lobe area is the "thinking" brain that we use to go about our daily business.

At the base of the brain, by comparison, we have our "ancestral" or "mammalian" brain. This is known as **"The Limbic System"**. Limbic means "root". This brain is primarily instinctive and **emotional**. It deals with **feelings** and holds and manages our emotional memories.

The Limbic System

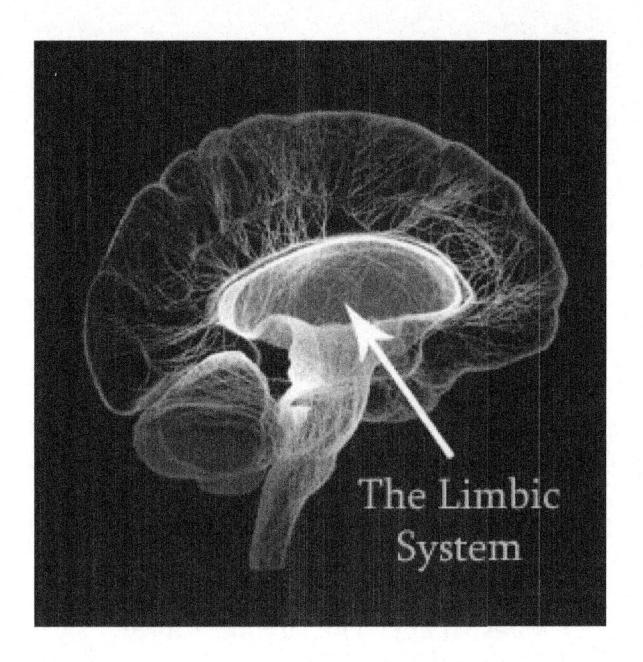

The limbic system is the small brain that served our earliest ancestors of two million years ago (who, incidentally, had a brain half the size of modern humans) and its primary concern has always been survival. It contains the instructions to shelter, eat, procreate, and avoid predators, poisons, explosions, falls, wounds, and venoms; essentially, to make new humans and avoid dying.

By nature, the limbic system brain is therefore jumpy when spooked.

When there's a perceived threat in the environment, it's considered unsafe to relax. We need to remain vigilant. Fear keeps us alive. It's the limbic system that creates the strong emotional responses that we experience as anxiety, panic, anger, and obsession, to name only a few items from the emotional repertoire. These are all responses that could save your life if your life was threatened. If there **is** a threat in your environment, you are going to **want** to be obsessed with that. Forgetting it's there, could, hypothetically, be fatal.

Ordinarily, this security system sits quietly in the background and doesn't significantly interfere with our day-to-day routines. For a non-anxious person, this emotional brain remains quiet unless a threat is detected.

Unfortunately, for those suffering from anxiety or other intrusive thought difficulties, the limbic system is super-charged by stress and it becomes overly sensitive, overly reactive, and overly imaginative in all the wrong ways.

An overly-aroused limbic system can see a threat in just about anything and if it can't find something obvious to pin the resident fear on, it will choose something.

Though the limbic system has no malicious intent toward us as individuals, it has a job to do. That's great when it's reading the situation accurately. It's pretty terrible when it's catastrophising, as an anxious mind is prone to do.

I know that "limbic system" is a clinical-sounding term. So, I've renamed it for this book.

Please meet, "The Zealous Guard."

> Er...We have an incoming contamination situation...
>
> Initiating internal lockdown procedures...
>
> Don't trust what this guy says. He's far too enthusiastic and a bit of a jobsworth!

As we proceed, I'll be using "The Zealous Guard" and "The Limbic System" as descriptions of this instinctive/emotion-based brain interchangeably. They are the same thing. Please make a mental note of that.

The Limbic System = The Brain's Security System = The Zealous Guard.

The Zealous Guard is not a bad actor. When there's a threat in the environment, he is there, guarding the ultimate treasure - your life. When in action mode, it's the guard that gives us that sense of urgency - the feeling of wanting to escape. We experience this as anxiety, often with screeching negative thoughts of doom and gloom.

*"Thanks, Zealous Guard! You have saved me many times. I'm just wondering whether going forward, you could be a bit more **smart**-guard and a bit less **zealous**-guard?"*

When it comes to anxiety, he's known to be too enthusiastic. Threats are over-estimated, he's too quick to react, and his response is disproportionately alarmist.

Our mind is trying to fight something that isn't there and it ends up attacking itself.

It's a similar principle to that of an auto-immune disease, where the body mistakenly attacks itself while trying to fight off a non-existent assailant. In the case of anxiety disorders, we could say that the mind/brain/security system also mistakenly attacks itself while trying to fight off non-existent invasions. Yes. It's ironic.

We know that when we are feeling threatened or alarmed generally, negative thoughts are more likely to occur, to be more pervasive in their reach, and become increasingly frightening. It's fair to say that things can get downright weird in states of high anxiety. High anxiety, by the way, is usually due to major stress levels in life. As stress rises, we lose some intellectual control and the Zealous Guard becomes increasingly dominant, bringing fearful feelings, wild anxious thoughts and catastrophic imaginary predictions.

We recognize that these imagined threats are treated as possible threats by the brain's security system. There's a great irony to the fact that the Zealous Guard is responsible for protecting us and yet it often is also **the cause** of the threat that we feel. The Zealous Guard generates fear in response to threat but it also responds to existing fear with more fear, meaning that fear of fear, known as secondary disturbance, becomes a new problem. This is not good in itself, but this fact also points the way out.

Fear of fear is often central to our problems with anxiety. Alarming negative thoughts are both a cause and a symptom of anxiety.

Be aware then, that it's unrealistic to expect to be able to solve just one of these problems without paying some attention to the other. These bedfellows, anxiety and intrusive thoughts cannot be completely separated. They are both linked within the limbic system brain, they are reciprocal, and we have to **calm the entire system down** to gain relief from these symptoms. Fortunately, if the majority of your anxiety is generated by your intrusive thoughts and/or safety behaviours like checking or avoiding things, then we can begin there.

Let's begin by understanding how avoidance of fear makes more of it.

Avoidance

Your desire to run away from these frightening thoughts, feelings, and perceptions is natural. If the threat was real, that would be the smart thing to do.

The problem is, here, the threat isn't real - it's imagined. Or, at least, it is overestimated.

With that established, let's understand why "avoidance" is a primary cause of further anxiety.

At first glance, this information is counter-intuitive. It's also difficult to believe or remember, in practice. When confronted with frightening and convincing negative thoughts, accompanied by the feeling of sickly certainty that something catastrophic is about to happen, it is not easy to recognise that the problem is with your brain, with an errant thought and emotional response, rather than the world itself. Every cell in your being may be screaming at you to take evasive action immediately. If we're inexperienced in these matters, that's exactly what we'll **try** to do...

... and that is a mistake.

The problem is, that being on the receiving end of this alarm (a terrifying thought plus an anxious feeling) can be alarming in itself so it's quite normal for the average human being to want to get away from those feelings and thoughts. Metaphorically, that results in running or fighting. Or, if you're not already in the danger zone, then why go there? That leads to avoidance.

This is the mistake. The guard isn't all that smart.

When you run from or fight anxious thoughts and/or feelings, it alarms the guard. When you avoid situations because you suppose that they are dangerous, your Zealous Guard believes you. It then increases the anxiety levels in proportion to your aversion.

The Zealous Guard is an automaton. It has ninja-level skills when it comes to defence. It will hijack your nervous system and have you down on the ground and out of the line of fire before you've consciously recognized that your muscles have moved. That's its job and it will do it better than your thinking mind could ever do. The thinking mind is too slow for millisecond emergencies. Instinct is king here. You've felt that many times. That's the jolt.

When it comes to figuring out whether such an extreme response is necessary though, sometimes it's erring on the side of caution by providing anxiety and then **it's looking to you for confirmation of the level of danger**.

What you do next, matters.

The Guard comes equipped with different alert levels. It's like the spam settings on your email. You have three options: -

High – Send all suspicious mail to the junk folder – you may find that emails you wish to keep are erroneously placed in your junk folder.

Medium – Send the most obvious spam to the junk folder.

Low – Some harmful messages may arrive in your inbox but you should receive most messages.

When our anxiety levels are high generally, the default setting will be **high alert** because the brain becomes hypervigilant in high-stress states. The problem with this setting is that we receive **false positives**. The security feature treats "safe" mail as threatening mail. As far as negative intrusive thoughts and anxious feelings are concerned, that's not a good setting for us. It is, by definition, the setting used by anxious, obsessive, and compulsive brains. They are finding false positives all over the place.

If our inner guard is constantly on high alert, we're going to receive a steady stream of these false positives. These, we will experience as our "What-ifs", along with a fresh dose of anxiety with each new arrival.

I've had anxiety so high before that the sun coming out from behind a cloud set off a full-blown panic attack. My hypervigilant brain registered the change of light level as an approaching army. That's a false positive. When anxiety levels are that high, just about anything could trigger the alarm. It is temporary. It will end when your stress levels are reduced.

That's the mechanics of it but meanwhile here is what usually happens...

What many people do is hunker down in fear, and hope that if we keep our eyes closed for long enough, it will all eventually go away. Sometimes, it does, for a while at least, but we may feel in our heart of hearts that it's not over. We've now had an experience of feeling overwhelmed, of losing control. Having experienced emotions that we didn't know how to handle we find ourselves with a negative precedent set against future exposures to anxiety. We assume that it is a battle that we cannot win and that frightening sense of vulnerability is the very opposite of the safety that is craved. It leaves us feeling vulnerable and under siege.

If the thoughts and feelings return when our stress levels rise again, as they will at times, we may feel that we are in no better position than we were previously to know how to eliminate them. That becomes a lasting worry that slowly erodes our sense of safety in the world. Under these conditions, avoidance of anything that might trigger overwhelming anxiety looks like a decent strategy. Don't wake the beast and hope for the best is the idea. It doesn't work.

The problem is, this approach sends the wrong message. As I said, the guard is a brilliant soldier but it's not intellectually smart. It's reactive. It's an automaton. It's trained to respond to what it sees. It's not a thinker. It decides what to do next by assessing what it sees on the field and checking that against its experience library.

Guess what you're doing as the scary thoughts appear?

If you're not running, you are searching for a hiding place or cowering in a corner with your hands over your eyes.

The guard sees that you appear to be terrified.

As any good defender of the realm should do, it sets about upping the level of defence in proportion to the perceived threat level. It figures that if you're afraid, then there must be something to be afraid **of**! Send in the jets!

But, what if it's only a false positive? What if your spam settings are configured to mistake safe mail for threatening mail? Well, the guard knows nothing about mail settings. It's watching to see what you do.

The more frightened you appear to be, the greater the negative anxiety response will be.

Now you can see why avoidance creates anxiety. Your avoidance reinforces the belief that there is something dangerous to be avoided and your guard believes you.

Challenging avoidance is one of the central pillars of this treatment. You'll be hearing plenty more about this as we proceed so keep in mind why we aim to welcome it with open arms. It leads to freedom.

Chapter Three – Why Do I Have Intrusive Negative Thoughts?

One question you may be asking is, *Why me?* Or, put another way, *How and why did **my** mind get itself into this kind of state?*

There is no simple, one-size-fits-all answer to this question. Intrusive thoughts and unwanted compulsions can be the result of numerous factors, some historical, some relating to your current circumstances, and others genetic, neurological, or medical. How you approach your solutions is dependent on having a good idea of what is causing your difficulty.

Here, I'm going to present the main causes in bite-size chunks that will help you identify the most likely sources for your anxious thoughts, obsessions, and/or compulsions. We will be returning to a number of these sources in more detail later. For now, just an overview.

Generalised Anxiety Disorder (GAD)

This catch-all category describes a state of free-floating anxiety that the sufferer experiences most or all of the time. It is usually triggered by either a single highly stressful experience or a build-up of chronic stress over time. Once underway, it can often appear not to have a definitive cause and tends to create a generalised feeling of fear, that then generates further fear. Although the cause is usually an overload of stress that can no longer be contained, the anxious brain will search for something definite to pin our anxious distress on, often erroneously, and these ideas can become a fixation, providing endless intrusive thoughts. GAD can affect people of all ages and at any time in life. Most people have a brush with it at some point during their lives.

As to the question of why obsessive/intrusive thought loops can be a symptom of GAD, the following rule applies: -

Stress and negativity overload will manifest as anxiety, and (free-floating) fear must find something to focus that fear <u>upon</u>. That, right there, is the intrusive thought/s or obsessional focus.

With GAD, it's common for the focus of our obsessions to be related to never feeling well again or convincing ourselves that we are fundamentally broken forevermore but that is by no means exhaustive. Anything could become a focus for GAD fears.

Solutions

For people falling into the GAD category, the expectation for a full recovery to a mind free from negative intrusive thoughts is excellent. Here, anxious intrusive thoughts are a clear symptom of anxiety. In practice, when anxiety levels are reduced significantly enough, the obsession/s will largely dissolve and vanish.

Stress and anxiety reduction generally may be all that is required to resolve this problem. Maybe you've seen this kind of recovery happen before in your life. A month of worry that suddenly evaporated? The most likely catalyst would have been a reduction in generalised stress and anxiety in your life. Can you connect those dots in your personal history? Think about it.

There are other causes for GAD but it's usually because our lives are being overwhelmed by stress in some way. Look there first. Make removing the overwhelming situations your priority and your mind should automatically return to a more peaceful state, free from obsessional concerns. This is an easier said than done generalisation I know but that's the essence of it. Anxiety relief gets a dedicated chapter later so we'll fill in more blanks there.

Trauma & PTSD

Most people have now heard of PTSD (Post-Traumatic-Stress-Disorder). This describes a mental/emotional condition brought about by traumatic events that leave a profoundly disturbing imprint in the mind. This imprint causes the mind to remember and re-experience the emotions relating to that event, even though it has passed. A loud noise from a falling object, for instance, may re-trigger PTSD in somebody who has been previously traumatised by an environment where loud noises signal terrible events. After the World Wars, this was known as shell shock, for obvious reasons.

Another response to trauma is numbness. This manifests as feelings of distance from your old life, a lack of pleasure, and feeling flat, isolated, and detached. It's a safety mechanism. It shields a human from the full weight of feeling the awfulness of their trauma all at once. Unfortunately, it numbs everything else too.

Lesser traumas also feature for many. Why do you get so touchy around a certain subject? What accusation or insinuation makes your blood boil? What rules do you live by that are completely inflexible? All of these items could point to a spot so sore that it's painful to go there. We mostly live around these.

Solutions

A solution could theoretically follow the following procedure: -

*   Find a way to bypass the brain's protective mechanisms so that we can make a meaningful emotional connection with the traumatic memory in a "safe" time and space. Therapy, Meditation, Mindfulness, Hypnosis, etc.

*   A willingness to re-experience the "unexperienced experience" from a place of safety and calm so that the brain can a) process the repressed emotion/s and b) review the material with a new perspective.

*   Successful completion of steps one and two allows us to continually re-assess our relationship to the trauma without the interference of the protective mind, those unwelcome visceral responses, in real life. What once was intensely negatively meaningful and relevant will steadily become a thing of the past. Our "beliefs" can change in a logical way allowing the trauma to pass fully into long-term memory where it will cease to be viscerally disturbing in the here and now.

There are some shortcut therapeutic tools for working with mild trauma and phobias that can work well. These include: -

- **EMDR** (Eye Movement Desensitisation and Reprocessing)

- **Rewind** (Visual Kinaesthetic Dissociative Technique).

Yes, I know, wordy.

Both EMDR and the Rewind can work well for straightforward traumas, and they may occasionally achieve results that appear to be miraculous, even with stubborn traumatic imprints. When we are dealing with deep and complex traumatic material that has roots in many places within a person, sometimes more and varied therapeutic work is required. The brain may refuse to relinquish its protection of these traumatic imprints with quicker fixes until it is convinced that it is safe to do so. If multiple traumas are indicated, the work will be approached in layers. We're unlikely to feel "safe" when we feel generally anxious. Sometimes, bringing that daily anxiety level down is an important component for the successful treatment of phobias and obsessions. Each success feeds the next.

OBSESSIVE-COMPULSIVE DISORDER (OCD)

Obsessive-Compulsive Disorder, often referred to as OCD, is a mental health difficulty that causes sufferers to experience repetitive negative thoughts that create significant anxiety. Some people have suggested that OCD should be understood now as a neuro-diverse condition rather than as a mental health difficulty. We will see how the conversation unfolds.

Often, though not always, these negative thoughts create a strong urge (a compulsion) to take either preventative (avoidance) or corrective action (a safety behaviour) to ensure that the perceived problem/threat has been eliminated or avoided.

The cliché example of OCD is that of a sufferer who experiences frightening thoughts about contamination; and the possibility of receiving/passing on a germ/virus-related disease. This will "compel" the sufferer to sanitise their hands, body, and/or environment repeatedly. The whole world is seen as a potential contamination threat. At their worst, OCD safety behaviours can take up most of a person's day.

There is also an OCD category known as "Pure O", meaning Pure Obsession. Technically, with Pure O there is no compulsion to follow up anxious thoughts with external behaviours. It's worth noting though, that despite the labelling, there often are compulsions present with Pure O but they take place inside the mind rather than in the external world. Somebody may, for instance, say a prayer/mantra, count their teeth with their tongue, or run a short "ritual" mentally. Efforts to mentally "solve" the concern are also considered to be compulsions. The focus of the ritual is usually for a form of resistance or reassurance.

These rituals don't automatically imply an OCD diagnosis. Many people have harmless "quirks" – tapping, routines, touching, counting, etc. They don't have OCD. It's usually something they've always done. It depends on how severe the intrusion is and how much it is bothering the person.

Typically speaking, a person will be diagnosed as being an OCD sufferer when the obsessions and/or compulsions create real distress, consume over an hour a day, and/or significantly interfere with a person's ability to function normally in society; that is to say, at work, at home and socially. Recent figures show that approximately 2-3% of the UK population suffers from some form of OCD. A higher proportion of people will suffer from mild obsessions and compulsions. These would not necessarily be diagnosed as OCD and could easily belong to the GAD and Trauma categories we just explored.

OCD symptoms can be as varied as one can imagine. We can become obsessive or compulsive about anything. Most OCD tends to focus on a theme of oneself or others coming to harm or being found culpable. OCD will usually attack our most vulnerable psychological spot, or put another way, our worst fears. It's common, for instance, for an OCD sufferer to feel that if they do not carry out an OCD-driven behaviour, a loved one will die or be harmed. OCD will leverage those fears to convince us that something awful is imminent.

Obsessions are defined as repetitive, involuntary, unwanted, often distressing thoughts, images, or impulses that commonly include but are not limited to: -

* Harming or hating – others, oneself, or loved ones.

* Fears about contamination - germs, dirt, viruses, etc. Worry about "infecting" others.

*   Excessive worry about illness and/or death of self or others.

*   Jealousy, envy, or becoming inappropriately overly concerned with another's life.

*   Violent or intrusive sexual thoughts.

*   Thoughts of impending doom or disaster.

*   Persistent, repetitive need to check potentially harmful elements for safety.

*   Irrational concern with form, number, or measure.

*   Extreme perfectionism/preciseness.

*   Upsetting thoughts of blasphemy.

*   Appearance – inappropriate attention to detail.

Compulsions are just as varied as obsessions, and they **attempt** to complete a cycle of anxiety reduction. A person who has obsessive thoughts about germs and contamination, for instance, may feel a strong compulsion to clean and disinfect. The working assumption is that if the germs are destroyed, then the anxious feeling will cease once the "threat" has been eliminated. Unfortunately, for OCD sufferers, completion of the behaviour provides only short-term relief. Anxiety returns and the mind soon demands that the process be repeated.

Germs and cleaning are easily linked but sometimes the obsession and the compulsion may seem unrelated. An obsession may create a compulsion to arrange ornaments in a certain way, sing a song inside one's head, tap seven times, or any other semi-superstitious remedy.

Compulsions can also be driven by obsessional thoughts of maintaining order and security.

Compulsions may include but are not limited to: -

*   Repeatedly checking gas is off, windows are sealed, plugs are unplugged, doors are locked, etc.

* Continually showering or washing (hands usually).

* Touching objects to make sure they are there.

* Arranging and ordering. Ornaments or collections. Lists and lists of lists.

* Counting. (Teeth, tiles, flowers, wallpaper squares, anything countable.)

* Cleaning and disinfecting (both for self and others.)

* Hoarding useless objects.

* Hair pulling and eating (trichotillomania). Spot/skin picking.

* Difficult cyclic routines that must be practised precisely.

* Restyling hair/clothes/makeup repeatedly before being able to leave home.

* Constantly seeking reassurances about self or worries.

* Repeatedly returning to the "concern" to check whether it's still "happening".

This is only a sample list of possible obsessions and compulsions. The list could be almost endless. It's important to note though that if you do have an obsession or compulsion listed above, it doesn't necessarily mean that you have OCD. The distinction and diagnosis are one of degree and although OCD is a serious disorder, it is an anxiety-driven form of what most minds do to maintain order in a disorderly world, namely, attempt to stay in control.

OCD could be said therefore to be "an anxious mind's strategy for attempting to control the uncontrollable." Or, put another way, to "have complete certainty and safety in an uncertain world." That's a survival imperative. Sadly, it is also an impossible wish.

OCD doesn't (fully) respond to the same therapeutic interventions that are used for anxiety alone.

OCD can be successfully "managed." It is rarely considered fully "cured" because it appears to have a neurological component, as opposed to merely a temporary disturbance of the brain/mind as is common with many emotional or anxiety-related difficulties.

The brains of OCD sufferers scanned in PET scanners have shown that the OCD brain exhibits damage or dysfunction in the basal ganglia region, located at the base of the brain. This causes the "error detection circuit" to become over-excited, leading to false positives when it comes to threats, and the brain behaves as if we are in terrible danger when we are not.

The "worry circuit" does not calm itself correctly and the feelings of dread persist even when corrective action has been taken.

OCD and severe anxiety can **appear** to be quite similar in terms of symptoms but the average anxiety sufferer will stop having obsessive thoughts when their anxiety has passed. This doesn't happen quite so neatly for OCD sufferers. They might still feel that something is wrong after taking evasive or corrective action, and while anxiety reduction will help, it may not provide the fuller solution that is sought.

Solutions

The treatment for OCD is known as "Exposure and Response Prevention (ERP)" or "Behavioural Therapy." There is more detail to come later on this but an introduction is as follows: -

*   We must recognise that the frightening feeling that something is wrong (anxiety) is the result of a problem in the OCD/anxious brain. The area of the brain responsible for letting us know that we are safe (now) is no longer calming our anxiety arousal levels as it should. Therefore: The <u>feeling</u> that this situation is dangerous is not based on fact. It is a perceptual mistake; the result of an error in the brain's security system. Thoughts that support fearful perspectives arrive bundled with these feelings.

*   With point one understood, we must refuse to "buy in" to the frightening or disturbing thoughts that accompany this feeling. We should treat them all as an error, that is, as inaccurate, overly-sensitised, or fully untrue, despite all the emotional signals telling us otherwise.

* We need to learn how to tolerate any frightening feelings that refusal to comply with anxiety's demands may bring, without giving in to the compulsions. Points one and two provide a sense of certainty that refusing to comply with the anxious thought's demands is the correct thing to do. This is very challenging for OCD sufferers. We begin, therefore, with exercises that challenge us only gently and then build from there, using the confidence we find along the way with small successes. When OCD compels us to "do" a behaviour, we must learn to resist carrying that behaviour out. Repeated successful refusal to carry out compulsive behaviours weakens OCD's grip over time by re-training the brain's habits and neural pathways[1] and demonstrating to the Zealous Guard that the danger is illusory.

With Generalized Anxiety Disorder, we look at reducing anxiety generally by tackling the big stressors in our lives. With Trauma, we look to the past and work on helping the mind relinquish its tight grip on historical horrors.

With OCD, it's all about the behaviours.

We could almost say that we need to forget about psychology here. This is less about you having mental or emotional "issues" than it is about you being the unfortunate recipient of faulty neurological wiring.

That doesn't mean that you don't also have your fair share of "issues" tied up in your OCD, or that the average human brain won't make similar mistakes. Just be clear that OCD is going to involve some brain re-training exercises as opposed to some deep and meaningful philosophical realisations, though they are never a bad thing either.

OCD sufferers must learn to use their frontal lobe area (remember… that's the "logic and reason" part of the brain) to continually adjust their perceptions. What should be automatic needs to be **manually routed**

---

[1] * https://en.wikipedia.org/wiki/Neural_pathway

using logic, control, strategy, and desire. In other words, you need to decide which thoughts you engage with meaningfully and which thoughts you discard as junk. With OCD, the filter isn't working as it should.

You'll have to filter manually for a while to show your brain how to make accurate connections.

With enough practice, OCD and anxiety sufferers can employ their logical brains to work around the bad neurological routing with new neural connections, establish new habits, and bring their OCD under control.

How is this possible?

BRAIN PLASTICITY

Did you know that there are people alive today with only half a physical brain who function just as well as the rest of us? Brains can adapt to imperfect conditions.

While brain injury is often irreparable, brains can **sometimes** recover some degree of function after damage. Specific functions such as speech, movement, and processing have a preferred location within the physical brain. When that area of the brain becomes damaged, that function is lost or degraded. Surrounding areas can, in time, re-configure themselves and pick up some or all of the functions using healthy brain matter. The same function may not feel the same as it used to because it is a new circuit that has been freshly built in the brain network. It's a "new" bit of you. Quite a thing.

The brain is less a solid object than it is a living fatty jelly, effervescent with activity; a hundred billion cells sending and receiving messages across a network of astonishing complexity. Each brain cell can connect with one thousand other brain cells at any given time, allowing for around sixty trillion possible connections. It's changing all the time. You are very literally not the same you that you were two decades ago. Most of your atoms have been replaced by other atoms, including your brain. It's a living miracle. Like you. Change is not just an idea. It's an atomic reality.

Information is processed in real-time, decisions are weighed, rules are followed, language is decoded, intentions are communicated, social cues are navigated, the past is considered, futures are imagined, and current tasks are completed. We might have many flaws but what our brains do for us is off-the-scale-amazing.

Crossed wires will happen sometimes.

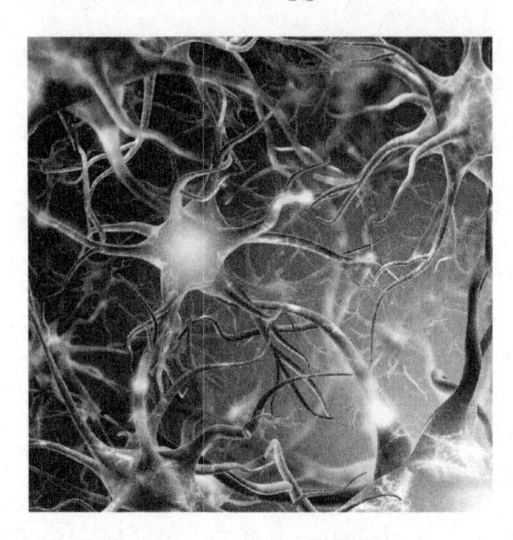

Each time you repeat a behaviour, it strengthens the particular neural circuit that is used to action that behaviour. Astonishingly, this isn't just a metaphor. Those busy circuits are physically reinforced to become more permanent structures in the brain. The brain coats the busy nerve connections (axons) with a thicker myelin sheath ensuring that the well-used circuits deliver fast and automatic signal transmission – an information super highway.

These established circuits are **hardwired**. They are coated in a myelin sheath for speedy transmission and permanence. These established circuits are what allow you to easily drive your car, ride a bike, play a musical instrument, write a postcard, clean your teeth, tie your shoelaces, or hold a knife and fork. It's all taken care of automatically for you, courtesy of your established brain networks. And that's how the brain likes it.

Consider that many of those brain networks have been established for some time. They are like thick mature trees in a forest full of saplings.

Heavily myelinated nerve fibres are surrounded by rings of the myelin sheath that look remarkably similar to the annual rings inside a tree trunk. The saplings are your hopes and dreams, ideas and networks that you're trying to establish, but the brain defaults to routing the majority of the signals through the established network. The brain won't cut those mature trees easily. They are solid. Dependable. They have received considerable investment already. Change is going to be hard work for the brain. It won't change established patterns on a hope, a whim, or a half-hearted suggestion. It will need to de-myelinate the old neural circuits and myelinate the new ones. In other words, it's resistant to change. Now you know why it's tough to change an old pattern and to make a new one stick. The brain will need you to repeat a new action many times before it will consider that new set of behaviours as worthy of a myelin sheath and "hardwired" status.

The good news though is that brains aren't set in stone at all. While it is understandably difficult to cajole your brain into de-myelinating unhelpful pathways and building new infrastructure, when you succeed, what was once a huge obstacle, now becomes your ally. Once advantageous pathways are established, they too benefit from the strengthening effects of repetition. Put another way, your new habits become the path of least resistance, and that's ease. What is difficult at first, eventually becomes the default way to do things. Going back to the old is unappealing.

It's through the repetition of these function-replacement exercises that the brain re-learns how to execute some or all of the lost functions.

The occurrence of intrusive negative thoughts does not indicate brain damage but the treatment for intrusive thoughts can be considered to proceed along similar lines because both recoveries share the principle of behaviour-induced neural plasticity to improve function.

We must adjust how we do things and stick with them for long enough that the brain learns and becomes comfortable with our new routines. That's the essence of how recovery happens. It's also how change occurs in our lives. We do something new until it becomes normalised. It's rarely comfortable at first.

Poor Mental Hygiene

Our first three categories, Anxiety, Trauma, and OCD, could all be said to be drivers of obsessional difficulties. They tend to be things that happen to us.

We'll define "poor mental hygiene" here as the psychological equivalent of dirty socks in the bedroom or weeds in the garden. They didn't happen. We left them there. Human minds have much to consider and the potential to be disorganised and inattentive is high.

We may permit circumstances that are hellish to live with. We may choose perspectives that are negative and depressing. We may ignore logic. We might court stressful beliefs and ideas. We might sell ourselves unnecessary drama or battles, be too hard on ourselves, or blame and shame instead of noticing what's commendable. The list goes on. And, there are reasons that we do these things and they are not always easy to see or rectify. This isn't a comment about a specific type of person. This is a comment about being human.

These mental dramas are all part of the rich tapestry of owning a mind connected to an animal body in sometimes tough and ever-evolving circumstances. We are driven by responsibilities, needs, instincts, superstitions, habits, fears and reactions. It's a lot to process and adjust for. Nonetheless, our ongoing well-being requires that we guard against inviting negative themes and events into our lives regularly. They might have mild entertainment value at the beginning but eventually, they take up residence. We may realise that we've created a mental monster only when it has already escaped our control.

We can ask ourselves whether in some way we have either invited our intrusive thought themes in or agreed to live with them? Sometimes we sign up for things in life that we later can't live with. It's okay to change one's mind. The lifestyles that create unnecessary negative mind-loops will require attention if we want to enjoy a peaceful mind. Endless negativity that includes unnecessary life dramas is toxic to our mental and emotional health.

To balance this, we must guard against "toxic positivity" at the other end of the spectrum. That's the notion that negativity is purely a choice and that we should just work harder to be more positive and see the bright side. Being a grown-up means fully facing your funky feelings. Real life involves bad days, bad weeks, and even bad years sometimes. Being told that you've failed in some way if you don't find a positive perspective can be very unhelpful when you are having a difficult time with your thoughts and feelings. *"What, you think I wouldn't prefer to be smiling right now?"*

Sometimes, we need to sit with our feelings and stop expecting to be full of joy today. We need to ditch the urgency for comfort and allow ourselves the experience of feeling what we feel, even when that's awful. We process by feeling. We get stuck when we resist. Bad days happen. Surrender. Don't fight them. Don't lament the lost time. Write them off as part of the expense of being alive and stay out of the struggle zone. Be Zen. It will pass. Then, we go again.

We can create the conditions for brightness to return but we cannot force wellness.

With toxic positivity to one side then, here we are talking about the kind of negativity we might indulge ourselves in. Here are some examples: -

* Consuming too much news and/or divisive social media. It's invariably negative. We used to live in tribes of fewer than a hundred and fifty people, without media. Now, we know about every negative event in the world. Doom-scrolling. It's too much. We can't process events on that scale. News is toxic to happiness. It can also be highly addictive. This includes social media and divisive politics. It's hard to see how much of a negative influence it has on well-being levels until you turn it off for a week. Remember, it's always been the end of the world, there have always been bogeymen, and the same dramas have played out countless times across history. Today's news seems urgent. It was always so.

* Playing the victim – blaming, shaming, moaning, groaning and never owning.

* Choosing pessimism – wilful resistance to more helpful perspectives.

* Failing to establish personal boundaries and giving beyond what is healthy for you.

* Accepting the first negative perspective that arises in the mind as the only perspective available and defending that position.

* Involving oneself in unnecessary dramas or battles.

* Frightening oneself with personal or global scares by researching websites of sometimes dubious content.

We have probably all been guilty of courting these stress-inducing behaviours at some time and we will, no doubt, do so again. We are not aiming for perfection here. We're just learning to be aware of what makes us feel unnecessarily anxious, angry, or depressed and then implementing some changes or practices that will shift us into a different atmosphere altogether.

Solutions

Solving the poor mental hygiene problem begins with a choice.

When the pain outweighs the gain, then it's time to make some changes. Saying no to more bad news, a drama you don't need, an awful relationship, a terrible workplace life, a pessimistic outlook, an urge to blame, an addiction that is hurting you, or any other compulsions that make you feel bad after you do them, requires **impulse control**. That means responding thoughtfully and deliberately with a pre-chosen response. It means making a new choice based on a considered decision. Not just once, but repeatedly, until the new choices become habits. All humans face these decisions. OCD and anxiety will force the issue. It's worth remembering that we don't have to tackle it all in one fell swoop. Just keep it moving in the right direction. Slow and steady wins the race.

MEDICAL CONDITIONS

Many medical conditions are known to increase anxiety, and since negative intrusive thoughts are part of that package, the same medical conditions may be implicated in the existence of obsessive symptoms.

Medical matters should be discussed with your doctor, and I'd caution against allowing your mind free reign to ruminate and obsess about all of the things that could be wrong with you. Dr Internet is not always your friend either. That does depend on how you use it. If you can do so, see your doctor, get a blood test, discuss your symptoms and please stop guessing. Basic blood tests will pick up many possible medical anomalies including nutritional deficiencies.

For reference though, here are a few possible culprits: -

*   **Malnutrition** – Mostly everyone now understands that nutritious food boosts good health at every level. Poor nutrition does the opposite. That formula includes the brain, mind, and emotions. A poor diet will struggle to support a healthy mind and body.

*   **Vitamin Deficiency** – Even with a good diet, we can still be vitamin deficient. It is worth being aware that some people don't absorb or convert some vitamins well, meaning that even if you supplement, your body may not be receiving what it needs. Pernicious anaemia, for instance, is an autoimmune condition that prevents the absorption of vitamin B12 resulting in chaos in the body. A blood test can identify these problems and there are solutions available. Supplements should be tailored for your needs specifically with the help of your doctor. Taking the wrong supplements can be more harmful than taking none at all.

*   **Hormones And The Thyroid Gland** – Hormones regulate the body's processes. The thyroid gland regulates the production and distribution of hormones. An imbalance in this delicate chemistry can create fatigue, brain fog, depression, anxiety, and other physical symptoms. Menopause is a recognised flashpoint for hormonal disturbance so if your anxiety/obsessions began with menopausal onset, that's another reason to speak with your doctor. Hormone Replacement Therapy (HRT), while somewhat contentious, may be worth exploring with the assistance of your healthcare provider. If you're holistically minded, you may be able to address this to some degree with diet and exercise. Men can also

suffer from hormonal imbalance, particularly after the age of forty. Men's testosterone levels drop considerably into older age.

*   **Gut Health** – As research continues, there is mounting evidence that our guts are inextricably connected with our brains. The gut produces the "happy hormone" usually associated with the brain - serotonin, and it is now understood that the gut is a system with similar organic complexity to the brain. It has even been proposed that the gut be recognized as a "second brain", such may be its influence on our lives. Bad bacteria can overwhelm our gut's helpful bacteria and we can feel dreadful as a result. Any illness that affects the gut, such as irritable bowel syndrome may be playing a role in your anxiety. Be careful when researching internet solutions in this area. There are many unsubstantiated claims and cures. Causes and resolutions may need to be tailored for you individually. A medical investigation should be your first stop if your gut isn't happy. Food intolerances could mean that a simple diet change or omission could be what's needed. *The gut microbiome* is the search term if you want to learn more.

*   **Diabetes** – Diabetes is a potentially life-threatening condition that requires careful management of blood sugar levels. When managed well, it may cause only minimal disturbance to a person's life but poor management will create illness eventually. Diabetes symptoms include mood swings, exhaustion, trembling, thirst, breathlessness, sweating and chest pain. Type one diabetes is hereditary and currently incurable. Type one requires regular insulin injections and strictly monitored blood-sugar levels. Type two diabetes is often linked to obesity and poor lifestyle and can improve or even be reversed with targeted diet and exercise.

*   **Chronic conditions** – too many to mention. Any chronic condition may be part of the problem. If you have one, it would be wise to research whether there are any known links between your condition and anxiety/obsessive thoughts.

Chapter Four – Shock And The Suggestible Mind

We've asked, and answered, "Why me?" In this chapter, we're asking, "How?"

I want to help you understand how the mind can absorb or generate anxiety-inducing intrusive thoughts when it is in a state of shock. Understanding this will help you to process what has gone before, but more importantly, it will explain how and why to avoid getting caught out at a vulnerable time of high anxiety. Such times could feel like they are happening daily for people in severe anxiety distress. Sometimes, that can feel like an ongoing panic attack.

If you are a person who experiences panic, you may be experiencing daily mini-shocks, generated by the anxious mind, all of which are sustaining the condition. Shock creates suggestibility. Then, negative thought themes stick, fear spreads, intrusive thoughts proliferate and more shock follows.

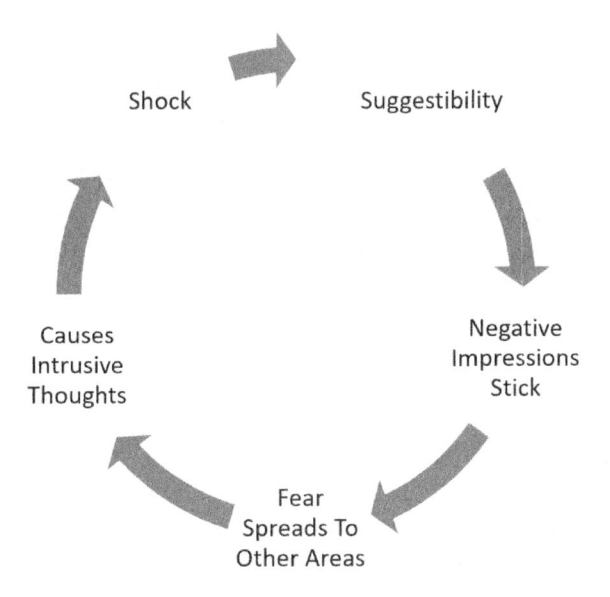

Shock → Suggestibility → Negative Impressions Stick → Fear Spreads To Other Areas → Causes Intrusive Thoughts → (back to Shock)

The question is, "How did these themes come about and why are mine different to others?"

Let's understand how our personal experiences may have hooked us into a world of fear.

Shock is the number one culprit.

A Scottish doctor named James Esdaile (1808-1859) employed hypnosis as a means of pain relief while operating on over three thousand surgery patients in Calcutta (now Kolkata), India. Many of these surgeries were amputations, at a time when modern anaesthetics were not yet in use. Though alcohol and opium had been used historically, Ether, the first Western "general anaesthetic", was only introduced in 1846, the same year that Esdaile published his hypnotic surgery results.

An interesting side-effect of his hypnotic intervention was reported. The post-operative death rate in his hypnotized patients dropped to just 5%, a dramatic reduction from the usual 25-50% mortality figures from patients who received no hypnotic help. This outcome, it was supposed, was due to the shock reduction experienced by the patients. Esdaile is quoted as saying, "The strain in pain lies mainly in the brain". It wasn't always the operation that killed the patients. It was the shock.

When he returned to Britain, he was unable to replicate his results conclusively. He was discredited as a charlatan but it seems that British scepticism may have played a large part in the poor results. As we now know, hypnosis requires a certain degree of buy-in from the hypnotisee. Indian culture was more receptive to such things. Most Westerners considered hypnosis to be hogwash at the time and may well, therefore, have resisted the intervention. Professionals know that the hypnotist is merely a facilitator, providing the correct environment. All hypnosis is self-hypnosis. It's not something done "to" you, so if you work at proving that it doesn't work, then you'll be right.

There are a few exceptions to this though and the one I want to highlight here is that: -

Human beings naturally go into a trance state when they are in shock.

I'm sure that you can relate to that statement. You remember your worst emergency-level incidents. They are etched into your memory with a clarity that few other memories are, sometimes, frame by painful frame. Because...

... what happens in trance... <u>sticks!</u>

This is relevant.

We recognize that a person in a traumatic situation is already in a state of automatic hypnosis (trance).

In practice, this means that their mind is wide open and in a state of **suggestibility**. Their "voice of reason" has temporarily lost its solution-creating abilities. From a hypnotherapeutic perspective, our patient is not fully in control of their mind because the protective brain has taken over; a process often referred to as "emotional hijacking." We are all familiar with this. Consciousness is narrowed. Rational thinking is overwhelmed by emergency procedures. We can include states of high anxiety and depression as being states of trance. There is little else in focus other than how awful the state is and what is to be done.

As James Esdaile demonstrated, the situation may be bad but it's the shock that does the most harm. You can see where I'm going with this, right? What can we learn from this understanding about how we manage the frightening thoughts and feelings in our minds? What is the priority?

In an ordinary non-hypnotised state of mind, our thoughts are "filtered" by the mechanism we call "the conscious critical faculty". That sounds wordy, I know, but the clue is in the title. It means that our consciousness is scanning incoming information with a **critical** eye. Anything that doesn't match our pre-conceived ideas about reality is simply filtered out or rejected. That's how our beliefs and perceptions are protected.

Trance is a state of mind where this mental scanning system is, to some degree, temporarily suspended from duty. In hypnotherapy, we use this understanding to deliver helpful ideas when a person's mind is filled with unhelpful ideas. Unfortunately, programming works both ways. We can also receive negative programming from a challenging event. This is how phobias are usually formed. The mind takes a snapshot and remembers to avoid that thing in future. To use different language, when we're in a state of trance or hypnosis, then words, phrases, ideas, thoughts, patterns, events and images can have a much greater emotional impact than they might do at other times and are more likely to endure in the mind.

In practice, this means that what you choose to focus on and give your belief to during a period of shock will become the overall lasting memory of that event. It may also amend your belief systems negatively. What your subconscious mind learns from the event will inform how it responds to any other similar situations, going forwards. The subconscious mind is quite black and white. It considers something as either good or bad. Then, the feelings match. When you have too many bad feelings about too much of life, then your world shrinks.

Positive perspectives can be displaced by negative perspectives and that's much more likely to happen when we are in a state of shock or fear.

This does present us with a bind. Since fear and subsequent shock are automatic, there's not a huge amount we can do in the moment to stop fear or shock itself from occurring. What we can do though is be aware of the potential of the moment as far as our thoughts are concerned and know how to not inadvertently worsen the situation.

Suppose I'm involved in a car accident. Nobody is injured but both cars are written off and it was a close call. My mind will automatically be producing big, dark, negative thoughts. What I do with those thoughts in the following minutes, hours and days will be crucial in determining whether I never drive again or whether I am back behind the wheel shortly afterwards.

Automatic negative thoughts will come at me. My mind will replay the accident. It will show me what could have been. I will feel alarmed, guilty, stupid and regretful. That's all to be expected. To some degree though, I have a choice. I'll need to be smart and disciplined about what I allow my mind to do now. It won't come easily. I know that this is a precipice.

Here's what I'm going to do: -

*   I recognise that the alarm and shock that I feel in my body and mind is entirely to be expected and is a direct result of something threatening happening. This includes unwanted replays of the event mentally and racing thoughts. I'll take that at face value and **choose** not to start concluding what this might mean to me at this sensitive moment. Those questions can be asked later when I'm calmer.

*   I recognise that the shock will last as long as it lasts. It's going to be uncomfortable. My body may shake. I might feel sick. My solar plexus area may lock up in fear. I may feel out of breath and tense. I will experience the feeling that something is badly wrong. I will allow my body to do whatever it needs to do... patiently. If it needs to shake, then I'll let it shake. If tears come, I'll let them flow freely. The world can stop for a while as my body processes the experience. I give the event and my body's response to it the attention and support that they are due. I am in service to myself in such times.

*   I recognise that the alarming thoughts and images that are present during this period of recovery from shock are an automatic part of the mind's response to danger. I refuse to engage with these thoughts and images as if they are an accurate prediction of the future and I will refuse to be bullied into giving up any part of my life to fear, as a result of them. No decisions about the future will be made right now. The shock state is not a trustworthy mind with which to make lasting decisions about my well-being. I will suspend any conclusions until I feel safer and can process the event rationally. Scary thoughts, tough feelings and confusion are the symptoms of an aroused limbic system (fearful/shocked brain). I'll expect them at a time like this. I will tolerate them, compassionately.

This needs to be anticipated but not feared.

Be aware that humans often make deals with themselves under severe duress, usually with statements like "I'll **never** do X again", and, "I'll **always** do Y again." I know that when my stress levels reduce, as they naturally will if I follow the steps above, then the frightening thoughts will also recede. If I've handled the situation mindfully, I am much less likely to experience a **lasting** emotional disturbance. If I allow my body and mind to fully "process" what has happened, it will do so in most cases, leaving a memory of the event but not trauma.

Being aware of the language that you use when you speak to yourself matters hugely in this context. You want to avoid shutting down a part of your life because fear has knocked your confidence. Don't make an "always or never" deal with yourself now that you'll regret later.

* If I'm smart about it, I might default to creating a much more positive set of thought patterns. For instance, I could choose to think: -

Okay. I know that these frightening feelings and thoughts are just a natural automatic response to what has just happened. I get that "you" (i.e. I am extending kindness to myself) feel afraid right now. That's entirely normal. I can allow the discomfort and shock to be there. My body and mind need some time to process this event.

I am in one piece. I have escaped. Accidents happen **but they are rare**. *Cars are replaceable. Insurance is there to help. I will be driving again soon. This will pass and my feelings will change. I will be safer in the future. Today will become another memory.*

....

This isn't just a nice pep talk. I'm consciously aware that I am **programming** my brain with these positive thoughts while I am in this highly **suggestible** state. I imagine myself six months from now, driving comfortably, as normal. I imagine myself as a better driver. I have learned from my mistakes. I have to choose these words and perspectives. Unless I have a well-programmed brain already, they will not come automatically. I will continue to repeat language and thoughts of this nature for as long as I need to do so and I will speak these words (to myself) without urgency. I don't want to be frantic. I also do not want to have a fear that if I don't get this right, at this moment, the results will be catastrophic. They won't. The direction is to halt any runaway negativity.

Any **urgency** will be "read" by the limbic system as a signal that something **is** wrong and the words that I'm saying could be rendered useless. I need to have some buy-in to the positive reassurance that I'm offering my mind. If you're reading this, you've survived every crisis you've ever been through. Remind yourself of that sometimes.

Even something as simple as that reminder is "buyable" because, for most people, that's mostly true. If we can buy the alarmist stuff, we can buy the truth too but we have to present it to ourselves first. You can be sure that it will be a lot more helpful than thoughts like, *Oh my God... I could be dead right now! I could have killed someone! I'll probably never drive again! I don't know how I'll ever get over this.* You may have those thoughts. That's fine. **Just don't attach to them**. They are phenomena. Nothing more. Don't turn them into negative programming and don't make them your own. You have a choice.

Here, I'm using an extreme example. An accident like this will shake the most grounded of people but if we can see what happens at the extreme end of the spectrum, then we can again understand that to a lesser degree, **any** shock or fear needs to be handled with a similar skill. This information will apply **most** of the time. I'll gladly concede that it may have its limitations but do remember that most of what this book is addressing are the imagined fears and thoughts that make up the majority of the human mind's intrusive mental material.

We need to become experts in the art of meeting shock and fear, particularly that which results from negative imaginings, with greater awareness. Then, it's less shocking. I'm referring here specifically to becoming adept at regarding anxious thoughts with a sense of quiet detachment, from the Observer position, instead of with fully involved panic and buy-in.

What is the Observer position?

It goes by other names – notably, **The Impartial Spectator**, and **The Witness**. It's the idea that residing within us is a part of the "self" who sees everything that happens from a detached perspective - simply witnessing, and recording. Call it a psychological point of view if that's less fluffy for you.

Remembering with hindsight gives us a taste of this perspective. When the emotion of the moment is removed, as in a distant memory, we can see what happened and understand it with the wisdom of detachment and the information that has emerged since the event. Then, we look back at that time and wonder how the heck we didn't see then what we see now. It looks suddenly as plain as day. Feelings and a lack of understanding were probably in the way at the time.

Mindfulness, meditation, hypnotherapy, and any other practice that involves slowing the brain down and clearing the mind can help to develop a better sense of the Observer position. It's a perspective beyond erratic emotion that is more easily accessible in the meditative states. We could try to describe it. It's better to understand it through experience. The aim is to practice this position and use it more often. The tools that you will learn later on in the book will capitalise on this understanding.

Chapter Five – Weird Worries

With OCD in particular, strange beliefs can establish themselves and it is not unknown for those beliefs to be graphic and bizarre. The high weirdness of the material can throw people into a shock-like state. With that critical brain temporarily suspended in fear, magical thinking is more readily acceptable.

Here are a few examples from my life as a therapist with details amended to protect anonymity.

* A person presented for help with diagnosed OCD. They were troubled with various intrusive themes but one of these was of note. They would "see" out of the corner of their eye, a small dog that would "run behind the sofa". When they "checked", they would find the space (unsurprisingly) vacant. When I pressed them on this, they explained that it was less a hallucination and more of a feeling. They still felt compelled to check, just to make sure.

* A person presented for help with an intrusive image that a baby might have escaped from a neighbour's house and crawled inside their washing machine in the garage. They were terrified that they might not notice and run a wash with a baby inside. Consequently, they were anxiously checking the washing machine regularly for stray babies, even when they had no plans to use the machine immediately. This obsession had been seeded by a magazine article about a baby who had crawled inside a washing machine.

* A person had become obsessed with a public figure who had been recently convicted and imprisoned for sex offences. They were not only alarmed by the thought that they might be like this person. Their obsession had managed to convince them that they might actually be **becoming** this person. They recognised that this was a ridiculous idea but still felt it as if it were true and would have panic-like sensations when they believed that they might be "becoming" that person. They had no inclination or history of abuse.

An OCD sufferer usually knows that their thoughts are irrational. They'd just prefer not to have them altogether. For the record, my clients here were not psychotic and were aware of the unreality of their perceptions.

Nonetheless, it's important to understand that obsessions can be strange at times. By being clear on this, we can be ready to come out fighting no matter how weird things have become. You're not the first to have strange ideas delivered by intrusive thoughts and you won't be the last. Don't let anxiety spin you the line that your anxiety is somehow worse, your thoughts are weirder than others, and that the proposed solutions, therefore, won't work for you. Rest assured, many have experienced high weirdness and still recovered just fine. As anxiety reduces, the sensations will dissipate.

How we manage the worries and anxieties in our lives is all about understanding that our brains can create inaccurate perceptions. Sometimes, the effects are extreme. Sometimes, they are subtle. They are all destabilising.

With this understanding, we need to learn how to **not** buy into these frightening ideas. Nail this and you're halfway there already.

Hopefully, you now have a few good reasons to go easy on yourself. Unfortunately, going easy on yourself may well be interrupted by the content of your obsessions. Many of those intrusive themes might focus on what a terrible person you must be.

Let's talk about that right now.

Chapter Six - Am I A Bad Person?

One of the most common experiences for intrusive thought sufferers is the feeling that they must be awful people for even having these nasty thoughts, images, and compulsions present.

We need to understand that the Zealous Guard lives in its own world.

Recently, my phone rang while my right hand was holding a wet dirty rag as I was cleaning the house. I put the phone on speaker with my left hand and held my hands away from touching anything for the duration of the call. On hanging up, two minutes later, as my attention switched away from my call, I noticed that the dirty feeling on my hands was still ringing away in the background. It was clear that it had continued to loop in the background, as a sensation, even when I'd been unaware of it as I focused on the call. It was a moment of personal insight into the nature of the "something is wrong" mechanism. In this case, it was the potential for contamination with dirt on clean things. It has a life all of its own. It's an unconscious process; a subroutine. The same thing happens if you're unlucky enough to get dog poop on you. You wash it off but it still doesn't feel clean and your mind returns to it repeatedly. This is how it is for anxiety and OCD sufferers. The feelings seem to just ring and ring.

So, let's begin there. It's not you. Okay? It's the safety mechanism doing its thing.

Most of us live with a sense of a clear boundary that reassures us that we won't suddenly do anything awful. Obsession sufferers also have clear moral boundaries. The difference is that they live with the anxiety that this boundary might not be solid enough to stop them from committing some atrocity, accidentally or otherwise. It's a fear of a loss of control. This doubt is repeatedly disturbing and it rings in the background, just like my dirty-rag hands did, just as anxiety does, just as dog poop does.

We all know that people who do heinous things usually end up paying for their crimes. The idea that one might, even unknowingly, be one of those people, terrifies sufferers. We need to undermine the whole premise of this idea and reveal it as the liar it is.

A common reassurance tool that is used therapeutically is to remind an intrusive-thought sufferer that the fact that they are so alarmed by the thought, is definitive proof that they **aren't going to act on it**. Unfortunately, most sufferers don't find sufficient comfort in this reassurance, partly because it still doesn't answer the question of why they have these images and horrors in their brains and what safeguards they have. Aren't the thoughts themselves evidence of malevolence anyway?

This is unquestionably one of the most difficult conundrums that harm-obsession sufferers deal with because there is, apparently, no guarantee that they won't cause harm in some way. Except that there is... sort of. The condition itself just makes that difficult to believe. I jokingly remind people that it's difficult enough to get someone to do what they do want to do, never mind what they don't want to do. Remember that. It's helpful.

Obsession sufferers are not only concerned about what they could potentially do but they are also questioning their intentionality. By the time they have sought help, they are sometimes convinced that they are hiding a dark and terrible secret, or a malignant character, even from themselves. The presence of unpleasant and/or disturbing thoughts seems to confirm this.

Why would my mind just flash an image of atrocity if there wasn't something fundamentally wrong with me? The assumption is that there is no smoke without fire. While that can be true in some contexts, here it is not.

I don't want to present this as a scientific position. It's a perspective born from my thoughts but I think it's worth sharing for you to consider.

Just over one hundred years ago, the average life expectancy was a mind-boggling thirty-two years of age. Long life has never been more likely than it is now. Our ancestors' lives were generally short and perilous – malnutrition, no antibiotics, anaesthetics or vaccines. Most people were dead by thirty-something and child mortality was rife. Worse still, it was a world in which plague, genocide, violence, torture, poverty and enslavement were considered normal, and few were safe from such fates. These days, many more of us escape the worst of these outcomes but our wariness is not irrational. Alongside human cruelty, pathogens and natural disasters have also been an ever-present threat. Safe is not a word one should use to describe history.

We carry the echoes of endless atrocities inside our bodies. Generations of horrors, both natural and human, have left their mark on our genetic expression. While we are creatures capable of enormous compassion and pleasure, we are anxious to forget the darkness that demands its place in the world.

That imagery and our instinctive repulsion to it resides in the collective memories held within our shared genes.

It's not only fears that can regurgitate themselves. We can also experience angry, blasphemous, racist, paedophilic, criminal, and just plain nasty intrusive content in the mind. *The worst image you could think of? No problem. Here's a vivid rendering of it for you. Have a nice day!*

Is that part of being human? Unfortunately, yes, but that doesn't mean that we nurse our darkness by default. On the contrary, the darkness within us gives meaning to our light and a reason for us to work at kindness. Our modern lives also provide a much greater scope to do so. With our core needs and essential safety in relatively better shape, we are in a collective position to be kinder than ever. Still, the echoes[2] of survival take up space.

History has been violent and sordid. Why should we suppose that our ancestors' thoughts about others were historically benevolent? Life was cheap. Time was short. Resources were scarce. We are programmed to survive. It has been survival of the fittest for much of our time on the planet. Corruption, scandal, murder, betrayal, power-grabbing, megalomania and war have nearly always been present.

---

[2] https://www.archaeology.wiki/blog/2015/05/28/first-interpersonal-violence-among-humans-documented/

The earliest (current) archaeological evidence of human-to-human violence is from about 430 thousand years ago[3] and that guy had his head beaten to a pulp with a club. Come along to the Middle Ages and we all know how insanely bloodthirsty those dark days were. Violent death was at least ten times as common then as it is now. Manners were not a mainstream concern until the Renaissance years. Civility has been bred into the systems that many of us live within today. It doesn't mean that the violent and defensive impulses have disappeared entirely.

Most people shake these moral clashes off and carry on. Those with obsessive brains can become confused and snagged, mistaking this dark content as a reflection of their personality and intentionality. It's not only personal. The echoes of experience, good and bad, are inside all of us.

A more clinical perspective can also help.

It's helpful to recognize the link between OCD and the condition called Tourette's Syndrome.[4]

Tourette's syndrome is classified as a disease of the nervous system and a neurodevelopmental disorder. Tourette's symptoms include involuntary physical and verbal (motor and vocal) tics. A tic, in case you don't know, is a repetitive movement or vocalization involving distinct muscle groups. With Tourette's, the vocal tics can be screech-like noises, repeated words, and/or famously, obscene language and targeted verbal insults. Physical tics can range from the tiniest gesture to limbs suddenly striking out.

Tourette's tics are not typically caused by anxiety. Tourette's people report that they feel the urge to tic build as physical discomfort until it must be released by carrying out the tic. Repression of the urge is possible, temporarily, but discomfort increases as the pressure to tic builds. Sometimes distracting activities can also alleviate tics temporarily.

---

[3] https://www.archaeology.wiki/blog/2015/05/28/first-interpersonal-violence-among-humans-documented/
[4] https://en.wikipedia.org/wiki/Tourette_syndrome

Friends and family of Tourette's people learn to disregard the **content** of these tics, even the truly hurtful personal comments when they are present because they understand that it is a neurological/nervous system condition. The person that they know and love is present independently of their Tourette's symptoms and holds no more malicious intent than anyone else. This is understood.

Inherent in that understanding is the recognition that human brains are full of wiring that can produce unpleasant thoughts independently of our intentions.

Dr Mansueto, the Director of the Behaviour Therapy Centre of Greater Washington in Silver Spring, MD, describes the frequent evolution of a "Tourettic nervous system" into an OCD mind in later life.[5] OCD adults were sometimes children with Tourettic nervous systems. The basal ganglia area of the brain is known to be implicated in both conditions and both conditions have been shown to have a physical cause. If you have had tics during your early life and later developed OCD, you have a link here to understand why you've been affected.

As with intrusive thoughts and OCD, Tourette's statements can sometimes focus on themes of paedophilia, rape, blasphemy, terrorism, sexual indecency, personal slurs and any other form of "inappropriate" that you can think of. Like OCD, Tourette's picks on the worst thoughts, and OCD, like Tourette's, also involves "tics" of a sort – involuntary movements - they're just not physical or verbal – they're more like thought-tics in the mind. Remember that OCD is a broad spectrum, so not every intrusive thought mimics a tic but the analogy is helpful. We can see intrusive thoughts as involuntary in occurrence but more importantly, **involuntary** in terms of **content.**

Involuntary means that **you didn't choose it, you don't intend it,** and you are not responsible for it, any more than a Tourette's sufferer chooses or means it when they blurt out, "fat pig" to the love of their life. Their love may be a little overweight. The fat pig comment might be tough to shake off but those in that world know that they must accept

---

[5] https://iocdf.org/expert-opinions/ocd-and-tourette-syndrome/

that it means nothing and says nothing about anybody involved. Everybody has a physical feature that could become teasing fodder. Tourette's will pick on it. "Big ears!" will do just fine too. It's not to be taken personally. There is no malicious intent. It's a medical condition. It's automatic. The content must be ignored by all.

Many obsessions focus on themes that involve harm to other people. While this fear draws on a personal desire to not harm, the instinctive fear that churns in the guts of sufferers may have its deepest roots in the fear of being found culpable. Historically, punishments have been harsh. If we are not imprisoned or put to death for our crimes, perhaps we will starve to death in isolation. Either way, upsetting the group or the authorities is a deeply engrained **collective** fear that forms the framework for so many obsessional themes – guilt, shame, blame, blasphemy, paranoia, and isolation, to name a few. Many obsession sufferers are terrified of discovering that they are, or may be revealed as, a criminal, a sexual predator or a paedophile – all positions that usually end in banishment, imprisonment, or death.

It is difficult to confirm what I am about to tell you as an inalienable fact but the generally accepted wisdom from the OCD community, sufferers and physicians alike, is that there are **no known cases** of anybody acting out their OCD fears in the real world. For clarity, that means that nobody suffering from OCD, either deliberately or in a moment of madness, stabbed anyone, ran anyone over, harmed a baby, molested a child, or undertook a murderous rampage. These things do happen in the world but they are **not the result** of OCD or intrusive thoughts. As far as these things occurring as a result of suffering from OCD, it just doesn't happen. By definition, it's the last thing a sufferer would **ever** do. Why? Because…

The best people have the worst thoughts.

"What if I'm a psychopath?"

Well, there is a statistical chance that you are. Psychiatry estimates that approximately one in a hundred people are affected by psychopathy but psychopathy is misunderstood by many. Not all psychopathic personalities intend to cause harm.

In modern parlance, we speak of psychopathy as a neuro-diverse condition that makes empathy difficult or impossible to feel for those who live with it. The psychopathic brain[6] is different from the neuro-typical brain, with studies showing significant impairment of brain growth and function in the amygdala - the fear and empathy region of the brain. In short, psychopathic personalities feel far less fear and are therefore less naturally attuned to societal pressures and norms. Chillingly, homicidal psychopaths have been known to report that they didn't know what that funny face was that people made when they died. That was fear. They didn't recognise it, never mind feel it.

OCD and intrusive thoughts are very definite indications of the presence of fear, making them the polar opposite of psychopathy.

The chances of being a strongly psychopathic OCD sufferer, theoretically anyway, are slim to none because social and moral norms are objects of great concern to OCD sufferers. The opposite is true for psychopathy. Those people may have to work to remember the expectations are even there.

The psychopathic personality will often outperform the neuro-typical personality in high-pressure situations because their reasoning is clean, their action is clear, and they move unhindered by undue emotional muddying of the waters.

It is unlikely that you will have made it this far into this book with a psychopathic disposition. This subject would be of little interest to you and you'd probably find all this talk on wooing feelings irritating, at best. The overwhelming evidence is clear on this. As a person who is disturbed by the thought of being malicious, even accidentally, you are one of the best people, morally speaking. Your concerns demonstrate empathy. You are, unfortunately, having some of the worst thoughts as a result of that.

---

[6] https://www.cambridge.org/core/journals/the-british-journal-of-psychiatry/article/neurobiological-basis-of-psychopathy/3B70FB0FF1E7195CCD59A690AAF554F9

Now, at least you have an explanation for where these dark themes originate from. In our collective history, everything imaginable has happened somewhere, at some time. We're all rooted in the same place. Our brains have evolved to remember the awful and make sure that it doesn't happen again. Fear is the chosen evolutionary mechanism to enforce that, and you are just the inheritor of that legacy. OCD often runs in family lines. Though we may never know it, there's probably a historical story or two in there somewhere that kicked the fear off in the family line. Plus, there are genes.

Chapter Seven - Dying To Live. Risk And Reward

We humans have a complicated relationship with risk but our ability to take some risks will decide the quality of life that we live. This examination of risk is important.

Obsessive-mind difficulties persist by presenting us with one massively destabilising question - the question of "What if?"

What if...

*   That bump in the road I just felt was a person or an animal that I have run over?

*   I have HIV/cancer/terminal disease and don't know about it?

*   My mother dies because of germs from me?

*   I am sent to jail for a crime I didn't commit or commit a crime I didn't intend to do?

*   Everybody secretly hates me and they are only pretending to like me?

*   I'm only kidding myself that I love my husband/wife/child/friends?

*   I have a panic attack in a public place and can't get home?

*   I see somebody vomiting in the street or start to panic and vomit myself?

*   I discover that I am a paedophile, a pervert, a disgusting, malevolent, or damned person?

*   I pick up an object and hurt somebody with it?

*   I lose control of my mind and do something terrible and irreversible?

*   I go "mad" and am committed to an institution?

* I am a bad parent?

* Somebody else brings contamination or infection into my home?

It's potentially endless.

The truth is that we live in a world in which little is certain. None of us has any guarantee that either we or our loved ones will be here tomorrow or that what we hold dear in other ways will endure. None of us avoid a fair bit of unpleasantness throughout a lifetime. That's a fairly unsatisfactory arrangement for human beings and the knee-jerk response to such uncertainty is to attempt to eliminate risk wherever possible. For many obsession-troubled people, this can involve taking extreme measures that will significantly limit freedoms and joys as normal situations are increasingly avoided or meticulously planned.

This process is both conscious and unconscious.

The **unconscious** part of the process is controlled by the Zealous Guard – the brain's limbic system. It might best be described as our "gut response" to a given situation. This response is primarily visceral and emotional – instinct presented in feelings. Trusting our guts is a double-edged venture. If our minds are healthy and balanced, then that little twinge of discomfort can alert us to the fact that there may be a threat that we have missed, consciously. That's our sixth sense and it can save us on occasion.

Unfortunately, where excessive anxiety, obsession or compulsion are involved, these signals are much more likely to be false flags and trusting your gut while you are filled with anxiety is murky territory. Logic is required here. During anxious times we are bombarded with "feelings" and our "assess the danger" meters are wildly overactive. We are likely to see dangers where there are none.

Certain activities in life are inherently risky; adrenaline sports, for instance. Dicing with death is a hugely thrilling experience for those who are cut out for it. It seems that for some, the higher the risk, the greater the rewards. The people who are willing to go into extreme sports are firmly in the minority. Few of us have the stomach for such things.

We do have a real problem though, when we find powerful negative gut responses in evidence during otherwise normal day-to-day functioning. We might perceive these fearful sensations as real, meaningful, and most importantly, permanent. So, are they set in stone forevermore?

In a word, no.

These immediate negative gut responses can be overridden by the conscious mind through a process of conditioning, that is, training.

Circus performers, BMX riders, skiers, snowboarders, gymnasts, high-wire walkers, climbers, racing-car drivers. None of them arrived at their mastery immediately. The first time they tried a stunt, a somersault, or a high-speed bend, you can be sure that their adrenaline was pumping and they felt fear. Most will be injured by their sport at some point too, and they know it but they don't give up. Their refusal to be forced away from the things that they love or want to do is what gives them their superpowers. They set out with the understanding that practice makes perfect and they continue to cultivate a willingness to keep trying until they are proficient. Any pain that might be involved in that process is accepted as part of the price of mastery.

People who approach a challenge with these levels of commitment rarely fail. They are willing to take the bad days with the good in pursuit of a greater goal. In practice, this means feeling the fear and doing it anyway. It also means being willing to endure pain because mastery is only achieved by getting it wrong a few times. Failure is not final. It is part of the process of success.

Famously, it is said that mastery requires ten thousand hours of experience. The number may be arguable but the point is that repetition and refinement lead us to excellence in what we do.

So, let's understand what the process of mastery looks like here: -

* The dangerous sport/activity looks insanely dangerous.

* We try the safer version first. I don't begin with a Formula One car. I begin with go-kart racing.

* In go-kart racing, my brain develops an intuitive understanding of the forces of gravity and momentum as I glide around the go-kart track.

* This intuitive felt-understanding becomes increasingly **automatic** with experience and I naturally improve at racing go-karts. In practice, that means that I do not have to **try** so hard to achieve a good result.

* After two years of racing go-karts, it no longer gives me the same thrill. My brain has "mastered" this activity. It seems dull. Too easy. I'm ready to move up to a more challenging type of driving.

The "unconscious" mind has learned to be confident in this activity and such confidence provides a natural antidote to fear. After two years of competitive go-kart racing, I now receive only a fraction of the adrenaline hit that I did at the beginning. Why? Well, simply put, my brain has become **confident** with the activity, but most importantly, my brain has become **comfortable** with it; used to it. It's time to upgrade to Formula One.

At one level, this relaxation of effort or stress in activity is about repetition.

Repetition creates new neural circuits and muscle memory, both of which build and improve skills.

Playing a musical instrument or riding a bike are skills that are not forgotten, once learned. Skills are behaviours that have been repeated consistently enough that they have become automatic.

With enough experience, the brain can draw information from a detailed mental map much more quickly than it can compute the speed, forces, eye-to-hand coordination and muscle movements required to complete a new skill. The key information I require to race go-karts expertly has been computed many times previously and is now mapped and drawn upon as instant knowing. The neural pathways are clear and direct. I have muscle memory. My internal experience, therefore, is very calm. I may appear to be hurtling around corners in a display of high-adrenaline screeching but I am not stressed and I am barely focused on the act of driving itself. My mind and muscle memory already know perfectly well how to drive at speed around corners and the task requires no effort on my part. My brain is now drawing from **experience** rather than computing every force involved in the moment. I now have the mental time and space to concentrate on taking the best racing line on the track to shave some milliseconds off my quickest time. The act of racing is no longer a chaotic blur. I have adjusted to it. I know where the boundaries are.

This natural conditioning process is a problem for adrenaline thrill-seekers. They need to go harder, faster, higher and riskier to get the kind of adrenaline hit they chase. Ask any advanced skier.

For the rest of us, natural conditioning offers a solution.

The basic formula is as follows: -

The greater our (successful) exposure to managed risk, the less anxiety we will have about further exposure.

Think about all of the things in life that you were once frightened by but which you now do without significant fear. How did that happen? Did you wake up one day and find you could just suddenly do them? Or, was it a process?

CHAPTER EIGHT – ROCK SOLID DEFIANCE

However unruly your negative brain is being, you're going to need to learn to put your hands over your ears and shout "La La La!"

Before you throw this book across the room in annoyance at this trite advice, do please know that I fully understand that if it was that easy, you would have done it a long time ago.

Later, we will be looking at the value of distracting oneself as a part of the formula for tackling obsessive feelings and thoughts. There **is** a place for that. Just to complicate matters though, we need to understand that there is a difference between consciously **choosing** to distract (an empowered approach) and being **driven** to distraction through fear and panic (a disempowered position).

Distraction looks the same from the outside but it's what's happening on the inside that counts.

If you're putting your hands over your ears in panic and running for the hills, that's not it. If you're putting your hands over your ears in defiance and sitting tight, that's something else altogether.

Which is why we're going to need a little detour...

I could have just said, "Anxiety makes you believe scary things that aren't true. You must stop believing scary things and you'll be just fine. The End."

Hmmm.

We **do** need to learn how to successfully challenge these frightening perspectives, but first, we need to know **how** we'll do it. We need a very specific mindset. Here's what a well-prepared anti-obsessional mindset looks like in practice: -

*   No matter how weird things get in my inner world, I flat **refuse** to believe that the shadowy world of dark dreams, anxious feelings, frightening perceptions/ideas, or horrifying thoughts gets to decide what my life is all about. **All minds** contain dark material. Life itself can be dark. I accept that weirdness as part of the package of being a human being on an animal planet. I can recognise that such perceptions increase when stress levels are high and that there are steps that I can take to minimise these discomforts.

Ultimately, I choose the philosophy by which I relate to life. and **I choose** a positively focused life. Life runs just fine without troubling obsessions. Thoughts and feelings that seek to undermine this position will not be willingly entertained as worthy of my energy from this point forward.

*   I have learned that "where attention goes, energy flows." If I keep my attention focused on a positive, constructive and empowered mindset and lifestyle, then over time, this becomes a deep groove that increasingly contains my existence more safely. There is science behind this. Human brains exhibit neural plasticity. It is possible to re-direct the neural networks in the brain through repetition. I may need to work on this. It requires ongoing maintenance but it becomes reliable once it's established. Even extreme disturbances can settle in time as new mental and emotional habits bed in.

We don't fight the bad. We make progress in the good.

*   I will be tested at times. 100% balance at all times is unrealistic. A bout of insomnia, a bereavement, an illness, a virus, a job loss or some other misfortune may unsettle me. I expect things to get dark and weird when I am unsettled. I trust that the balance **will** return eventually if I follow the rules above. Some things just need to be ridden out in life. Sometimes that process takes time and I will need to be patient and consistent. I've had enough experience in life to know that this is not merely a hope, it's a reliable expectation… if I follow the rules.

*   I recognise that having a short period of anxiety, depression or an OCD spike is very similar to catching a virus. It's not contagious but I treat my stressed, low or worried periods with the same level of **acceptance**. I didn't ask for it. It's unpleasant, it's inconvenient, maybe even painful, but I'll suffer more if I rage against it or make a victim of myself.

If I could have stopped my anxiety from arising before it happened, I would have done so. I didn't get that opportunity on this occasion. That makes it outside of my control and therefore, by definition, something I should not be punishing myself for in any way. I am not a bad or stupid person. I know that resistance will not fix this. Acceptance will help me to tolerate it and self-soothe more effectively. Eventually, it will pass. Maybe I'll learn from it? Maybe it will force some change that I need? I'll need to adjust my expectations for immediate comfort until it does and take the correct action and approach to minimise my symptoms. Most importantly, I must remember that nothing is truly wrong. It's just one of those things that happens sometimes. We can make space for bad times. They are part of the package of living. Unexpected positives usually emerge too.

*   I am committed to doing whatever it takes to support my anxious brain back to great health. That includes reviewing what I'm thinking, doing, and consuming, as a minimum.

*   I know that it's a mistake to "get into it" with my brain when it's sending me new things to worry about. I am willing to sit with the discomfort that frightening thoughts will bring but I refuse to engage with that content as if it is true.

Notice then, how these points support the position of defiance as far as scary thoughts and feelings go. I need to teach you how to find a mindset with similar protections built into it. To do that, I'd like to tell you a bit about how successful therapy happens, in practice.

Anxiety is a trickster. Sometimes, it's a bully. We can become wise to its ways. When we're in those dark places, it's like a black hole. It's dark, we can't leave and no light enters. From that perspective, it's almost impossible to believe that things could be better again. We may even forget what better feels like.

Somehow though, slowly, things do get better, sometimes by our efforts, and sometimes because time passes. When they do, we look back on the black hole experience and wonder what on Earth just happened. It was like a fever. Emerging from the black hole feels like no less of a relief than recovering from the flu. Many clients have, over the years, expressed this point to me repeatedly. I've lived it a few times myself.

The therapist knows this. The therapist understands that the patient is in the black hole. They know that the client can see no light and lives in a state of perpetual worry.

The experience of anxiety is saturated with the feeling that something is badly wrong. As a result, worrying feels so right.

Naturally, our clients are afraid to fully believe us when we tell them that they are safe and will emerge from this awfulness. Even our counsel is tainted by the doubt of anxiety. It's here that therapists are tested. It's not an easy job. Here's the dilemma.

Nobody can give a guarantee on the outcome. Our client's anxiety knows this too. Anxiety, by its very nature, is a Doubting Thomas, so we play a little game of "Yes... but..." The therapist presents a solution. The client's mind finds a way to block the solution. It's why they are here in the first place.

"Yes... but... " We're going to encounter these two words again and again. "Yes... but... " is the central mechanism that allows negative thoughts to worm their way into our minds and take up long-term residence. You know how those thoughts argue.

Here's an anxious thought sufferer who is booked to stay with friends: -

Thought: "What if you sleepwalk in the middle of the night while staying at your friend's house and do something terrible without knowing it? You could end up in their kids' bedroom!"

Response: "Don't be ridiculous. I don't sleepwalk!"

Thought: "Yes... But... there's always a first time! What if you do but you don't know about it?"

Response: "OMG. You're right! How can I **know** that I won't? Or, that I already have but don't know about it?!"

The above response is a fail. We get nil points for that one.

The correct response is: -

*This is an **anxious thought** that bears no direct resemblance to my current reality. I refuse to be dictated to by fear. I want to go to my friend's house and stay over the night. This is normal life. If I suddenly lose control and commit a heinous crime, (it's 99.99% certain that I won't by the way), then so be it. I'm putting my stake on the table and taking the risk. I'll deal with that if it happens. Until then, I'm getting on with my life, even if I have difficult thoughts and feelings while I am doing it. I need to make a stand now.*

Adjusting a thought such as this won't change things straight away, and naturally, after a few attempts to adjust our thinking without feeling any immediate gains, we may fall foul of impatience. It's through continued adjustment that we gain incremental ground.

There is a philosophical position here too.

Fear threatens to ruin us if we don't do as it says. That's bullying. We have to take a stand against this.

We claim safety and a sense of security by being willing to go through some pain to defend it, should defence become necessary. Your inner self knows that you're willing to do whatever it takes to self-protect and appreciates that deeply. It makes the unconscious mind feel that you're in control.

As I already said, this isn't easy. The thrust and parry game that I sometimes had to play with my client's anxious mind was a test. Their anxiety was testing me to see whether I could be forced to admit that there might be a chance that they would be the exception. Would they be the one who was truly beyond help? Did this therapist's assurances have meaning? Their anxiety tested both of us. I'd done this before, many times. I knew that if we held our ground, eventually, things would improve.

One way or another, I had to "prove" to their anxious minds that I could be seen as a trusted source of experience and information and that when I said, "You can recover", it wasn't just lip service. Their anxiety would throw hopelessness at me in twenty different ways and I would send back hope, strategy and reassurance in twenty other ways. They wanted to know that I wouldn't quit on them when things got tough. Ultimately, my job was to teach people how not to quit on themselves. I could become that rock-solid support that they needed for a while but after we had parted, they would reprise that role. Some minds learned to trust me quickly. Others made a sport of testing my counsel. The goal was always to model the success mindset though, so that they could do it for themselves. This book has the same goal.

The role of the therapist is to be a "rock" - un-swerve-able, immovable, and most importantly, <u>consistent</u>!

The message must never change. We might need to deliver the message in twenty different ways until we find the key that fits the lock, but the central message is always the same - "You are safe. You are recovering. There has been a misunderstanding that has caused you to feel very threatened by things that don't need to be feared so intensely. Let's understand the mechanics of this and the history. Then, this can be corrected. I won't just tell you that this is so. I will show you the evidence. Here is a way."

The means for this is tailored for each individual. Some people respond better to soft and meditative approaches while others might prefer a set of clear boundaries along with good stern motivational instruction – army style! The outcome of holding my ground, in the great majority of cases, was that my clients got better.

What was it that got results? Was it my bedside manner? My clients' commitment? The most important thing of all was the building of **certainty** that one way or another, this problem could be emptied of its energy. We aimed to get a foot in the door, to change something, however small.

The giant is not too big to fall. We just need to be smart about our aim.

My client's anxiety would attack this message in different ways. My job was to hold this message **consistently**, no matter how fiercely their anxiety said otherwise and keep helping them to make small improvements in the areas where we could see progress in the meantime.

Changing what can be changed will result in an increased sense of control.

Honestly, this could be as simple as committing to some daily exercise. It's the act itself that improves the internal sense of control. An improved sense of control reduces overall anxiety levels and that in turn reduces the strength of anxiety's arguments. At a certain point, eventually, the anxiety no longer has a leg to stand on, so to speak, and with a little push, it can finally come crashing down, revealed as the liar that it ultimately is.

Once a person has experienced the slaying or slowing of a giant, something changes. What has, until now, seemed like an invincible opponent, suddenly reveals its weakness - an Achilles heel.

It's made of lies. It always was. The mistake was that you gave those lies power by believing in them.

Defiance is the key.

Later, there may be new giants. They may seem fiercer, meaner, and stronger. If we've been away from the battlefield for a while, we might take a couple of sideswipes initially, having enjoyed much peacetime. We may find ourselves reeling. Doubts will arise. What if this time is different? What if I can't beat it again?

This is how it is, especially in the beginning. Ultimately though, we regroup. Then, we push on through and eventually, we emerge, winners once again. It is testing, it is unpleasant, and it might seem endless at times but I promise you that over time you are becoming wiser. Eventually, these cycles will become shorter and less intense. You begin to understand the rules of engagement. You learn to be a skilled planner. You learn what helps you and what hinders you. You'll see the enemy coming from a long way off and plan accordingly.

Eventually, you become the rock for yourself.

Chapter Nine - The Hydra

Intrusive negative thoughts fight dirty. It's in their nature to target our most vulnerable aspects.

It would be easy to assume that you are being personally attacked by a minded invader who is determined to take you down. That's not how it is. It just looks like that because the material that is prevalent in your obsessional concerns is drawn from your fears and vulnerabilities and that makes it seem personal like someone curated it just to give you a bad time.

In this book, I have, so far, deliberately used language that paints this task of recovering from obsessional mind difficulties in combative terms. I used the language of war to highlight the fact that we have to approach this task with a bit of fighting spirit. Both anxiety and intrusive negative thoughts are tough adversaries and half-hearted or wishful approaches to recovery are more prone to failure for the reasons I've just explained.

But even with battles won, can we ever really be free of the torment?

Let me tell you the story of the Hydra.

The Hydra is a venomous multi-headed mythological beast from Greek legend. Hercules, famed for his great strength, fought the Hydra in the second of his twelve labours but was initially defeated when the Hydra re-generated two new heads for each that he removed.

He needed a new approach and enlisted the help of his nephew, Iolaus, to cauterize the decapitated stumps so that no new heads could regenerate. The last head was immortal however and he buried this head under a great rock, putting the hydra out of action for the foreseeable future. He then dipped his arrows in the Hydra's poisonous blood and this poison became a power that he used in later battles.

The symbology of the last head being indestructible is a nod (excuse the pun) to the fact that these destructive forces are **contained** rather than defeated.

The poisoned arrows symbolise taking what one learns from each battle and using it to progress in subsequent combat situations; another helpful metaphor. The Hydra is a perfect symbol for our intrusive negative thoughts.

My clients would joke with me, "Couldn't you just get rid of all the germs in the world for me?" Life would collapse into goo were that to happen but we know where they were coming from. Let's just suppose for a moment that I could oblige their request. "Poof! All germs are now gone!" Do you know what would happen? They'd say to me, in their best pile of goo voice, "Er... thanks for getting rid of all the germs. The thing is... now I can't stop thinking about heart attacks."

The problem, you see, is not germs. Or heart attacks. The "theme" is a focal point for an anxious mind.

These are the heads that you hack at, but that immortal head, the one that must be severed and contained, is anxiety itself.

Are you worrying today about precisely the same things that you were worrying about this time last year? Some things, maybe, but have some new ones crept in while others have fallen away? Aha! A clue. That would be just that your priorities or even simply what's on your mind has shifted.

When I say that intrusive negative thoughts fight dirty, this is what I mean. They'll go for the things that frighten us, currently. The mind will hone in on the thoughts that attack our most vulnerable spots. That could be different at different times.

Here's an example of a top-five list of potential worries. Fear of: -

1) Losing a loved one.
2) Being diagnosed with a terminal or debilitating illness.
3) Being found to be a terrible person.
4) Germs and/or contamination.
5) Ageing.

Who wouldn't relate to our number one worry? I mean, losing loved ones is just about the worst thing imaginable for the average person. It's not a minded attack though. There is no little man with evil intentions trying to undermine us. It's simply a case of a mind with a hierarchical structure of potential horrors.

It's going to go to your number one worry and pick on that because that's the thing that poses the greatest threat to your well-being and existence.

As you can see, there is enough here in the top five worries to keep any of us busy with worry for the rest of our lives, and that's the point. If we could eliminate any possibility of losing a loved one, our number one worry, then the anxious mind would simply move on down to number two and so on. It's potentially endless.

As the myth of the Hydra illustrates, worries, by their very nature, are **immortal** foes because being alive involves a constant stream of challenges, thoughts and feelings. Worries naturally follow but **they can be contained and managed**.

Balance is tricky, and with the best will in the world, we won't get it right all the time. Life's cycles tend to be a law unto themselves and our journey through time, psychologically speaking, is not linear. It's cyclical. Its spiral-like patterns repeat.

The trick is to be ready when the same old stuff comes around.

With experience, we make increasingly short work of extricating ourselves from the sticky moments in life without spiralling into the dark depths. This is especially relevant to you if you're experiencing anxiety or intrusive thoughts for the first time in your life.

So yes, in practice, negative thoughts and feelings will always be a part of human life but the first cut is also usually the deepest. It's a shock when your mind turns on you but there is a well-trodden path that will lead you back to safety and flourishing. You'll become familiar with it.

Eventually, you'll master this, as many have before you. It helps to know that.

Chapter Ten – The Superstitious Human

Intrusive thoughts and compulsive behaviours often involve themes that most of us would call superstitious.

We, humans, like to know why things are the way they are. We want to know why A leads to B. By recognising causal links, we can make great stuff happen repeatedly and reduce or eliminate the occurrence of the not-so-great stuff.

When we can **attribute** a symptom to a cause, then we tend to feel less worried about the symptom, particularly if we can recognise that the cause is a non-threatening passing condition like a common cold.

For example, many people who begin a course of treatment with an SSRI antidepressant drug may find that it increases their anxiety levels in the first few weeks of use. The prescribing doctor will advise the patient of this possibility, along with the reassurance that the anxiety should reduce and give way to more beneficial effects within one to four weeks. As uncomfortable as that may be, most people can tolerate the situation because they can **attribute** the discomfort to an **expected** temporary side-effect of the medicine. As a result, they are less likely to worry that something must be wrong. Any dissenting thoughts about being permanently broken as a person can rightly be held at bay with the proviso that better days should be arriving soon.

Penicillin, our first effective antibiotic mould was "discovered" in 1928 by Alexander Fleming but there is archaeological evidence that penicillin has been used by human beings as a remedy for illness for thousands of years, particularly in healing septic wounds. In ancient Serbia, Greece, and China, mouldy bread was pressed against infected wounds as a remedy. It is rumoured that this practice was accompanied by rituals of appeasement to the gods and spirits responsible for illness and suffering. Did our ancestors **attribute** successful healing to the antibiotic properties of penicillin or the gods of mouldy bread?

In the absence of hard scientific understanding, we humans tend towards superstitious thinking. The English Collins dictionary gives the following description for superstition: -

"Irrational beliefs, especially with regard to the unknown."

Irrational beliefs may not be without value.

The rationalist position, determined to remove any magic from the world, will point out that there is no scientific evidence to support the logic of superstitious perceptions. We can also say that some superstitions, even in the absence of scientific rigour, may be helpful at times.

If a person takes their lucky charm to an interview and it makes them feel good and they get the job, then it's been a help, right? The rationalist might say that the charm had no bearing on the outcome but that's not strictly correct. It did affect the person who believed in it and that gave them a sense of confidence that helped them to perform better at the interview.

Superstition may also add other elements of value to our experience. It may be that we sometimes choose superstition over scientific logic because we remain connected to the ancestral lines of hope that flow in our blood.

Over many generations, superstition, ritual, and appeasement of gods have appeared to save countless lives. Whether the rituals made any difference, scientifically speaking, we may never know for sure, but the point is that they seemed like they did to the people who performed and witnessed them, at the time. The good fortune was attributed to the ritual, and as such, became established as a truth, something one can "believe" in.

Belief is the stuff that our subconscious minds draw upon to decide how we feel about something. If it feels good, we do more of it. The echoes of those miracles reverberate in our being to this day. Whatever you believe and however much it is debated, superstition is in our blood and it is probably here to stay. We've done it for as long as anyone can know and we are still doing it today.

Many of us are told what we should believe in from an early age, and once in place, this stuff is difficult to remove, particularly for those who suffer from obsessional thoughts. I have met a few sufferers who have struggled with their early religious indoctrination. Though they had chosen to disavow themselves of their unwanted religious conventions, particularly the guilt-filled ones, thoughts and feelings of shame, guilt, and blasphemy continued to haunt them. This is not laziness or lack of insight. Their core programming is hijacked by anxiety and OCD. They didn't get asked whether they wanted it or not. That's true for most of our cultural programming.

The cause and effect of superstitious behaviour may not ultimately stand up to scrutiny but many would rather not take the chance.

Just touch the wood already!

Touching wood is the UK's most popular superstitious act and a survey carried out by Professor Richard Wiseman at the University of Hertfordshire suggests that almost three-quarters of Brits do it![7]

I've already mentioned that unwanted intrusive thoughts and feelings will intensify as our anxiety levels rise. Unsurprisingly, anxiety will also increase our susceptibility to superstitious thinking. Professor Wiseman's report, rather brilliantly, asked some incisive questions that produced illuminating insights. We learn the following: -

*   50% of "worriers" report being somewhat/highly superstitious compared to only 24% of non-worriers.

*   42% of people who have a strong need for control in their lives report being somewhat/highly superstitious compared to only 22% of people who indicated a low need for control.

*   38% of people unable to comfortably tolerate ambiguity indicated that they were somewhat/highly superstitious compared to 30% for those who manage ambiguity easily.

---

[7] http://www.richardwiseman.com/resources/superstition_report.pdf

* 91% of those who felt anxious after they broke superstitious rules described themselves as needing high control levels and having a low tolerance for ambiguity.

* 15-18% of respondents used either a lucky charm/ritual or avoided breaking a superstitious rule at some point during that last month.

To summarise then, people with a high degree of need for control, difficulty tolerating uncertainty, and a predisposition to worry are also likely to be the most superstitious among us. Most importantly, they are also likely to be the ones who respond with anxiety when the rules of superstition are broken.

Is your superstitious brain asking you to follow seriously ridiculous rules and threatening you with unpleasant consequences if you don't follow those rules? Superstition then ceases to be a harmless quirk and becomes a menace to your peace of mind. Moving forward, those are myths that will need to be dismantled.

Correlation And Causation

There is a difference between correlation and causation. Correlation refers to when two subjects (variables) appear to be affecting each other. For example, when employees receive a pay rise, then worker morale increases.

Let's suppose that our workers also receive great news at home around the same time that they receive their pay increase. Then what? We can't be certain that their improved happiness levels have been **caused** by the pay increase. The two events have occurred simultaneously but that is not enough information to be sure that they are necessarily linked. That may be merely a coincidence.

I apologise for informing you that people die by becoming entangled in their bedsheets. This chart is only one among hundreds of variables that demonstrate similar spurious correlations. In this one, we see that cheese consumption and bedsheet deaths have followed the same relative rise over a ten-year period.

Per capita cheese consumption
correlates with
Number of people who died by becoming tangled in their bedsheets

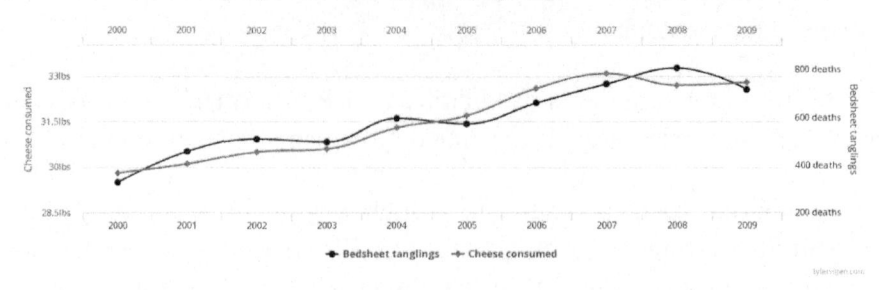

Thanks for the information and graph to: - http://tylervigen.com/spurious-correlations (Creative Commons 4.0 licence.)

Is it possible that cheese consumption and bedsheet deaths are linked? I guess if you are willing to go to some extraordinary lengths to conflate the two, then you may be able to make a case for that, but it would be the exception, not the rule.

The more steps you need to use to make the "causative" link work, the more likely it is that the link is coincidental rather than causative.

Let's just suppose, that as an obsession sufferer, your brain has decided that "death by bedsheets" and "cheese consumption" are linked by the "evidence" that this graph presents. You will ban cheese from your life. You will be anxious when you go out to eat. You will examine your food to make sure there is no cheese hidden within it. You may even have medical information that supports your theory that cheese disrupts melatonin levels which could cause a person to dream heavily becoming entangled in bedsheets. Your brain only needs to **believe** that there is a link. Remember, the obsessive brain will try to eliminate **all** risks. Even if it's a tenuous link and you know it, the obsessive brain will opt for *better safe than sorry* when left to its conclusions.

So, are you a fool? No. You are responding to feelings created by a brain that is doing its best to keep you safe but achieving the opposite. Let's get away from any notions that we are gleefully making associations between unrelated variables because we are too lazy to think. That's not how this works. We don't get to choose what the obsessive mind decides to focus on, nor the connections in the brain that it automatically makes. The brain has billions of data points that it draws from to decide how to respond. We shouldn't be too surprised when wires get crossed. We are where we are at any given moment, and we have to work with that. Just recognize that confusing correlation with causation is a well-researched and widely understood error in human thinking.

If you suffer from obsessional difficulties, you're going to find it very difficult indeed to extract yourself from magical thinking if you don't or won't take seriously the notion that your brain may be providing you with faulty logic. It's real. It's a thing. It needs to be understood, and finally, you need to make your recognition of it a part of your overall strategy to recover.

Could something wild happen? Sure! Is it wise to back the outsider though? It makes no logical sense, particularly when you realise that what you get if you win the bet is an even more deeply engrained obsessional problem.

It's your life and nobody should be telling you what to think. The counsel here though is that the smart money goes on the **most probable** outcomes. Will you sleepwalk and harm somebody if you "dare" to go to a friend's house for the night? Will you suddenly pick up a knife and harm someone if you "dare" to keep knives in your kitchen? Will someone die because you didn't do your safety behaviour correctly? Will you be cursed to have bad luck or sentenced to damnation because you had a nasty thought? Any of these could happen, theoretically. Nothing is guaranteed in this life but in the absence of certainty, we must use the next best thing we have to work with and that is statistical probability. And a bit more trust in ourselves.

How many times have you done the ritual or behaviour before? How many times have you done it imperfectly? Did Grandma die every time you weren't sure that you did it right? If it didn't happen **every** time, then it's not causative, it's a correlation. At some point, Grandma will pass away because it's her time. The fact that you happened to do your ritual imperfectly on that day is not causative, it's simply a correlation.

Unless you share your thoughts with someone else, nobody (except you) will be there to police them.

Critical thinking skills are something you must take ownership of. It's great to have the mental privacy to think whatever you please but it's also a potentially dangerous freedom if you are prone to obsessive difficulties. In discourse, another person can point out the errors in your logic. If you have no discourse with others on these matters, there are no such checks and balances except those that you deliberately apply.

As I hope I have highlighted, brains, especially obsessive brains, can lead us astray. We have to be on guard about this: not anxious about it, just mindful, aware and wise about it. If you have a lucky charm and it makes you feel better to take it with you, go for it. If believing in fairies brightens your world, go for it. If your brain is telling you that you'll need to do seriously time-consuming behaviours before you leave the house in the morning or suffer some terrible fate, then the error is with your brain, not the danger in the world.

Know the difference.

Chapter Eleven – Certainty, Truth, Lies, and Doubt

OCD has been rightly dubbed "The Doubting Disease."

Doubt is difficult to tolerate at the best of times but it's worse when anxiety levels are high. The anxious mind doesn't tolerate uncertainty well.

Thinking things through is how we derive order from chaos. Thinking something through methodically, therefore, is likely to deliver peace of mind when we find solutions. Unfortunately, not all of our thinking **is** methodical. Much of it is circular, repetitive and negative, leading to rumination and the formation of looping faulty beliefs and anxieties.

Anxiety-fuelled beliefs can be irrational but they can be powerfully persuasive nonetheless because they are directly linked to our feelings. Unless you're wise to the potential that your feelings and thoughts have to mislead you, then it's easy to become a staunch advocate for irrational ideas.

"I feel it, therefore it must be true" is a very alluring position.

Beliefs

We must remember that with anxiety and OCD, we do not **choose** to receive intrusive thoughts.

Here, I want to make a distinction between what you think and what you believe. Although thoughts are linked to beliefs, thoughts themselves are automatic.

Our personal beliefs require a degree of "buy-in", that is, agreement. It's worth noting that belief can be arrived at consciously, with your full awareness and support, and unconsciously, meaning that it happened without your awareness of how and why that belief came to exist within you. Beliefs are sometimes opinions and opinions are frequently second-hand. You'll still support it because it "feels" right. Most of our beliefs come from our environment – mentors, culture, family and peers. Life has a humbling way of revealing how wrong we have sometimes been about something as time reveals new information.

Robert Anton Wilson famously wrote: -

> "What the thinker thinks, the prover proves."

Or, in other words, reality will eventually conform to your thoughts. Your outcomes are the results of micro-choices made along the way. Those choices are informed by your thoughts and feelings.

We will also get more of what we believe in because beliefs drive actions and actions drive outcomes. We are invested in our beliefs. We are motivated by our beliefs. Many are willing to die for them. We get more of what we give our time, attention and energy to – for better or worse.

> **What we are doing in the privacy of our minds becomes the prevailing reality that we experience.**

If you believe that you are not loveable, your feelings will bend reality to conform to your expectations. Your mind will discount the acts of love that come your way as meaningless flukes or platitudes and look only for evidence of your lack of worth. As a result, you may be defensive (hostile) in your interactions with others causing them to not want to spend time around you. The belief that the world is hostile is then confirmed and your position never changes. You get more of what you believe in.

Perhaps you are a reasonably talented singer determined to become a popular artist. You don't have a single doubt that you can find a meaningful audience. You believe in hard work paying off. You refuse to fail. Your dream is delivered. Eventually.

> **Beliefs drive feelings. Feelings drive actions. Actions drive outcomes.**

When beliefs are positive, reinforcing our sense of control, self-worth, gratitude, and safety, then feelings are relaxed. If we believe we are endangered or worthless, our feelings are dark, churning and obsessive.

Belief is not a thing that we have a great deal of immediate conscious control over either. Beliefs are housed in the **subconscious mind** and they are automatically assigned "protected" status. They cannot be easily erased or amended.

Why?

Well, how would you feel about waking up tomorrow morning and finding out that all your beliefs have magically vanished? You wouldn't know who you are, what the world is about or what you stand for. So, beliefs are like the glue that holds our personalities and worldviews together. Without them, we would be adrift. That's why the subconscious mind affords them protected status.

Beliefs don't have to be correct or verifiable to be protected. Our emotions react aggressively to any attempts to undermine our existing beliefs, regardless of their objective validity because an attack upon our beliefs can feel very much like an attack upon our person and security. Instead of enticing us to reconsider our position, such challenges tend to cause people to either shut down or double down on their beliefs and nothing can be achieved. Plus, there's pride. That's a shame because we all stand to benefit from some upgrades to our belief systems.

I highlight this to illustrate that our beliefs are powerful and enduring. We shouldn't expect them to adjust overnight because we or anyone else asks them to. Brains don't work that way. They resist change. They need some encouragement. We have to give them compelling reasons to change and then…

…we must entice our beliefs into healthy positions, wooing them by example.

We have to **demonstrate** to ourselves that committing to new perspectives brings a net benefit, despite being hard work. Before we can commit to tackling these invasive negative themes, we will first need to be in **conscious** agreement that the beliefs in question are not helpful and that **we want them gone**. In other words, we need to want change and be willing to challenge our old beliefs. That means, "Don't side with your illness. It's not your friend."

We've already mentioned that we'll need our unconscious mind to agree with our revised assessment of any danger to us if we are to successfully challenge our intrusive negative thoughts but we won't even get off the start line unless we also have **conscious** agreement that our thoughts are unnecessarily manufacturing fear. The subconscious knows very well when our heart isn't into something.

This poses a genuine problem for people afflicted with these doubting diseases. It is often the case that the line between what's rational and what isn't has become increasingly blurred, especially if an obsession has had time to become a familiar habit of thought or behaviour. To complicate matters, not everything fits neatly into the categories of safe, unsafe, true or untrue. There is sometimes room for genuine doubt.

True Doubts

I have had many occasions to agree with a client that their specific obsessive difficulty is a perplexing one. Not everything we worry about is irrational. Health anxieties, for instance, are particularly tricky because, without ongoing medical tests, there is no way to be sure that we do not carry an undiagnosed illness. Sometimes there may be a genuine reason that an obsessive worry has formed - a real-life contamination threat for instance. Or an unexplained symptom. A test may be wise.

The problem is, for those with an obsessive difficulty, one test will never be enough. This week it was spittle on a window ledge. Next time it might be a takeaway meal or a sneeze on the bus. The mind can easily use a convoluted string of faulty logic to argue that infection has occurred. Where does it end?

These situations are typical of how obsessive themes focus on **difficult-to-disprove** scenarios. If there are verifiable elements in the mix, such as "it happened to someone" or "last time I didn't do the compulsion, my cat fell ill", then it becomes more difficult to refute. That still doesn't make it true. It just makes it a good fit for an obsessional concern.

A very helpful phrase I kept in mind as a therapist was as follows: -

> **"If you fight for your limitations, then you get to keep them."**

It is a useful soundbite to help us remember that little is likely to change if we continue to fight for limited perspectives in the face of greater evidence. Make sure you're clear about who your number one enemy is. It's not the existence of strange diseases.

Dr Schwartz, the author of Brain Lock, gave us a great line to help with this problem.

If you think that it <u>might</u> be OCD (or an obsession) **then it <u>IS</u> OCD** (or an obsession).

For clarity, that means that if you are worried that your house will burn down because you left an appliance plugged in before you went out for the day, that's not reality, it's an anxious thought. If you're convinced that you have cancer because you feel fatigued, that's health anxiety.

Why?

Because it's a **might**.

Did you receive a phone call from the fire service about your home? No? So, what leads you to fervently imagine that your house is burning down at this very moment then? To feel panic about that? It's not that your house is burning down. It's anxiety. It's the OCD. Therefore, it's obsessional, not factual.

Here's another: -

The obsession is that you might be a horrible or damned person. What is this based on? Maybe that time you got caught stealing penny sweets in the corner shop when you were ten? How forgiving is God, exactly?

Did you do the crime? Yes. Are you a bad or defective person? No. Nobody lives a life without making mistakes or doing things they are not proud of. That's how we learn what we don't like, or what hurts others. If you have learned from it, then it's done, no matter your age. That's all we can do. Don't forget to factor in the thousands of acts of kindness and selflessness you've put in too. That's not nothing.

You have anxiety-fuelled intrusive thoughts about a matter that is forgotten about by everyone but you. The condition will find something to pin the fear on. That will do it. If it wasn't that, it would have been something else. Is it worthy of your attention? Absolutely not.

Logic will be your first adviser. This remains true even though we acknowledge that the intrusive thoughts and/or anxious feelings make this feel almost impossible. "Almost" and "feel" are the key words. It's not absolute and it's not a fact.

Claim your certainty. Pick a side. Stick to it. Your position is your power.

Is it an intrusive thought? Yes. Did you choose it? No. Are you inviting it in for a glass of something? No? Then, don't be interested in what it has to say. Like a bad lover, letting it in always leads to somewhere worse than where you are today. Resist the urge to bite, however enticing it seems. The minute you engage with interest in such a conversation is the moment you are **legitimising** what the obsession has to say. And you're back in the loop.

The better advice is to listen to what you choose to be in life, not what OCD or obsessive fears tell you that you are.

It's going to do that until we give it something else to work with. That something else is not winning the argument with intrusive thoughts, it's a change in the way that you do life. You start behaving **as if** those fears are lies.

You will demonstrate that you're not buying it any more.

We understand that the unconscious mind operates on a "better the devil you know" preference. Expect therefore that your feelings will create resistance when you start telling your obsessive brain that it's working with bad logic. Our first job is to escape the circular, repetitive thinking that sustains the anxiety, and that is habitual at this point. We need to begin by taking a cold, hard, **clinical** look at the situation and we need to do this with a willingness to demand evidence before we give our belief-power to scary ideas.

Is Ignorance Bliss?

Conversely, one of the perils of owning a sharp, perceptive mind, is that we can have **too much** knowledge - the curse of the intellect. An anxious mind overthinks and an over-thinking mind can generate anxiety.

Do you have a well-thumbed medical encyclopaedia? Just be aware that it's dangerous territory for an anxious mind. You could convince yourself that you have twenty diseases that you didn't know existed. We all know this by now.

I had clients who bought themselves a blood pressure monitor. They were taking readings multiple times per day and frightening themselves silly with varying readings. Obsessively checking your blood pressure is going to cause stress because that constant "checking" sends a message back to the guard that there must be something wrong. Your guard will respond to that with fear, which sends your blood pressure skyrocketing, usually as you are checking it. The same can happen at the doctors. It has a name – "white coat syndrome." Can you see how tricky this is? We want to be informed about the things we need to know about but not so full of maybes that the merest heart flutter convinces us that we are ripe for a heart attack.

This covers the basics as far as anxious minds are concerned, but not every obsessive thought, misattribution, or avoidance behaviour is rooted in past experience, nor necessarily, generalized anxiety. Approximately 2-3% of people are affected by OCD – Obsessive-Compulsive Disorder.

Chapter Twelve - OCD Or Anxiety? What's The Difference?

Anxiety, in all of its forms, will cause a flood of negative thoughts, and when repetitive, they could be rightly called "obsessional". Often, these will take the form of anxiety about anxiety. An anxiety sufferer may spend significant time ruminating about feeling anxious and worrying that the feelings may never go away or that life will never be right again. Alongside this, anxiety sufferers can experience more specific worries and fears too, that become inflated in proportion to their overall anxiety levels.

When anxiety is severe, the anxiety sufferer can easily become fixated on a particular theme or concern, and fears can become overblown or irrational. To the untrained eye, this can look remarkably similar to OCD. Symptomatically, they are similar because both involve a mind filled with negative rumination and both create similar emotional disturbance in the limbic brain.

Severe anxiety can look like OCD but they are not quite the same thing.

I'll explain the difference.

One treatment for anxiety that can be particularly effective is releasing and healing past trauma. Historically, I have used regression-based (analytical) hypnotherapy as my tool of choice for doing this. There are other methods.

My client and I would follow the feelings, to travel within the mind's eye to the source of the specific anxiety my client wished to resolve, usually a past event. We'd work to meet and release the repressed emotion, change the belief system created by the event, and watch the specific anxiety resolve. How? We'd proven it untrue at the unconscious and conscious level. We'd see a significant anxiety reduction, and in time, that person would see their obsessional focus melt away. It would become irrelevant, since the original trigger had been recognised as incomplete, or fiction and the subconscious library had successfully updated accordingly. The mind lets it go. This is true belief change.

OCD is different.

My therapeutic mentors had told me that OCD would not collapse into solution with the use of regression therapy. My experience has confirmed that my teachers were correct. OCD will not yield to "healing" experiences in the same way that specific anxiety will. If a person was **only** "anxious", their obsessive worry would often collapse into solution once the root cause had been identified and resolved. If they had OCD, it wouldn't.

Now, here was a clue.

OCD often doesn't appear to have a single, fixed root.

OCD will simply **attach** itself to any concern that happens to be nearby. As explained earlier though, it will usually use a hierarchy of fears to do its worst. For example: -

1)   *Fear of learning that I'm a closet paedophile.*

2)   *Fear of becoming infected with HIV.*

3)   *Fear of being attacked.*

4)   *Fear of developing cancer.*

5)   *Etcetera...*

If you knock out number one, it will simply re-attach to number two and so on.

Some 2014 research from the John Hopkins University School Of Medicine identified a genetic marker in OCD sufferers that might be the culprit. OCD tends to run in families. Anecdotally, I can confirm this. From taking many client histories, I learned that there are often other sufferers in the family line. It seems that OCD is truly a **genetic/neurological** condition, while anxiety is, generally speaking, a

psychological condition. If that's wordy, let me add a couple of definitions: -

Neurological – The science of the nerves and the nervous system (including the brain), especially of the diseases affecting them.

Psychological – About the mind, especially as a function of awareness.

In other words, OCD may be a neurological problem with roots in brain configuration, and anxiety is more often a temporary mental/emotional disturbance that could affect anybody. Both have their roots in the body because they both involve chemical configurations that create symptoms but "neurological" implies an existing and **enduring** state within the brain/body's physical configuration.

Psychological/emotional difficulties tend to be more fluid, relating to **temporary** emotional arousal and imbalance in brain chemistry which can be reset and rebalanced with attention to stress levels and well-being factors.

This explains why an anxiety sufferer's intrusive thoughts will diminish or disappear when they resolve their overall generalised anxiety but the OCD sufferer's troubles will continue. The OCD sufferer's intrusive thoughts, while exacerbated by anxiety, are not, strictly speaking, **caused** solely by anxiety. There is a deeper problem.

A part of their brain is not functioning correctly.

The credit for the following understanding goes to Dr Jeffrey Schwartz. His book, "Brain Lock" is recommended reading for any OCD sufferer.

Dr Jeffrey Schwartz is a well-known name in OCD-related circles and is recognized as a treatment pioneer. He headed a team that carried out extensive OCD research at UCLA using PET scans. Being an OCD sufferer himself, his interest was more than academic. He set out with the notion that OCD could be greatly relieved with the correct use of "mindful attention" and went on to prove his case fairly conclusively. Not only did his patients experience a significant reduction in their obsessions and compulsions, but their brain scans showed that the previously overactive areas of their brains had cooled and normalised as a result of the treatment.

Let's take a look at the OCD brain and understand what Dr Schwartz has shared with us.

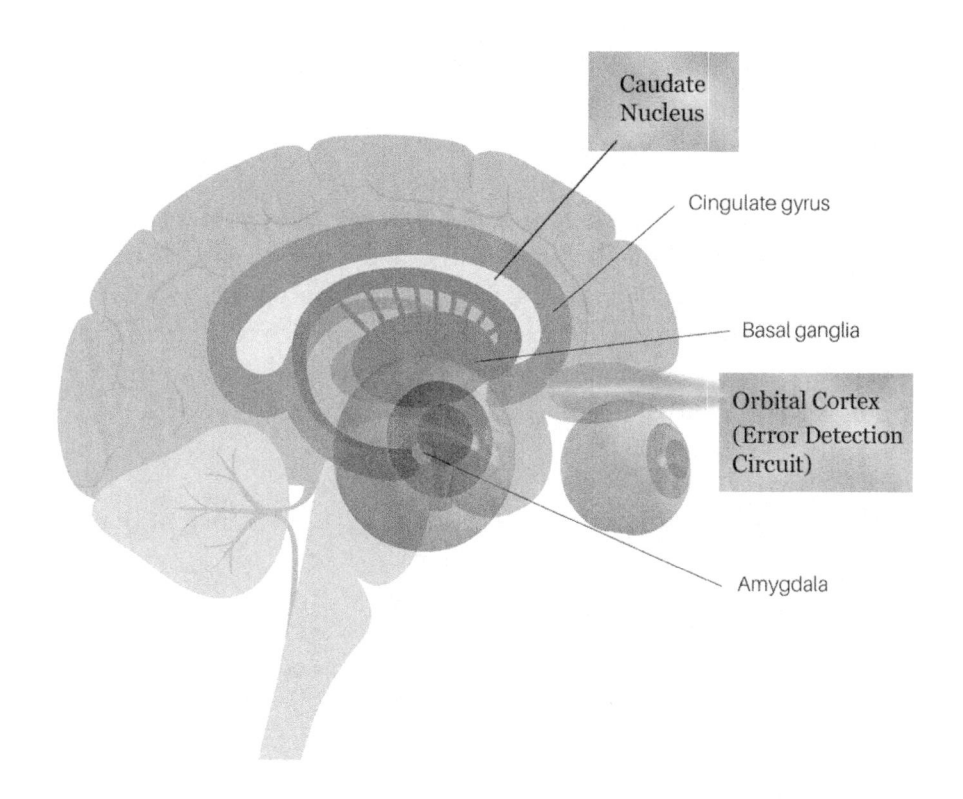

Caudate Nucleus

Cingulate gyrus

Basal ganglia

Orbital Cortex (Error Detection Circuit)

Amygdala

*   **The Orbital Cortex** – This frontal brain area is involved in the initial perception of danger. It detects whether something is "right" or "wrong".

*   **The Anterior (Front) Cingulate Gyrus** is activated by the detection of fear and causes our mood (feelings) to respond with fear sensations such as a churning stomach and anxiety.

* **The Caudate Nucleus** is contained within the basal ganglia area. It is the filtering station for the signals that come from the Orbital Cortex. It is involved with "automatic transmission", which means that this is the part of the brain that switches from one thought or behaviour to another.

It looks complicated but it is worth understanding.

Dr Schwartz tells us that in OCD sufferers, the Caudate Nucleus is not functioning correctly. The Caudate Nucleus is like a switch. It has an on position and an off position. "On" means an action is required. "Off" means everything is okay.

In a non-OCD person, when a fearful perception (something is wrong) comes in through the Orbital Cortex and is passed to the Caudate Nucleus for "filtering", it is usually dealt with appropriately (we act) and then the Caudate Nucleus, having responded, switches from "on" (action required) to "off" (action not required). Thus, the gate closes and the automatic transmission shifts gear back to "ordinary" awareness as the worry state recedes.

It is believed that in OCD sufferers, the gate gets stuck in the "on" position.

"On" becomes the default setting. The urge to act defensively continues. Hence, we have repetitious rounds of "compulsions"

The feeling that something is **still wrong** is detected by the Orbital Cortex which then begins the cycle again; each part of the brain continually arousing the other. The Cingulate Gyrus and the Amygdala are also aroused by this activity, supplying as they do, when negatively aroused, additional feelings of dread and panic.

How do we "get" OCD?

If you are an OCD sufferer, you may be asking "Why me?" The answer may be as simple as, "It's in your family line." We may less get OCD than always have had it. Sometimes, it appears in early life and it's well known for developing fully in the late teens to early twenties.

Just to complicate matters, many other conditions overlap with OCD. Autism, physical tics, learning difficulties, ADHD, and Tourette's syndrome are all examples of conditions that can include obsessive and compulsive components. These conditions require **different** treatments and general handling from OCD alone. Many have their roots in neurology and will not respond solely to psychological or behavioural interventions. Some are conditions that are technically incurable at present. These are specialist areas and beyond the scope of this book. The understanding presented here may be of use as an adjunctive therapy but please do speak to a healthcare practitioner for advice in these other areas. The approach you use to improve your situation will need to be tailored according to your needs.

Assuming that you do not fall within these categories, then the following applies to you.

While we know that there is an involuntary cognitive (perceptive/thinking style) distortion involved, OCD is usually classified as an **anxiety disorder** (as opposed to cognitive) since most sufferers (80%) will already be aware that their thoughts and compulsions are distortions.

These thoughts are not the result of incoherency in the personality. Rather, they are the result of faulty anxiety signals in the brain.

Cognitive therapies (those pertaining to the way that we perceive and process mental information) are ordinarily concerned with the recognition and correction of unreasonable and irrational thoughts – CBT being the best known of these. We have learned that the most effective way to bring this negative cycle of fear to a close is by **refusing to behave in accordance with the threats** that the thoughts and fears provide. Behavioural adjustments are required for recovery.

Successful treatment should also include some practical methods for reducing anxiety generally. When emotional arousal (anxiety) is reduced, it becomes much easier to correct erroneous thoughts and challenge anxiety-driven behaviours.

Interestingly, brain scans in OCD sufferers have also shown that the amygdala, which is an almond-sized part of the brain near the brain stem (and part of the "limbic system" you learned about earlier), becomes over-active when compulsive behaviour in OCD sufferers is denied expression. We see the same response in anxious people. That means that refusing to carry out a compulsion usually results in a feeling of discomfort, anxiety, or panic. This is understandable. When a brain is telling its owner to take evasive action and the brain's owner (i.e. you, the sufferer) does not do so, it ramps up the pressure to comply by increasing anxiety. It truly believes that you are in danger.

With OCD treatment, we tell the brain, "Your message of alarm is in error. All is safe."

Ultimately, you need to be able to separate yourself from the symptoms. This is central wisdom in OCD treatment because much of an OCD sufferer's distress will be created by the mistaken belief that the thoughts or compulsions are in some way indicative of a twisted core identity.

You are not your anxious thoughts or your OCD.

If we feel threatened by something, then the mind moves into a hypervigilant mode and invariably begins to "notice" thought patterns that relate to that threat in some way. Whilst acknowledging that OCD has a neurological factor, let's just have a look at how obsessive behaviours could begin in somebody who is anxious but OCD-free.

Here, we are using an older person as an example. It's not typical for OCD to develop in later life but I wanted to give an example of how a person with latent obsessional tendencies might find obsessional concerns dominating. While many will know about their OCD early on in life, we should be aware of the possibility of stress and anxiety triggering an obsessive problem at any age: -

Margaret lost her husband last year. She has become anxious and starts to worry excessively about security. She has sleepless nights, noticing every creak in the house, and imagining terrible things. In her waking hours, she feels an overwhelming need to eliminate any threats or dangers and feels compelled to repeatedly "check" that the windows are secure, that doors are locked, that plugs are unplugged, that hands are clean (germ-free), etc. She is checking windows at three a.m. She is in a loop but she can't seem to stop. She feels like she is losing control. Outside doesn't feel safe. That frightens her more.

Then, another thought crosses her mind. Having lost her husband, she begins to be troubled by the thought that she might not be able to cope if anything were to happen to her daughter.

What if? What if?

She begins to imagine scenarios where she might have some unwitting part in her daughter's demise, injury, or estrangement. Having such vivid thoughts and visions begins to make her wonder if she can even trust herself. Day by day the imaginings become more vivid and detailed. Her anxieties increase.

Notice how she has begun to confuse her anxieties with her sense of self. She is now worried that there is something potentially seriously wrong with her as a human being.

Central to the workings of hypnotherapy is the recognition that the imagination is an extremely powerful tool. It can be used positively to create foresight and innovation which can inspire us to positive action or it can be used negatively to create worry and anxiety which can paralyse us with fear.

The instinctive mind responds to what we **imagine**, as well as what is. The now hypervigilant instinctive mind, seeing these dreadful happenings (in the imagination) assumes that this lady must be in terrible danger and increases the level of vigilance and security. Now, the mind, believing the world to be a hostile environment filled with dangers seen and unseen, switches to red alert and begins to "notice" even more things that are a cause for concern – sometimes silly things, irrational things. In the presence of such great disorder, such a great loss of control, then perhaps there is some other way to create order.

Margaret now adjusts the ornaments on the mantelpiece to be millimetre perfect. It's never quite right. She does this repeatedly but it brings no real rest.

She soon finds that to enjoy any semblance of peace, she needs to know that her daughter is okay and starts to phone her repeatedly to make sure. Her daughter, Lizzie, seeing her mother's obvious distress agrees that it's okay for Mum to phone, but occasionally, despite her best intentions, her irritation leaks out on the fourth call of the day.

Margaret feels dreadful about worrying her daughter like this and becomes frustrated with herself... starts to hate herself a little. *Perhaps everyone would be better off without me?*

Then, depression and hopelessness set in. Now, she worries about her relationship with her daughter. The very thing she most feared, losing her daughter, is in danger of happening, it seems, and she feels that she may be the architect of it. She is also withdrawing from the world. More anxiety ensues. There are further attempts by the mind to "fix" it... and so on it goes. Exhausting reading, isn't it?!

Lizzie is not about to quit on her Mum but Margaret's brain has lost sight of this.

In this example, please note how the main contributing factor to the creation of this difficulty (outside of the life event) was an overload of negative rumination. Mum didn't know the rules about anxiety and this was the result. It's easily done. Keeping a close watch on unruly worries is an ongoing job. It's harder during times of upset.

When obsessive thoughts or compulsions are running riot, we know that it is difficult at first to have any measure of intellectual control. If the condition forces a withdrawal from everyday life, that will also reduce our sense of control generally and that might create a share of anxiety and/or depression. We want to reverse this trend of withdrawal, so we are going to work practically towards lowering negative emotional arousal levels and encouraging a fuller re-engagement in normal life as part of the strategy for recovery. Margaret must be allowed to grieve but long-term withdrawal will make things worse. Life engagement is required.

One piece of advice that is sometimes absent from OCD literature is the counsel to work on reducing anxiety levels generally either before or alongside the prescribed treatment for OCD. Put simply, reduced anxiety levels restore control to the frontal lobe, and the logical brain, and that's the brain we need to be using to tackle OCD efficiently.

Please excuse the plug here but anxiety reduction is a big subject. It's dealt with fully in my book *Anxiety Relief*.[8] I can't cover all of that here but we'll understand a few of the basics next.

---

[8] https://www.youcanfixyouranxiety.com/anxiety-relief

Chapter Thirteen – Anxiety Relief

In this chapter, we'll cover the basics of general anxiety relief.

When fear appears to produce positive results, from a survival perspective, then the brain adopts anxiety as the best strategy to make your life safe.

Here's the process: -

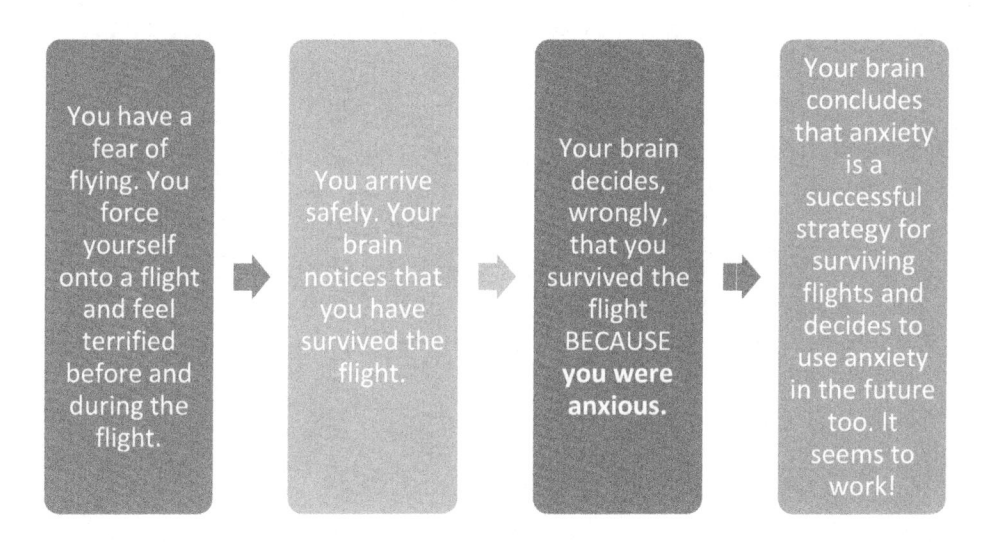

| You have a fear of flying. You force yourself onto a flight and feel terrified before and during the flight. | ➡ | You arrive safely. Your brain notices that you have survived the flight. | ➡ | Your brain decides, wrongly, that you survived the flight BECAUSE **you were anxious.** | ➡ | Your brain concludes that anxiety is a successful strategy for surviving flights and decides to use anxiety in the future too. It seems to work! |

A fear that considers that it is protecting you means that the Zealous Guard has no reason to not do fear. If we leave the conditions as they are, then "fear is good" continues to operate as the primary driver of thoughts, feelings, and behaviours. We do buy into this sometimes. We instinctively trust that the fear must be telling us the truth because all this intensity and urgency can't be without reason, can it? There **must** be *something* wrong?

An anxious brain can even become anxious about not being anxious.

Yes. You read that correctly. The logic is that if I'm not anxious, then I'm not being hypervigilant to threats and I am therefore unprotected.

This was something I learned as a hypnotherapist and it's worth sharing. The first part of a hypnotherapy treatment plan involves teaching relaxation skills. I sometimes had my client hooked up to a Galvanic Skin Response (GSR) monitor – a small digital gadget that allows you to measure stress responses via tiny electrical pads on two fingertips. It's part of the kit used in lie detectors. As I invited them to relax with calming language and focusing, I could watch the number on the monitor going steadily downwards, indicating that they were relaxing nicely. Then, suddenly, maybe five or ten minutes into the session, the number would shoot up and I would know that they just had a big emotional response even though the session appeared calm. I could see this on the monitor and I was able to ask what happened to alarm them.

More often than not, they'd say that they realised that they were super-relaxed and at that moment, they suddenly felt panicked. For them, deep relaxation didn't feel safe. It was unfamiliar and therefore full of uncertainty. The evolutionary imperative to always be on guard for dangers doesn't trust relaxation when relaxation itself is unfamiliar. Anxiety's logic is that if you are too relaxed, then you won't notice the ambush. The Zealous Guard orders a jolt of stress-inducing adrenaline. "Wake-up! There's danger. You're asleep on the job!"

This didn't mean that they couldn't **learn** to relax. From a therapeutic perspective, the fact that they got jumpy as the guard came down, shone a clear light on the problem.

The Zealous Guard needs to learn that relaxation is safe and pleasant.

Otherwise, it won't happen. And, if we're incapable of being relaxed, then there's only one other position available, which is "on guard", and obsessional focus is the result. Think of **learning** relaxation as preparing the ground. Your body and brain need to learn how to be comfortable with relaxation. That requires that you introduce this novel concept to your Zealous Guard. We think of it as a skill and a practice, that, when repeated, like most things, becomes easier and clearer. The body learns by doing.

Relaxation

Many former sceptics will now rave to anyone who will listen about the positive effects of meditation and mindfulness on obsessive thought management, mainly because to their surprise, when they did it, things got easier.

Relaxation doesn't only help us in the moment that we do it. It de-arouses the whole emotional system and has a lasting positive effect on our overall well-being. It's not necessarily that relaxation zaps negative intrusive thoughts. It's more the case that relaxation calms **everything** down. A less-aroused brain is a less obsessive one with a greater sense of control.

We've focused, so far, on what upsets the Zealous Guard. What I haven't mentioned yet is that even the Zealous Guard can be lulled into comfort.

Relaxation is known to activate the parasympathetic nervous system. That's the body's *rest and digest* state. This slows the body's processes down and that includes the brain. The Guard takes a metaphorical nap during these times. In a relaxed state, the brain slows down and so do your thoughts and anxiety levels, generally speaking. There are exceptions.

There's also potentially a spiritual approach to be explored here. Meditation, while certainly not exclusive to Buddhism, does lead us towards thinking about that discipline. Interestingly, Buddhism has a lot to say about restless minds.

Buddha is famously quoted as saying: -

"Your suffering is caused by your clinging and your aversion."

There is a lot to unpack in that short statement. The distillation of it is that life includes difficult experiences to tolerate but there is peace to be found in working on reducing our disgust at what we don't like and also in learning to be less afraid of losing the things that we love. The position is that reality exists on its own terms and we might as well work on getting okay with that, including the bits that we don't like.

That will lead us to philosophical perspectives about the nature of duality and our impermanent experience here. Buddhism, which is not purely a religion but a set of tools for accepting reality on its own terms, considers this our great work in life. It's worth noting that we are much better at acceptance when we are calm. That's something that meditation aims to facilitate.

Acceptance of pain is not a welcome message because our instincts are to struggle against the unpleasant. It has been said that pain is inevitable but suffering is optional. If we leave it to chance, we are likely to continuously repeat the loop of disturbance and clinging, sometimes leading unsatisfying lives as a result.

The promise is that by deliberately developing acceptance of life's inherent heartbreaks, we can become less repulsed by pain, death, and loss. Less repulsion equals less fear and wasted worry energy, and that allows us to be more in the moment, fully appreciating the here and now. This becomes a philosophical approach to life.

Ironically, being fully alive means fully accepting that tomorrow, we may not be.

We have accepted that the moment will not last forever, and gratitude for now, as opposed to fear for the future, then follows. The past is gone, the future is not guaranteed. Now is the best place for our minds to be and meditation is the perfect tool for being right here, right now. When the mind focuses only on the breath, the only thing that matters is the next breath. We are no longer in the past or the future.

As the mind slows down, stillness can develop, and in the stillness, we can become aware of an okay-ness beyond our feelings. We learn that we are not solely our feelings. Nor our thoughts. We have existence and awareness beyond them, a calm and quiet space that we can visit. To the uninitiated, this sounds like woo-woo but once experienced, it is perfectly self-evident. The main hurdle is that you have to make time and space to practice it.

How's Life?

Next up, we all have an idea of how we would like life to be. Anyone who's lived a while on the planet will know that when you arrive at your destination, you don't just put your feet up. New goals emerge. Our pleasure is not solely in the completion of our goals but in the journey too. We feel better when we are being constructive and heading somewhere hopeful.

Solution Focused Brief Therapy (SFBT) is a therapy that focuses on creating practical, real-world solutions to current difficulties. It flips the idea that by fixing our minds, we will fix our lives. Instead, this is the principle that a healthy life will create a healthy mind. There are, potentially large changes to make but SFBT begins with small things.

Is it possible to do a couple of extra walks? Could you eat better quality food? Drink less alcohol? Anything that might make you feel generally healthier and can be implemented without undue stress and strain is a good place to begin. It's unlikely that any single change will vanquish anxiety alone but doing **something** is your statement to yourself that you mean business. The real value comes when all of those small tweaks add up to a positive change in the landscape of your life generally. Yesterday, it was four walls. Today, you're in the community. That's significant.

Don't try to take on the world. Just one little improvement at a time is great. If you have the energy, organise an area in your home, chuck out your junk (if that's not an obsessive area for you), get up to date with paperwork, and fix that shelf or paint that wall. Make an **extra** effort. Schedule your intentions. Follow them through. Go beyond the usual and you will know satisfaction. Lace up your trainers and step outside. When we don't do the things that we know in our hearts are healthy for us, apathy weighs on our minds.

It's about setting up the landscape of your life so that you have a sense that your world is opening up, not closing down.

This takes time and patience but when you combine it with the other improvements possible here, then results should follow.

One of the best ways to stop feeling awful about life, whatever the cause, is to go and help others. Volunteering is the obvious route. If you have health and resources that allow it, do consider it. The benefits for you can be vast, and you're relieving suffering. That's our best defence against a hostile world. Make it better. Be the change.

MENTAL HYGIENE

We can start pulling back from habitual negativity by choosing to notice how and when we might inadvertently collude with intrusive thoughts that are mean, limiting, irrational, disturbing, or anxious. It's not easy, especially if you are in the dumps already. It requires challenging your own mind's inane chatter when it's being unhelpful.

CBT provides a system to identify these thoughts, recognise that they are distorted or erroneous, and adjust our perspectives, reducing anxiety. It also formalises our intention to start the work of noticing and adjusting those distorted and alarming perceptions that turbo-charge anxiety levels. CBT's aims include becoming aware of moments when we dwell unnecessarily on the negative or see the situation through a purely negative lens.

We ask if there is a more positive way of viewing a situation. Negative perspectives create negative feelings. If your mind tells you that something is the end of the world, look for a reason to dispute that thought. You've been through worse, probably. Plus, feelings are transient. They are always on the move and much as it is tough in the moment to self-challenge, perspective is everything. Make it a personal challenge to see if you can flip a situation from a negative to a positive. What has been learned? How might this unfortunate experience save you a ton of trouble somewhere down the line? Who else benefits from your experience? A challenging situation is difficult by definition. Many bring gifts too. Look for them.

In CBT, this desire to get to the heart of an issue is known as Socratic Questioning. Socrates, the famous Greek philosopher was known for his irritating lines of enquiry: -

"Yes, but WHY do you think that? Do you have any evidence that it is so?"

He was considered a "gadfly", a colloquialism for people who questioned the status quo. Like a biting fly, the gadfly hovers around, destroying the peace and threatening the culture's reassuring but dysfunctional structures. He had to go. He argued that his anarchic presence was an asset to the Athenian society but they killed him anyway when he refused to atone for his position.

Before he got into trouble with the law though, he was a great philosopher, and the following examples of Socratic Questioning are drawn from the wisdom he left us.

1) When I'm not feeling this way, do I think differently? How?
2) What would a more helpful thought look like?
3) What evidence do I have to support this thought, feeling, or belief?
4) Am I blaming myself for something that is outside of my control?
5) If my friend was thinking this way and asked for my advice, what would I say to them?
6) What evidence do I have that contradicts this thought?
7) How likely is the worst-case scenario? Am I feeling like it's inevitable? Is it?
8) If the worst happened, how would I resolve it - eventually?
9) Are there any positives in this situation that I am not seeing?
10) Are there any strengths or lessons that I can bring from past difficult experiences that can help me today? How did I get through it?

It's logic. It challenges faulty emotional processing and guides us toward greater objectivity.

Changing Your Thoughts

The Zealous Guard is a livewire to our visceral gut responses – instant, automatic feelings. These instinctive responses require no thoughts at all to activate. The recognition of a threat (real or imagined) in our environment is all the guard needs to spring into defensive action.

Beyond this **automatic** anxiety, however, there is the possibility of generating endless anxiety through the process of rumination, that is, re-visiting and **buying into** stress-provoking patterns of thoughts and behaviours.

Remember, we have already established that the presence of intrusive negative thoughts is an **automatic** phenomenon. You didn't ask for these thoughts. CBT recognises that. What you do have control over though is whether or not you ultimately regard these thoughts as true and/or accurate. Inadvertently, humans can nurse negativity.

CBT is a process designed to help us to choose more helpful thoughts and behaviours.

It leverages logic and rational perspectives to challenge the brain's negative self-talk. It's not a philosophical therapy. It is all about practical thinking skills applied in the moment at the point of need.

As well as working on negative thoughts, CBT recognises that **behaviours** also feed back into the mind and emotions. The Zealous Guard sees what we do in each moment and those behaviours either instil a sense of calm and control or demonstrate doubt and powerlessness, both of which are candidates to increase anxiety and misery.

There is something in the old maxim, "We have to fake it to make it." Confidence, the slippery thing that it is, is in the mind. It's about how we hold ourselves and how we see ourselves. To a degree, that's a choice. It's also something that can be modelled. Our Zealous Guard watches this carefully. Sometimes, we have to put on a show for the Zealous Guard and step onto the stage despite our sweaty palms and thumping heartbeat - you know, find the lion within.

Courage isn't only something you have. It's also something you do.

In this book, we are drawing from a small selection of CBT tools, albeit slightly tweaked, but CBT itself is good medicine for a wide range of psychological difficulties. You can apply it to almost any situation, usually on the spot. It's easily learned with or without a therapist. It's widely available online for free and while it should not be considered a cure-all, it's certainly a handy piece of stress-busting knowledge for all humans that should have been taught to us all on day one. For instance, did you know that words like have to, must, should, and ought to can eat away at your peace? CBT looks at things like that. It's worth understanding why.

We know that when hopelessness sets in, we can fail to recognise that the conditions that made us captive in the first instance are no longer as they were. This is called **learned helplessness**. Though our chains are now severed, like the characters in Plato's cave, we remain transfixed by the shadows on the wall and stay put.

Life is in constant flux and what wasn't possible then may be easier now.

Tolerance

As is duly covered shortly in this book, our suffering increases in proportion to our inability to tolerate discomfort.

Suffering is pain resisted.

In CBT, this is addressed under the heading of "increasing frustration tolerance" which is as it sounds. Remember how the Zealous Guard looks to you for confirmation of the threat level? If you are resisting the unpleasantness of your feelings and thoughts with any sense of alarm, that translates as bad news to the brain's security systems, and anxiety increases. Studies confirm that people's subjective experience of pain increases as stress levels escalate.

Relaxed people tolerate pain better.

The antidote to tension in the presence of pain is having psychological tools that allow you to be in the presence of the alarming material without setting off the brain's sirens and lights, and not losing your nerve.

We do this by using meditative compassionate attention.

We deliberately bring kindness to the parts of ourselves who experience fear.

This is quite different from resistance. It is acceptance. Shortly, I'll teach you how to use it.

Mindfulness/Meditation/Hypnotherapy

Meditation

Here's my favourite explanation of how meditation helps the anxious mind.

Imagine a glass of clear plain water. This is the mind. Take a scoop of earth and stir it into the water. You now have muddy water. How will the water clear again? We must let it settle. Gravity will clear the water but only if we do not further agitate the glass.

Meditation provides the best environment for the mud to clear. When there is no agitation, the water is still and the view is clear. It's a pleasant state that feels uniquely reassuring. A simplicity. Just being. It's time out that leaves a pleasant afterglow.

This muddy water model is a fitting metaphor for anxiety too. The energy that anxiety episodes release into the human nervous system takes time to settle down. Days, sometimes longer. When the Zealous Guard is on red alert, our job is to be calm and still. We must aim to agitate the inflamed nerves as little as possible. Meditation helps with that.

Mindfulness

"Be here now." is the rallying cry of mindfulness.

Most of us live distracted lives. Mindfulness is about making time and focus to be fully present in the here and now. It has roots in Buddhist meditation and aims to calm and focus the mind, reduce the mental chatter, and notice one's thoughts and feelings without attachment, judgment, or overreaction. That sounds like a big ask but that's why mindfulness is popular. With a little practice, these changes tend to occur easily in a meditative state.

With this exercise, you intend to focus solely on your breath. The idea is to create a single point of focus. The breath acts as an ever-present anchor for the mind. The only request is that your attention remains focused on the sensation of breathing.

We are invited to notice the feeling of the air as it fills our lungs, and as it leaves. We can become aware of the exact transition moment that inhale becomes exhale and vice versa. We can notice how the air feels cooler on the nostrils on the inhale and warmer on the exhale. We can feel gratitude for the air that feeds our bodies. We can imagine breathing in calm and breathing out stress. These are ways to remain focused on the breath and although they are a form of mental activity, they're acceptable as a means to keep the focus. They are not the end goal, just a stepping stone, and a pleasant one at that. The busy mind (that's your thinking mind, by the way) will find it an acceptable form of distraction. Think of it as giving the Zealous Guard a job to keep them quiet for a while.

Except that, while you're developing a quieter atmosphere for yourself, things are happening in the mind and body that don't happen during distraction and action. For starters, the parasympathetic nervous system (PNS) becomes dominant. This is the "rest and digest" state; a state of calm. Your Zealous Guard will take a metaphorical nap for a while, having been lulled into serenity by the hypnotic focus on breathing. Thoughts slow down. A quiet arrives.

In meditation, the breath is always there. It's regular. It's observable. It's the obvious focal point. It also slows naturally as we relax, which is good feedback too. We know we're doing something right when the breath slows down and everything feels quieter.

Switching to a place of peace takes a bit of practice. What almost all busy minds do, when sitting, doing nothing, as beginners, is they get busy. Sometimes, they do the cha-cha. Most of us are mentally busy with work and vocation and many of us are distracted by screens or audio when we're not. Time on our hands, our minds are not sure how to handle. At first, it feels alien. That's all the more reason to do it. We remember Dr Sukhraj Dhillon's quote from *The Art Of Stress-Free Living*: -

"You should sit in meditation for twenty minutes every day - unless you're too busy; then you should sit for an hour."

Sitting. Doing nothing. It doesn't make a great deal of sense to the restless and busy mind. Why bother? It's boring. Rest assured, the urge to think about the ironing, the shopping, or what you're having for dinner is normal. As is the urge to suddenly attend to a task, too. *Anything to distract from this boring sitting.* Thinking that you're doing it wrong is also normal. These are just a few of the ways that the mind initially attempts to avoid being inactive with itself.

If you have intrusive thoughts, they may well jostle for your attention as you attempt to be still and silent. This is the brain doing familiarity. It wants to hold onto busy. It knows busy. Busy is safe. This relaxation business... not so much. Remember the law of reversed effort. If you try too hard to relax, you introduce stress into the situation, and that's not relaxation.

My best meditational experiences happen when I'm able to get out of my way; to stop trying for anything. I focus on learning to be with what is, good and bad, to notice what arises and then I aim to let it go, witnessing without judgment. These are practices that flex the muscles in the emotional mind, creating resilience. Meditation is training the mind to be steady in the presence of unwanted phenomena and to respond calmly to **whatever** is being experienced. This is called equanimity – an equally composed response to all that happens. Thus, we are neither unduly disgusted by the darkness in life nor deliriously excited by successes.

Meditation is something we do when we don't do anything and nothing can be something worth doing.

You focus on the breath and let the body and mind do the rest. Notice what unfolds. Usually, at some point, maybe five minutes in, more for some, there's a recognition that breathing has deepened and slowed. Thoughts are fewer and gentler. Emotions are less intense.

Hopefully, you'll find it a pleasant state to be in and become aware of the benefits, with practice. We'll be learning basic meditation later.

Hypnotherapy

With hypnotherapy, it's the hypnotherapist's voice that is used as the single point of focus, instead of the breath. As Thai massage is to Yoga, so hypnosis is to meditation. You could call it lazy meditation because it's guided, just as a Thai massage does the stretching for you. It also has the advantage of using specific language that is tried and tested for soothing and directing people into deep relaxation. If you're curious now, well that's great because I'm including a hypnotherapy recording that I made especially for this book. Please do check it out. It can be used as part of the anxiety-busting plan. Here's the link.

https://www.youcanfixyouranxiety.com/calming-thoughts

This recording is deliberately general so that it can be applied to many different obsessive situations. It allows your mind to fill in the blanks. I will repeat the link at the end of the book. You can use it right away if you wish but when you've finished the book, you'll understand all of the references in the recording. To be clear, you can use it repeatedly, as needed or desired. You can stream or download from the linked page. Enjoy!

CONTROL

It's stressful to you when you try to control the uncontrollable.

It's also stressful to you when you fail to exert control in the areas that are important to you.

It helps to be clear about what can be controlled and what cannot. Let's examine this: -

What you can control:

1. Your thoughts: You can choose and direct your thoughts. This includes what you focus on and how you choose to interpret the meaning of the thoughts themselves or any given event.

2. Your actions: It's your decision what you ultimately do. Never forget that there are many ways to change a life. You can take action any time you wish.

3. Your attitude: You control the direction of your attitude. You are free to choose how you wish to approach and perceive different circumstances.

4. *Your beliefs and values:* As discussed, beliefs don't change easily but they will ultimately be shaped according to our values. Your values are your choices.

5. *Your effort and commitment:* You can commit to goals, undertake projects, work on your relationships, and set your compass for personal growth. That is within your control. It might require investment and learning.

6. *Your self-care:* Your physical, mental, and emotional well-being is vital to your success in life. You can do this. Or not. Self-care could very well include seeking therapy. The choice is within your control.

7. *Your boundaries:* Maintaining healthy boundaries in your relationships, work, and personal life is also a form of self-care.

8. *Your learning:* If you don't know how to get things done, there are no excuses these days. There are books, videos, podcasts, and courses for everything. You're reading one now. Gold star!

What you can't control:

1. *Other people's thoughts and actions:* We cannot control how other people think or behave. We may have influence. Often, their drama encroaches on our world.

2. *External circumstances:* The weather. Global events. Leaders. Remember, the world's needs outweigh your personal ability to supply. Nobody can be all things to all people.

3. *The past:* We can neither change nor control the past. Dwelling on it stirs up unnecessary negative emotion. Longing for it is no better.

4. *Other people's opinions and judgments:* Honestly, someone else's life may have been so completely different from our own that it is pure folly to suppose that they might see everything, or even anything, as we do.

5. *Natural processes and outcomes:* Ageing. The passage of time. Illness. Death. All are currently beyond human control.

6. Other people's emotions: We can maybe influence their experience but their emotions may be beyond their control, never mind ours!

7. Random events: Humans can't control volcanoes, hurricanes, fires, floods, pandemics and accidents. To name but a few.

Unfortunately, we often worry about what we cannot control. That is natural. It's not skilful. Learning to refuse to fret over what cannot be controlled is a skill. It needs practice. If you are fretting about something that is **outside of your control**, start reminding yourself how unreasonable it is to blame yourself, every time the thought appears. You wouldn't let someone else tell you to do something that can't be done. You wouldn't speak to a loved one in that way either, so don't stand for it from your thoughts. Those attacks are below the belt. You deserve to be treated as well as any friend. Demand that.

Food, Drink, Drugs, & Exercise

The slip into poor health is often a slow and subtle one. So slow that as the years pass by, we may not notice a decline. *A new ache. No problem. Oh, there's another one. Well, that's just life.* The thing is, it isn't always just life or ageing. Sometimes, we are operating below our physical and mental potential, at whatever age, because of what we consume and how sedentary we are. A healthy body will support a healthy mind, and both together will support a good life. It's not only about avoiding illness and death either, it's about the quality of our life experience while we are having it. A poorly fuelled engine gives a bumpy ride, limiting possibilities.

Diet requires attention. Please don't overlook this. Nutrition will support your recovery powerfully. **Good food is medicine.** Poor food can be poison, literally, including for the brain. Please do learn the basics about nutrition – protein, fibre, sugars, fats, simple and complex carbohydrates, and your body. Don't let the fast-food industry feed you. Your health is not what's most on their minds. It's a life and death matter, eventually. The healthiest balanced diet on the planet is the Mediterranean diet. I recommend beginning there.

Drugs, including medications, also require processing inside the body. Approximately sixty per cent of people in Western society use alcohol, so it deserves a mention here. When you're unwell generally, it should be remembered that alcohol is toxic to the body and the brain. The latest research is now suggesting that no amount of alcohol is beneficial to health. Adding toxicity to stress will cause more stress. The body and the mind are not separate. When the body is under toxic stress, we will find ourselves less emotionally and mentally resilient as a result, leading to unnecessary feelings of being overwhelmed. Problems are not resolved by alcohol use. They are still there the next day.

Repeated hangovers or even regular low-level alcohol use can have a significant negative impact on overall well-being levels, with symptoms similar to depression because alcohol is a depressant. It's not only the next day's hangover that affects us. Alcohol use disrupts many delicately calibrated internal systems, including the endocrine (hormonal) system that regulates the entire body, and, importantly, our moods. Even once a week drinking can scupper last week's recovery before it's complete meaning that we never reach peak health or well-being but lose a little bit of steam with every physical insult that's not repaired. It's easy to mistake this malaise for general life gloominess but a period of healthy living might open our eyes to new health and happiness possibilities.

While alcohol use isn't problematic for everybody, be aware that cutting down or stopping might create positive conditions that you weren't aware were available to you. I know it's a big job to get started but don't underestimate the transformative power of a healthy diet and cleaner living. It can provide a new lease on life, and for many, does. Try a month if you feel you can commit to it. You can assess then whether the benefits you feel make it worth continuing or not.

Coffee and caffeine. "Seriously? You want my coffee now?!"

Sort of. Maybe. Sorry. Just for a while...

If you're a big caffeine user, you should be aware that caffeine can increase anxiety significantly and that it is much more likely to do so when you are anxious. It's a stimulant. If you're anxious, you need calming, not stimulating. Therefore, regular coffee users may discount the effect that their current caffeine use is having on their anxiety levels because it's never caused anxiety before. That'll be because you weren't anxious then. Be aware that drugs do different things to people according to their baseline state. What was great yesterday can be awful today.

If you are a big caffeine user with high anxiety, make it a priority to reduce your caffeine use to determine whether it is contributing to your current discomfort. If you have five brewed coffees a day, replace one or two with decaf. A week or two on, replace one more with decaf. Note if there's any difference in your anxiety levels and stick with what helps. Remember that drinking caffeine later in the day can prevent easy sleep well over six hours later, and sleep is an anti-anxiety medicine, so late caffeine intake is best avoided. Instant coffee averages around 70mg of caffeine per cup, roughly the same amount as a cup of tea. Brewed coffee is four times that strength at 250—300mg of caffeine per cup, so pay particular attention to the brewed coffees. Caffeinated energy soft drinks and some cola drinks as well as some medicines also contain high levels of caffeine so check the ingredients and know what you're consuming.

Exercise is now formally recognised as one of the best natural antidepressant activities available. Even a short walk every day can improve things here. Exercise releases feel-good chemicals from the body's internal pharmacy. If you're out and about in the world each day, make choices that work your body appropriately. Assuming you're fit, don't take the elevator, use the stairs. Walk the last mile to work. Need something at the shops? Don't take the car. Walk instead. Waiting for the water on the stove to boil? Do twenty push-ups against a wall. Later that day, do twenty more. With these small changes, you can fill a reasonable exercise quota that will keep things moving without it being a huge deal.

Chapter Fourteen – Stiff Upper Lips

There may still be a place for a bit of British stiff upper lip.

If we treat ourselves as if we are terribly fragile, then we never really toughen up for difficult or shocking experiences. Resilience is a good thing and it's cultivated by throwing oneself into the world, with all the knocks and bruises that brings.

We need difficulty to grind against. It's not always pleasant but it keeps our mettle strong and our edges sharp. If we tell ourselves that general unpleasantness is to be avoided at all times, we'll create a mindset that lacks resilience, fears change, has weak boundaries, takes no risks, and achieves less.

Confronting and embracing difficulty is part of learning to be a resilient human being in a rough and tumble world. It's also how we build things. Need encourages solution-building. Without work and challenge, nothing happens, personally or collectively. The same principles apply to mental patterns too. Like muscles, they grow stronger when we use them, and they fade when we don't.

Welcoming challenges, moving beyond the comfort zone, and embracing the inevitable hardship in our lives are part of what leads ultimately to satisfaction and well-being. It's not that life is always great. It's that we aim to be acceptant of what hurts while maximising what brings fulfilment, courageously. The courage part usually creates something of value in the world.

We must therefore guard against giving every negative experience or feeling a label as an illness, a disorder, or an injustice. Sometimes, life is unpleasant, and it's not always fair. Life also appears to be indifferent to our misfortunes. There is nothing to rail against and nobody to blame. In the end, if we allow frustration to run rampant, we end up hurting only ourselves.

If we call all of life's pains illnesses, we send ourselves the message that something is always wrong.

Let's not assume though that this is a good reason to suggest that everybody who is experiencing overwhelm is being an entitled wimp. Most people struggle on silently, bearing great strain without complaint. Robin Williams said it best, "People don't fake depression. People fake being well." That's true for most people.

This chapter is a clarification on the matter. Call it a commentary if you wish. It needs addressing though because how you feel about these matters will dictate how much empathy you're able or willing to apply back to yourself.

Many people are carrying trauma but don't recognise that they are. Many of us are so keen to **not identify as victims** that we will not entertain the notion that we may be experiencing the effects of trauma. We struggle on and tell ourselves that this is just how life is, never daring to hope that we could be free from the constant dread in our guts. It's admirable in spirit but unnecessary. Things can be better.

It's a common misconception that trauma only affects people who have been in warzones, kidnappings, terrorist attacks, assaults, or accidents. It's not as simple as that. Trauma is subjective. What you laugh off may haunt another for a lifetime, and the events that might appear to be the most traumatic on paper may be the ones that affect you the least. A car crash may be frightening or damaging but the real trauma in your life may have been the constant disapproval you received from parents, peers, or an authority figure. Or, it could be your current unbearable job circumstances. I recently heard somebody suggest that trauma may be caused not only by what we received in life but also by what we didn't receive. It's a recorded fact that neglected children don't develop well. Quantifying trauma and its causes are not exact sciences and few things are more intensely subjective.

In recent years, we have seen a dramatic improvement in the awareness of post-traumatic stress disorder (PTSD) as a real and involuntary mental health condition. It is not a weakness. It is the brain's natural response to threat, shock, loss, and horror.

Unprecedented numbers of war veterans have come forward in recent years to tell of their enduring mental torture long after they left the battlefields. The US government estimates[9] that about 30% of personnel serving in the Vietnam War have suffered from post-traumatic stress disorder. We are currently seeing levels of 11 to 20% of veterans from the Iraq and Afghanistan wars suffering from PTSD in any given year. We should remember that these figures are applied to trained military personnel; people who placed themselves in the line of danger and received training designed to toughen them up for such events. These figures are living proof that a high proportion of human beings are susceptible to trauma, even when they have an inner certainty that they are ready to face the worst. Put simply, we have limits to what we can cope with. Some experiences are not easily processed.

Trauma is a strange phenomenon. It can creep up on us many years after the initial sensitising event. We often rationalise our traumas away. A terrible event happens. We do whatever we need to do to get through it. We are in emergency mode while it is happening. We find that we have access to an unusual degree of inner strength. If the situation is public, people may rally around us with support. We cope admirably. We think we are fine. In most visible ways, we **are** fine.

Years pass by and life goes on. The support and comradery for our tough times have long since passed. Then, one day, we notice that we've been avoiding something. We're stressed but we don't know why. We over-react. We lack patience. Life has lost its shine and fear or regret has taken up residence within us. We start to realise that something feels broken. When our minds remember those darker days from our past, we feel dread and repulsion. This could be simply a touch of the blues but equally, these could also be the subtler faces of trauma.

Yes, trauma might involve extreme anxiety, de-personalization, night terrors, triggers, and flashbacks, but that's the cliché. Sometimes, trauma eats away at us slowly as it drips back into our consciousness, obscuring our light over a longer time. Like water running over rocks, it can slowly cut a groove in us, even with a stiff upper lip.

Sometimes though, it's something else entirely...

---

[9] https://www.ptsd.va.gov/understand/common/common_veterans.asp

Chapter Fifteen – Do We Do It To Ourselves?

I'm usually the first person to point out that people with mental or emotional health difficulties need and deserve empathy. Regardless of the cause of the problem, feeling mentally unwell is one of the most challenging difficulties that a living being can face. It's equal to physical pain.

We should remember that even our pets can suffer from anxieties, depression, obsessions, phobias, and fears. That's hardly down to mismanagement of life circumstances on their part. So, let's not be too quick to assume that mental health problems in humans are always due to personal mismanagement. We all have histories and much of what has happened to us, particularly in early life, was beyond our control. Much of that set the scene for future difficulties. Some things will still feel out of control. Some of us didn't get what we needed to become immediately rounded and healthy-minded individuals. We have to collect those skills while we are in the world.

Nobody chooses to have a mental health problem. Mostly, we don't even know what one looks like until we recognise that life isn't what it ought to be, and then, somebody, usually a doctor, explains that we have one and gives it a name. People who have never had mental health difficulties usually find the whole subject baffling. Once we have become aware that we are suffering from a mental health disorder, we have two choices. We can accept that as our lot or we can figure out how we got here and how to make things better for ourselves.

The real reason for this preamble though is to get to this point.

Sometimes, we cause ourselves unnecessary suffering.

The last thing I want is for anyone to feel like they are getting a lecture from me on this so I'm going to tell you about some of the ways that I can cause my own suffering. I'm much better with this stuff these days, mainly because I'm older and more experienced. I'd be lying if I said I was completely free of it though. It comes with having a brain, and a past, and it needs to be tackled when it arises.

The first of these disturbances relates to money; a common concern. It still is. A good chunk of my life has been lived not more than a couple of months away from being broke. Early life was no frills. I'm sure most readers are or have been in the same position. Understandably then, I spent a lot of time feeling nervous about where the next bit of money was coming from. Being self-employed for many years has only increased that uncertainty.

However, when I finally had an emergency fund, the feeling that financial trouble was just one small emergency away didn't remove itself in line with the reality of the situation; the feeling of danger persisted. That's years of programming doing what we'd expect it to do, that is, run the poverty programme. As the years have gone by, I've had to repeatedly adjust my thinking to remind myself that the world will not come apart if I don't meet my own arbitrary financial goals. I don't have future security but I have the immediate concerns covered. The feelings still come though.

The key point here is that I have been known to **willingly** entertain these anxious thoughts and feelings about imminent destitution even though there was no immediate rational reason to do so. And then feel wound up and anxious. I know this is the case because I **consciously** chose to believe that I **had to** make that amount of money, even while knowing at some level that it was an anxiety-driven **preference** and not an immediate pressing **need.**

The feelings of scarcity are a product of my unconscious mind. The decision to think and behave as if those feelings are accurate is a product of my conscious mind.

I agreed with the anxiety.

Now, when destitution fears arise in me, I ignore them by reminding myself that they are anxious projections, not accurate perspectives on current reality. I remind myself that if the worst occurred, I would start again. It happens. People survive it. I don't try to get rid of the feelings. I just keep adjusting my perspective consciously. I have been known to spend money that I shouldn't, just to put two fingers up to my poverty programme. Defiance. I do take my own medicine.

Let's see a different example.

Another insistent visitor for me is also rooted in my personal history. If you know my story, you'll know that I experienced severe anxiety and depression in my early twenties. A bungled spiritual search turned into an anxiety nightmare. Depression followed.

Despite only ever being well-intentioned, the outcome of my youthful misadventures was a catastrophic and sustained period of ill health. This later led to a constant feeling that whenever my health failed in any way, it was **my fault**. The immediate default to self-blame was automatic. While that intense lifestyle had ended many years previously, the feelings of personal culpability for all and any health problems I might experience subsequently, persisted, regardless of the change in circumstances.

If I contracted a common cold, then it was my fault. If a muscle pulled, it was my fault. If I had a mouth ulcer, it was my fault. If I didn't sleep well, it was my fault. If I was anxious or low, it was because of something I had done or hadn't done.

In this example: -

The feelings of self-abuse are a product of my unconscious mind. The decision to behave as if those feelings are accurate is a product of my conscious mind.

Again, I agreed with the feelings. I'm close to one hundred per cent better with this now.

And, finally, the old faithful - "I may have upset somebody" theme.

The feelings of fear of rejection are a product of my unconscious mind (past rejections). The decision to behave as if those feelings are accurate today is a product of my conscious mind.

The first part, I have little immediate control over. The second part, I do.

The feelings and thoughts of rejection or injury are involuntary, unwanted, and intrusive. I'd prefer to feel loved and confident. From that perspective, they are part of a neurosis, a fear, a phobia, a trauma, and a difficult history. Some patterns of thought have been with us from the earliest days of our lives. Not all fears and traumas are caused by abuse or accident either. Some are just terrible misunderstandings of perspective – feeling more abandoned or threatened than we were, for example, often because we didn't have enough information to understand what was going on at the time.

These symptoms are generated **automatically** by the unconscious protective mechanisms of the brain, as explained earlier. At this level, we are not doing it to ourselves. Our brains are simply doing what brains do, reminding us of past instances of damage, and we are on the receiving end of those powerful instinctive signals.

We are causing our suffering, however, when we **collude** with these false destructive narratives and apply them back to ourselves as ongoing truths. My financial example above is an instance of such a mistake. We should note that these narratives are appealing to the obsessive brain. They're familiar. Homely, even.

Have you ever seen somebody making life unnecessarily difficult for themselves and wondered why the heck they're doing that? That's likely to be this principle in action. What you are seeing there is a person whose thoughts require them to go to sometimes extraordinary lengths to ensure that the said belief system is not challenged or that their safety behaviours are actioned.

Here are some examples of self-visited harms that might be relevant to people with **low-level** anxiety: -

One

Intrusive thought/feeling: *I can't afford to...*

Behaviour: Extreme and irrational thrift. Willingly enduring unnecessary hardships such as wearing holey shoes, refusing to buy a bottle of water when thirsty, refusing essential repairs, or making do with equipment that no longer functions properly when the funds are available to rectify that.

Two

Intrusive thought/feeling: *What if I get lost?*

Behaviour: Avoiding - new places, travelling, job interviews, party invitations, meetings, explorations etc.

Three

Intrusive thought/feeling: *I'm not clever enough to use a computer.*

Behaviour: Avoiding mobile phones, computers, the internet etc.

I've used these three examples deliberately to illustrate **low-level** anxiety because generally speaking, these types of difficulty will collapse quite easily if they are challenged with logic and/or support.

I want to differentiate between extreme OCD-like difficulties and these types of floating anxieties. While the list above could apply to extreme OCD-driven concerns, I intend to illustrate those difficulties that **may** exist because we've failed to challenge them properly.

I already touched on number one in the examples I gave from my own life. Let's assume that the worrier in this case is not poverty-stricken. We know that hoarding can be a serious disorder and I have no wish to trivialise those experiences but mild hoarding may be a hangover from thrifty patterns born in early life. Then, it's a case of unwillingness or inexperience in how to challenge unhealthy patterns of thought and behaviour.

It takes courage to get down to this kind of work. It's going to be uncomfortable. If it wasn't, we'd already have made the change. Thinking hard takes energy and this requires continued adjustment. When negative thoughts and feelings arise, we must dismiss them as junk and remind ourselves of our reasons to ignore them and determine our change. It helps to have those reasons to hand, so here's a nice tool for creating a more objective perspective.

It's called a **cost-to-benefit analysis** and it is drawn from Cognitive Behavioural Therapy (CBT). As simple as it may seem, it can be surprisingly powerful in action.

Take a sheet of paper and draw a line down the middle, splitting it into two columns. Add a horizontal line an inch from the top of the page to create two header boxes and write "Costs" on the left and "Benefits" on the right.

Now, be clear about what it is that you are analysing. In this example, it's the **costs** of spending money on items I need versus the **benefits** of spending money on items I need.

Here's my take on this one: -

Costs

* I will have less money in my bank account and that will make me feel less financially secure.

* I will feel anxious when I spend this money because my programming sees spending as inviting later suffering.

* I may genuinely regret spending this money if I need it for something else at a later date.

* I may have to endure irrational feelings of being wasteful or irresponsible.

Benefits

* I will no longer be experiencing the stress of having to engineer around a problem that would be easily solved if I were willing to invest in the tools/skills/assistance necessary to complete the task/meet the need.

* I will eventually realise that I need this tool/item/service and buy it anyway. What is the point of struggling on without it now when I could be using it today?

* I may learn that it is a pleasure to have the use of said tool/skill. It is likely that the pleasure will far outweigh the anxiety of having less money in reserve.

* I could die tomorrow! Then, I would have suffered needlessly. It's there to be spent on making life enjoyable and user-friendly. That's for now, not some imagined future that may not come.

* By challenging my fears, I am taking a positive step forward in making it easier to do so in the future. The chances are that I will enjoy my purchase and suffer no actual hardship from spending the money, re-conditioning my belief system positively. This will make me **less anxious** about spending in the future.

* I can guarantee that I will suffer if I do not spend this money because I am already suffering as a result of not having what I need. I am only **imagining** that I **may** suffer if I spend it.

* Any savings I have are losing value all the time. If I buy it in three years, it will cost me 10-20% more!

If my fear is creating anxiety about spending because it believes that it is trying to keep me from (financial) pain at a later date, then clearly it has its facts wrong. By preventing me from spending on what I need now, it is causing the very suffering it purports to be trying to save me from - poverty. I am behaving **as if** I am broke when I am not, to prevent the possibility of being broke later. I'm already getting what I fear, **now**. The same money will be worth less later and the goods will cost more too. It's bad logic from numerous angles.

We could go on. Hopefully, the point is made though, that through analysis we can quickly arrive at an almost unarguable conclusion that spending the money when we need to is a no-brainer, whatever our feelings say on the matter. The benefits outweigh the costs. If our feelings say differently, then we've either missed something in our calculation, or our feelings are proven to be wrong.

The costs, mostly, are imagined. The benefits are very real.

A proper analysis shows this clearly.

I invite you now to make your assessments on the remaining two practice cases – "I might get lost" and "I'm not clever enough." Don't do it in your head. Grab some paper and a pen and get it down in front of you in black and white. It will take you ten minutes and it will familiarise you with the exercise. See what you can learn from the examples, and then apply the formula to any areas of your own life where a good dose of logical challenge might help you to collapse and disempower an unhelpful belief.

As basic as this task seems, please don't knock it until you have tried it. I was once brought to tears of relief and understanding when I completed a cost-to-benefit analysis around an important emotive family issue that had left me morally confused for weeks. I learned that my fears had been over-ruling reason. I just needed to see it in black and white, in front of me. I'm no great fan of reams of therapeutic paper homework but this tool can be a lot more powerful than it may first appear and it will take only a few minutes to complete. Please go ahead and try out some cost-to-benefit analyses on some of your most limiting feelings/thoughts/beliefs. You may find that illuminating too.

...

Next, I want to move on to some examples which are more likely to apply to those people who have OCD. These need to be viewed through a different lens. It's in the nature of these types of difficulties that they **will not resolve when logic is applied.** These are examples where we are **not** doing it (causing suffering) to ourselves.

One

Intrusive thought: *I might be a paedophile.*

Behaviour: This person may avoid spaces where there are children. He or she will refuse invitations to stay at a friend's house if there are children present. They may have a passion for teaching or child-related service but feel unable to work in a young person's environment. Anything with children involved will be avoided.

Two

Intrusive thought/feeling: *I'm fat and ugly.*

Behaviour: Obsessive checking of appearance in the mirror before leaving the house. Refusing invitations for fun stuff. Avoiding contributing to conversations. Avoiding the swimming pool or the beach. Never eating in public. Never buying clothes from a shop in person.

Three

Intrusive thought/feeling: *I am or may be contaminated with something nasty and be likely to infect other people.*

Behaviour: Compulsive cleaning/disinfecting of the local environment and/or own body. Avoiding handling meat. Avoiding eating at restaurants. Avoiding physical contact. Panicking if in the presence of somebody known to have a cold or stomach bug. Avoiding children/schools/doctors/hospitals. Avoiding public transport or shared spaces. General anxiety around food.

...

I'm deliberately treading gently here. Being on the receiving end of these types of thoughts and feelings when they are OCD-level-disturbing is a challenging experience for sufferers. The last thing anybody needs is to be told to pull themselves together and apply a bit of logic.

However, I will say this. Logic applies to OCD sufferers too. Logic **alone** will not be enough to resolve an OCD-level difficulty but it does form the backbone of treatment, so if you're in that category, please take note. You'll need this too. You'll also need a bit of extra structure to work with said logic and we'll be coming to that shortly.

There are diagnostic criteria that doctors, psychologists and psychiatrists can use to distinguish OCD from generalised anxiety. I hope that you will now have enough understanding to be able to make a reasonable preliminary appraisal of your position. Remember, a formal diagnosis is a doctor's job though.

When describing my own unhelpful mental and emotional chatter, I suggested that catching my mind in the act of leading me down a thorny garden path required brutal honesty. I'm attempting to make your life easier by including this chapter. Your difficulties may require just three essential tools for a solution: brutal honesty with yourself, a willingness to endure the discomfort of challenging your old patterns and assumptions, and a keen application of logic.

I'd advise beginning here, with a cost-to-benefit analysis, whatever the nature of your negative thoughts. For some, it will be enough to regain control of unruly thoughts and feelings. For others, it won't. Don't sweat on this. With further structure, which I'll be explaining shortly, you'll have more robust tools at your disposal should you need them. Get clear here and you can bring what you learn to the work we'll be setting out in the next section of the book – **Action**.

PART TWO – ACTION

The tools and techniques that I am about to deliver to you in this book are neither secret nor revolutionary. They don't need to be.

What they need to be is... understood.

Plus, they need to be applicable. If the proposal is too much bother or too complicated, the chances are that you won't do it, or won't stick at it.

Real-world therapy needs to be made simple for the recipient. There's a rule in hypnotherapy that the hypnotherapist should avoid using language that a twelve-year-old wouldn't understand when delivering hypnotic suggestions. In a hypnotherapy session, just two words might be powerful – "You could." Simple can be effective.

Learning happens best when we have an emotional connection to the subject – an interest. If it's meaningful for us, we pay attention, and if the right elements are absorbed, then we retain that learning and it expands our options as we face similar future situations.

The intended outcome for this book is that as you read the last page, you will be left with a clear sense of **what** to do, **why** to do it, and most importantly, **how** to do it. If I've done my job properly, it won't be because you think that you "should" do the exercises, it will be because you've recognized why they're going to help you and you'll be excited to get started.

Anxiety cares nothing for you. It doesn't have a minded agenda to either punish you or fix you. It doesn't have an agenda at all. It is the result of genetics, environment, trauma, misunderstandings, ongoing stress, and/or neurological dysfunction. It's much more like a runaway train than it is an evil force that has come to make your life a misery. Do the wrong things and anxiety increases. Do the right things and it will improve. It doesn't care.

Next up, you have one life. Time waits for nobody and all sales are final. Cause and effect are a fact of life. Pain is passing. The achievements of effort are solid, remaining after the work has been done.

It's in the unwritten rules of being a Human Being that if we don't take some risks, we won't reap many rewards. If we take risks, we are going to lose sometimes. It's probably going to hurt.

But, what hurts more?

Not living.

That is what we are faced with when our mental health is in a rut. *Do I stay safe and live at thirty per cent of my potential? Or, do I take the bull by the horns and say "You know what? I might get hurt but if I don't do this, I might not live at all!"* It's an existential invitation to all, though nobody is obliged to take it.

To my mind, this is a philosophical position because much as it makes logical sense, the power that initiates movement is not derived from logic. Logic does not drive many of our actions - feelings do, and here, I'm referring not to OCD or anxious feelings but how we feel about our life, self, and others. If I am to make the jump into action, I need a power source capable of driving that action for long enough to succeed and that requires that I either need or want that change more than I fear the pain of doing nothing. I'll need enthusiasm and the desire to get it done.

Determination follows desire.

If I want it badly enough, I'll pay the price for it.

Or, if it's a dream that drives you, then it's all about being unwilling to live with the limited options that your circumstances currently provide. Sometimes we need to be angry about the situation before we are willing to take the necessary steps to change it.

It's an atmosphere. It's a decision. It's a determination. It's a line that we draw in the sand.

And, it's risky.

How do these suggestions sound?

You can't go to the park in case you encounter dog poo or vomit. Go!

You can't eat from the barbecue your friend made in case you get sick. Eat!

You can't visit your friend's house because you might say something inappropriate and everyone will know that you're a secret pervert. Visit!

You can't walk through the supermarket without reading every sign that you see. Walk!

Defiance!

That is how you will overcome these difficulties in the long term.

What are you risking? Germs, humiliation, fate, death even? So be it! It's that or not living. When fear dictates our lives to us, that's blackmail and we can't have it. That's the line that cannot be crossed, and it is anger, incredulity, and outrage that can generate the power necessary to tolerate the risk and do it anyway. What is life if it is not being lived to the available capacity? We have one life, and a right to strive to live it fully. The world isn't always fair and so that may not be a position we can enjoy at all times but let's be clear that it is a positive and determined existential agenda to hold.

Obsessive illness will seek to undermine such a message but that is exactly the point. Why listen to frightening thoughts that rob us of autonomy? That's a rhetorical question, by the way. We know why you listen. It's hell if you don't but let's be honest, it's hell when you do too, right?

Through it is then.

Recovery is going to involve risk.

You will risk discomfort, doubt, and disappointment. At times, you may feel like you are risking your life. It would be easier to chicken out. Or, would it?

Having a baby carries risk. Surgery is rough but we do it when we have to. Asking someone out on a date is challenging but we do it. Moving home, changing jobs, seeking therapy, travelling, marrying or divorcing, and having children, to name only a few of life's big events are calculated risks that human beings tolerate to enjoy fuller lives.

Living is risky and living fully is riskier.

This is not to suggest that people who suffer from anxiety or obsessive-mind difficulties are incompetent in life. On the contrary, most sufferers manage the majority of life's complexities admirably, and my OCD clients often had the greatest sense of humour and irony as well as keen, highly perceptive minds. Low intelligence was not the problem, at all.

Is life worth dying for?

We risk it every day and as uncomfortable as it may be, risk will be involved until the very end of our lives. Philosophically, we must each decide whether it's worth the risk of being willing to die to live. Nobody is asking you to gamble with your life. We just want to be able to go to the barbecue and eat the perfectly safe food that our friends and family make for us. It's a philosophical position, not a death wish.

There are two points to take away from this.

The first is that through repetition of new actions, our brains can become desensitised to perceived danger (real or imagined) and achieve confidence within our chosen pursuits. Those chosen pursuits don't need to be Formula One racing. Specifically, the new actions you will be undertaking will involve an ongoing refusal to live your life according to the demands of anxiety and compulsions.

The second is that we find the force to endure the discomfort of apprenticeship through a bloody-minded determination that we will either live fully or die trying (philosophically speaking – life-threatening ventures are not advised.)

In any other situation, I probably wouldn't choose those words. When it comes to obsessions though, death is often a central fixation. You're not being advised to die trying. I will counsel you later not to try too hard. Sometimes you will need to give yourself a break. This will sound like a contradiction. It isn't. You're just being asked to meet what your mind throws at you with a steely **longer-term resolve** that won't be bullied into submission at the first sign of resistance. The words "die trying" are just a shortcut to that resolve.

At a certain point, we look back and see that we **are** different now. We are made of wiser, stronger stuff. What once held control over us, no longer has such power. We have mastered it. Our brains are routed differently now. It's hard to believe it's possible before it happens. When it does, it makes perfect sense because you are no longer who you were.

Once that vital ingredient of determination to live a better life is present, even if it's still just a seed right now, then with understanding and application, great things can and will be achieved.

Maybe you just have to risk it to find out?

Chapter Sixteen – The Heart Bears Witness

"A problem shared is a problem halved." At least, that's what the proverb states.

If you are lucky enough to have a trusted friend or family member to share your inner life with, you'll already have some idea of how valuable it can be to have someone around to witness your joys and your pains. It's human to need to share our stories and we are each an important part of the stories of others.

Under normal circumstances, a light sharing of minds is all we might need to keep ourselves balanced in this regard. When we are in pain though, our experience is concentrated. Then, that need to be deeply heard will intensify. When we feel truly "heard", our experience is validated. To a degree, the burden is also shared.

Being heard can involve more than somebody merely listening though. Listening can happen through the ears but it can also happen through the full being of a person. That's harder to come by.

In our day-to-day lives, we are busy, not only physically, but mentally and emotionally. Your loved one may look and nod as you speak but as often as not, they are, shall we say, distracted. That's okay. They may be stressed. They are living their own busy life, complete with pressures, moods, fears, and conflicts. We can't expect our loved ones to deliver an endless stream of focused compassionate attention. Some people may manage to do so but they are the exception, not the rule. Yet, we do need compassionate attention, and that need increases when we are feeling poorly.

Where do we go to get this? Who is available to really "hear" us?

Our loved ones can't realistically also be our therapists.

If you have loved ones who help you, that's great, but the point here is that they are neither trained nor sufficiently impartial to give us all that we need. It is a firmly accepted part of therapeutic training that we should not work therapeutically with loved ones. It's a messy dynamic. When therapists are at home, they're just Dad or Bill or Mum or Wendy. If therapists can't be therapists to their friends and families, it follows logically that we shouldn't expect our loved ones to fulfil that role either.

Conversely, when therapists are at work, they are no longer Bill or Wendy. They put the professional hat on and they do what they are trained to do – provide sustained, focused, compassionate attention and guidance for their clients. That is primary and it's something that most therapists will give 100% of themselves in delivering.

Nowhere else do we experience similar attention upon our emotional well-being from another person. Please don't misunderstand me. Our loved ones may give us a form of sustained and kind attention but it's not the same thing. Therapy time is all about you and your well-being. The quality of attention you'll receive from a therapist is a truly unique situation. In this setting, you don't need to feel guilty about saying too much, being a drain on someone, or being indulgent. It's a shame-free space to learn specific tools for specific difficulties.

We have a deep need to have our experience witnessed and validated. We've already noted that therapy may be one resource that can deliver on this request but there is also another way.

We can do it for ourselves.

To my mind, **self-witnessing**, with the heart, is more powerful than having someone else witness you but it's not something that everybody practices, mainly because without instruction, it's not something that a person would necessarily stumble upon intuitively.

Luckily, great therapeutic minds have been at work and they have shared their discoveries with us. It turns out that you can have a conversation with your deeper self that can make a huge difference in how your body and mind respond to life. You just need to know how to do it.

In my experience, having someone else witness my pain is wonderful in the moment but the relief passes quickly. Why? Somebody **was** with you but now they are not. With self-witnessing, the witness stays with you afterwards because the witness is... er... you. And, wherever you go... there you are.

In addition to this, there's another advantage to self-witnessing. We know in our hearts that as kind and understanding as someone may be, they can only relate to our pain through the filter of their own experience. I can have a pretty good idea of what you're experiencing as we all use similar hardware (a human body) but there can be no question that everybody's experience of existence differs, sometimes hugely. It is satisfying when you know that you've been reasonably well understood but it can't match the 100% identification you receive when you choose to self-witness. That witness **knows** the pain, first-hand. The inner witness was there. That kind of understanding cannot be found anywhere else. It is when your recognition of the raw emotion of that time or event synchronizes with the memory, that the feelings start to flow freely and healing can begin.

And, finally, self-witnessing is a surprisingly effective way of soothing difficult feelings. If you think about it clearly, you'll recognise that **feelings** drive obsessive worries and compulsive behaviours. Thoughts are often bundled with and are sometimes the sole cause of these feelings, but the feelings still have a life of their own that we must manage.

If we could tolerate difficult feelings without permitting them to make our decisions for us, then we would become unstoppable.

We would choose our destiny and keep doing what we need to do until we're where we wish to be. Some gifted humans make this look easy. The rest of us are usually hindered by our feelings.

An OCD sufferer does not go through hours of daily checking or ritualising because they think it's a good idea that leads somewhere great. They do what they do because they are frightened of what their feelings will put them through if they don't do as they are told.

If you can master the skill of tolerating a difficult feeling without submitting to its demands, you will have the necessary tools to achieve pretty much whatever you wish to do, including beating your obsessions and compulsions.

Learning to self-witness and self-soothe was, for me, a game changer. After six years of feeling completely unable to handle the awful feelings that anxiety and depression dished up for me daily, I was at my wits' end when somebody finally demonstrated to me that I'd been doing it all wrong. I had, naturally, spent six years trying to be free of the anxiety and depression; to not feel it. That was my mistake. Don't do that. It doesn't work.

What message are you sending to yourself if you exist in a state of urgency to not feel what you feel? Don't think of pink elephants. You're thinking of pink elephants.

Trying to not feel what you feel is nonsensical to the human brain. Instead, set your expectations for slow and steady improvement by focusing on what you can do, not what you can't.

Lasting mental and emotional change mostly occurs slowly enough that it is almost imperceptible.

Three weeks after you begin working on your anxiety with tools that work, you look back and realise, *I haven't had that awful feeling for a while.* You may not have recognised that anything else had changed at all. You may have plenty of other difficult feelings still. That's good. This is a change that hasn't alerted your Zealous Guard to start interfering. The change has been accepted at the subconscious level, which is where you need it to happen. When you continue this practice for long enough, a few weeks later, you realise that you've been enjoying an activity you wouldn't previously have considered and you didn't go through a huge drama to do it.

In practice, this is how things continue to improve. We move incrementally from one mental state to another, over weeks and months, until there have been so many incremental changes that they've all added up to a great big one which is the change we've been hoping for. If we make changes to our diet and lifestyle, those improvements will be even more noticeable. This is the change that lasts because as you can't expect to go rapidly from a chronic negative emotional state to a lasting positive one, it also works the other way around.

Healed minds and bodies don't collapse overnight for no reason.

Please understand this and remember it. Patience is key. Every step forward counts.

I've written extensively on the method I'm about to present to you, in my other books, and although I'd prefer to deliver unique material in each book, this understanding is so central to the resolution of emotion-related suffering, and in particular to this programme of recovery that it cannot be omitted. I must ask readers of my other books to permit me this repeat information for those who are using this book as a standalone resource. The tool is tweaked specifically to be used in the context of obsession-busting and I hope that understanding the process in a different context will only deepen your understanding of this important area of human psychology.

A few words of clarification are needed still before we proceed.

In this section of the book, I am going to introduce you to two main therapeutic approaches **that will appear to contradict each other**. Please pay attention now as I need to explain a crucially important distinction between these opposing approaches if we are to avoid confusion later.

One approach (this one) will suggest that you attend to your deepest feelings with patient and compassionate attention. The other will suggest that you adopt a detached, logical, and clinical position with the things that you think and feel. Hmm… sounds confusing?

If we were to use modern clinical terminology, we would loosely call the first approach Acceptance and Commitment Therapy (ACT) and the second, Cognitive Behavioural Therapy (CBT). Other fields have also used these ideas. You are going to need both of these skills to successfully work with your anxious thoughts and feelings using the model I'm presenting but **they both do different jobs in different contexts** – head and heart is one way of thinking about it.

The acceptance and commitment approach (compassionately witnessing your thoughts and feelings), is an approach that will teach you how to support yourself compassionately when you are experiencing difficult emotions like fear, panic, discomfort, and vulnerability. It's also a form of resilience training for your brain.

As we go forward with this endeavour, having access to this tool is important. If you are unable to tolerate the initial anxiety of challenging your patterns of thoughts and behaviours, you are more likely to give in to fear and make little progress.

Acceptance can teach you how to tolerate difficult feelings in the pursuit of a greater goal.

If you can hold your nerve and refuse an avoidance behaviour when your brain is screaming at you to take evasive action, you will succeed. As I explained earlier, this is a desensitisation process. That means that the hardest part is the first part because it's scarier to do something new for the first time than it is to do it for the twentieth time. As you become more practised in applying compassionate attention to your feelings, you will gain new confidence in saying "no" to the demands of your obsessions and compulsions. You will self-soothe so powerfully that you feel safe even in the presence of difficult feelings. Eventually, your brain will adjust and the anxiety will diminish. Do it for long enough and you may forget all about the anxiety. This is the heart part.

The second approach (the CBT) can be thought of as the **structure** that will contain the **process** of desensitisation. This is the head part. Here, the aim is to remove excessive emotion from the situation and witness your thoughts and feelings from an emotionally cool, **detached** position. This detached position aims to increase objectivity (logic and evidence) and decrease subjectivity (your own brain's catastrophic untruths) when assessing whether your thoughts and feelings are helpful.

To be clear then, the acceptance and commitment tool outlined here will help with tolerating difficult feelings and the cognitive behavioural tools will help with knowing exactly what you need to do in each moment to stay on track with your obsession-busting practice.

In this chapter, we are concentrating on method number one for now – how the heart can bear (soothing) witness to our distress, with acceptance and commitment.

...

We discussed "the law of reversed effort" earlier. It states that the harder we try, the more likely we are to fail or get the opposite of the intended effect because trying too hard introduces tension into actions that would normally be automatic.

For example, if you start worrying about how you are breathing and **try** to control it, you'll simply get in the way of your body doing what it knows how to do already. That will make you tense and create an anxiety loop that messes with your breathing pattern bringing about the very symptom that didn't exist until you started worrying that it might! You'll mess up the carbon dioxide-to-oxygen mix and the body will create the first pangs of panic. You start believing that you can't breathe properly. That's a psychosomatic problem.

I know that body monitors are now on people's watches and fit-bits. Unless you have a genuine medical or fitness-based reason to do so, please don't start obsessively measuring your body temperature, heart rate, blood sugars, or blood pressure daily or hourly. These will vary naturally and if you start "trying" to control these things you will introduce anxiety unnecessarily which is likely to give you the very symptoms you fear - in this case, high blood pressure.

"Trying" to escape from difficult feelings also increases your anxiety.

The harder we try, the more urgency we introduce, and that generates more anxiety. For now, then, let's just understand that if we try to "escape" from these thoughts and/or feelings, we end up giving them more power over us.

The correct position then is to witness the thoughts and feelings that are present, willingly and calmly.

The basic premise of this approach is that by demonstrating a willingness to be present with your difficult feelings, you are sending a message to the Zealous Guard that this feeling is **tolerable**. If it's tolerable, then it can't be a major threat.

When you "sit" calmly with your difficult feelings, you send a message to the guard that says, "I don't agree that I am in danger. I've got this." Then, the guard relaxes. Eventually. Once trained.

That means less anxiety and a calmer brain. We can go further than merely tolerating these feelings though. We can learn to **support** the parts of ourselves who feel alarmed by them.

What follows, may at first glance appear to be a set of complicated instructions. Please let me assure you that it isn't. I am providing a detailed explanation as we go, to deepen your understanding. The basic format will be summarised as follows: -

*   Still the mind. Create focus and calm.

*   Sit willingly with difficult feelings.

*   Self-soothe and offer factual reassurance.

For ease of comprehension and application, I am going to break this down into three separate practice sessions. Once you understand and have practised all of the steps in the process, it will be something you can apply at any moment, literally in seconds. You will have this tool available for life. While you are learning this process though, I would recommend initially learning the three steps separately, one at a time, until you are familiar enough with all of the steps to bring it all together into a single practice. By the time you are implementing the third step, you will naturally have built up to an all-in-one format anyway.

STILLING THE MIND

First of all, I want to provide you with instructions for a five to ten-minute exercise that will help you to experience a state of relative mental calm. (Stilling the mind.)

1) Make time and space somewhere where you won't be disturbed for ten minutes.
2) Sit comfortably and close your eyes. Take a few nice deep breaths and then just allow your breathing to find a normal, steady rhythm. Give it time to settle. It might take a minute or two.
3) Focus on the sensation of the breath moving into your body and the sensation of it leaving with each inhalation and each exhalation. Don't try to influence your breathing. Just notice the sensations.
4) Stay with this for as long as you wish. Usually, a few minutes will be sufficient to "settle" oneself.
5) You may find that your mind feels swirly, unfocused, or actively distracted. That happens. If you notice that you've forgotten to focus on your breath, that's fine. It is not a failure. Just gently return to noticing the sensation of breathing.
6) Don't "expect" too much. You are not aiming for meditational Nirvana. Just focus. Stay with it for five to ten minutes and when you're ready to close the exercise, gently allow your eyes to open. Notice how you feel now?

What you have here is the most basic formula for "meditation" or, as some people prefer, "mindfulness", that is, choosing to direct your awareness to a single point of focus. In this instance, the breath provides that focal point.

If a person is very anxious or uncomfortable generally, it may initially be challenging to sit still and do nothing. Don't "force" anything. The intended result of this exercise is simply to learn to bring your usually externally focused attention into a state where it becomes internally focused. We are closing our eyes to the outside world for a few minutes. Usually, but not always, you will notice that the mind will begin to settle after a few minutes of doing this. Thoughts and feelings may become less hurried and intense, your breathing may become slower and deeper.

Once you have practised this a few times, you will hopefully now have an understanding of two things. Firstly, when you sit quietly and focus on your breath, your brain becomes a little calmer. Secondly, you can focus your attention inwardly, regardless of having a busy brain.

If neither of these things happened for you, rest assured, that's neither a failure nor a surprise. Our minds are often accustomed to a lot of busyness. It's completely normal to experience some resistance to slowing down. Be gentle with yourself. Think of it as a skill that can be developed. Try at another time too. Mornings suit some better and evenings others.

Once you have a little practice at achieving some basic inward focus, you're ready to move on to the next step.

Sitting With Difficult Feelings

This time, repeat the steps above to create a state of internally focused awareness and then use your awareness to mentally scan your body, from the top of your head to the tips of your toes. Notice, as you scan, what kind of feelings you are experiencing in this moment. Is your body relaxed, or do you feel tension? Do you have sadness in your chest, anxiety in your guts, anger in your throat, or any other emotional sensations that draw your attention? If you have none, that's probably a good sign. It indicates that you are either relaxed in this moment, or that your resting state is one without significant anxiety or negative feelings. For everyone who finds tension in attendance, here's what you do.

Wherever you notice emotional tension in your body, bring your entire awareness to that place in your body and be curious about it. It can help to ask yourself whether it has a colour, a texture, or a shape? Is it heavy or light, still or moving? Does it have a form? If it does, this just helps to keep the focus. If it doesn't, that's okay too. Just remain with the feeling.

Imagine (mentally) diving into the feeling to explore it. Don't try to force anything. Bring softness to this interaction. Be a friend to yourself. Show interest. You may already notice that your relationship with the feeling begins to soften. Usually, such difficult feelings may be perceived as monstrous. With **curiosity and softness,** you get to come at it from a different angle, that of "interest". You like it when people show positive interest in you, right? Well, so do your feelings, especially the ones you usually flee from. As far as they are concerned, when you willingly pay attention to them, it is an act of friendliness. They tend to respond favourably. You are also sending an "I am not afraid" message simply by being courageous enough to attend deeply to difficult feelings without the expected drama.

As you move into the feeling, permit yourself to feel it deeply. Be courageous. This may seem like a challenging instruction but here is where everything may be about to change for you. If we have been at the mercy of such feelings for a long time, it is to be expected that we have come to feel fearful about the feelings themselves. One aspect that we might feel is that if the feelings are this bad when I'm avoiding them, how much worse could they get? Surely, I will be obliterated if I allow myself to feel them?"

This is fear of fear.

Now, up close, when you willingly go into your difficult feelings as opposed to running from them, something interesting usually happens.

We discover that the feelings are <u>less</u> intense when we give them our full attention than they are when we are trying to escape from them.

If all goes well, you may be genuinely surprised by how significant the reduction in discomfort can be. This can be a watershed moment. If you can learn to be in the presence of difficult feelings without yielding to panic, you are already halfway back to health. This is a vehicle that can achieve this with relative ease.

You will now have a tool that allows your negative feelings to exist but no longer feeds them with the fear of the fear that they have thrived on for so long. You are no longer trying to evade these feelings urgently. You have learned to "sit" with them, calmly. When you do something different with your feelings, their response must also change.

Begin by practising this simple technique a few times until you find the value in it. Ideally, I invite you to embrace this tool and make it your own. It's all very well somebody telling you that something can help but the real Eureka moment happens when it clicks for you. That's a personal experience and everybody will have their subjective impressions of how or why something is useful. If you find it useful and have your reasons for that, they are completely valid. I'm confident it will help. Recognizing why it helps **you,** specifically, can only help more, and it may take a few attempts before you have your own take on it. Just give it a chance and pay attention to the subtle aspects of your experience. They count too.

When you are ready to do so (take as long as you want), just open your eyes gently and give yourself a moment or two before allowing your attention to gently return to the external world.

Self-Soothing & Reassurance

Okay. The final part. Here, we need to make a distinction.

You may have a problem with the notion of being kind to the awful feelings that have been a source of real pain for you. You can relax. That's not what you are being asked to do here.

This step requires that we differentiate between the negative feeling you experience and the **part of you** who experiences it.

The fact is, that through the process of natural selection, we are the inheritors of a nervous system that is highly attuned to self-preservation. The cautious have survived. That makes some degree of anxiety a virtual inevitability for a significant proportion of people. Our brains see danger everywhere. That's a negative feeling. It won't kill us but it's wearing stuff, particularly when those feelings are intensified by chronic anxiety or OCD. Surely then, we can find some compassion for the suffering parts of ourselves?

I'm appealing to your empathy towards yourself here. We are not setting out primarily to be kind and compassionate to the feelings themselves, though that will do no harm should you feel so-minded. We can be kind to our feelings without believing that they are telling us the truth if we wish, but here, they are considered phenomena. They are not who you are. They are what your body and brain are doing right now, on autopilot, and in error, we might add.

As far as feelings are concerned, indifference is probably about right. They are seen, in this context, as part of the machinery of being a human being. They exist but they are not representative of an unadulterated truth or reflective of our intentions. How many times have any of us had insecurities that turned out to be entirely baseless? Is your jealousy always justified? Was your anger misplaced? Did all your worries come to pass? When it comes to obsessional difficulties, there's every expectation that there are inaccuracies, and often, outright lies.

For now, the agenda is to be kind to the parts of yourself who experience distress in the presence of these thoughts and feelings.

This part of the exercise asks for a little more than just the application of a "technique". It asks you to be personally and meaningfully involved in sending sincere kindness from the most robust and settled parts of yourself (here, represented by your compassionate heart) to the most vulnerable parts of yourself (those parts of you who live in fear). If it feels difficult to find kindness, that's fine too. Just set your intention towards kindness and maybe, as you deepen your communion with yourself, you'll find that kindness begins to trickle in. It's a common experience. We hold ourselves accountable for so much. In this space, it's often possible to have a moment of softness where we see that something has been outside of our control and we've been too hard on ourselves. That usually softens us and kindness begins to flow.

This may all seem a little abstract at first. I want to make sure that you've got the full picture before you jump in and practice it. I'll explain the process in its natural order, with detailed considerations, and then provide a summary at the end of this chapter for quick reference. Please read the whole section before you leap into action…

Do you remember when you fell over and scraped your knees, as a child? The world had ended. Then, Mum, Dad, or the school nurse cleaned and dressed your gravelly wounds and in minutes all was okay again. What was it that made you feel better? Was it the antiseptic? A sticking plaster? Well, that was comforting. Mostly though, we felt better because somebody cared enough to attend to us. Nothing has changed. We still need that.

We will begin this third step then, by repeating the first two steps of stilling your mind and then sitting with the feelings, as explained. You don't need to close the exercise in each stage now that you're on the final part of the exercise. The idea is that once you have practised each stage individually, you can then roll it all into one process. As we are learning step three now, we can do it all in one go. If all has gone to plan, at this point you should be able to sit more calmly with those difficult feelings and they should also be feeling less intense. If there is just one feeling to focus on, stay with that. If multiple feelings are jostling for attention, focus on the one that feels the most urgent, first. You can repeat this process with each feeling individually later.

Now, we ask a question. "If this feeling could speak to me... if it had a voice, and I asked it what it is feeling right now, what would it tell me?"

Don't try too hard to find an answer. No urgency, please.

Relax, be patient and pay careful attention. Give it thirty seconds at least. Allow your body and mind time to absorb the question, and then pay attention to the response. In this context, feelings can be information. Be still. It might be subtle.

Your feelings contain the answer.

They will speak what they feel. If you can feel the feeling, then you can name it.

The feeling you are focused on now has an opportunity to respond. Here are some examples of what you might expect to receive as a reply.

* "I'm not sure. I think I feel really scared."

* "I feel really low. It feels like there's a great big weight on my chest."

* "I'm worried about the future. I'm not coping well."

* "I feel like I'm going mad. I'm so tired of fighting all the time."

* "I feel like there's no hope anymore."

* "I feel like there's something wrong all the time and I don't know why."

* "I feel I'm a danger to others."

* "I'm worried about my family. I keep thinking something terrible will happen to them."

We are compassionately **witnessing** what is happening at the feeling level. Compassionate witnessing does not include beating yourself up or making instant judgments about yourself. That's not loving, is it? Keep in mind that you are aiming to extend kindness from your heart to the parts of yourself that feel unsafe or vulnerable.

Witness these feelings with the same kindness that you would witness a child presenting to you with cut knees. Assuming that you're a compassionate human being, how would you feel towards that child in need of help? This is the same principle. Simple, uncomplicated kindness.

This feeling of concerned empathy is the most important part of your response.

Words can be empty if they are not accompanied by sincerity. Your compassionate attention should include sincerity, and your care will be directly communicated to the anxious parts of yourself when you **feel** care towards yourself. Remember what we said about self-witnessing being more powerful than somebody else witnessing your pain? Well, here's where that understanding comes into play.

Ask yourself a question now. Do you behave with kindness and compassion towards that part of yourself or do you scold them for being weak, stupid, or any other form of not good enough? Perhaps your intrusive thoughts take care of that for you?

Imagine being on the receiving end of being told you're weak, stupid, or bad for suffering from anxious or obsessional worries. How does that feel?

Presumably, you want these parts of yourself to toughen up, to be more resilient, and to think more clearly? Consider then, whether treating the vulnerable parts of yourself with admonishment will encourage them to be stronger and more confident? Imagine the school nurse telling you that you're an idiot for scraping your knees. It doesn't work, does it?

What **does** work is kindness.

Kindness, attention, understanding, and at the very least, a desire to help. All of this can be easily communicated in a meaningful way to our most vulnerable selves when we begin from a place of inner focus.

Since we associate the heart with love, I'll ask you now to bring your awareness to your heart area and take a few moments to remember how it feels to give and receive love and kindness. Think about the selfless things people have done for you and what you have done for others. Tune into the sweetness you will have felt from such exchanges and bring that to this moment. Do your best to feel how it feels to give and receive freely.

For this moment, your heart is the therapist, the listener, the healer.

I have a wise friend who once told me that the greatest journey a human being can take is the one "from here to here." As he told me this, he motioned with his finger from his head to his heart. This is a similar idea.

With your mind now focused on kindness, compassion, and giving, you imagine sending that love, that caring, from your heart to the place in your body where you are "holding" those difficult feelings. I mean literally where you feel them. If there is anger in your head, you send it there. If there are butterflies (anxiety) in your stomach, you send it there. If there's grief in your throat or chest, you send it there. You send as much love as you can muster, directly to the places in your body where you feel distress and you keep sending it, in waves, with certainty and conviction. Kindness, caring, valuing, empathy, attention. You intend to make that love available to the parts of you that are often ignored or feared. You are **including** the distressed parts of yourself in your life and letting them know that they too deserve kindness, love, and attention. Until now, they have been ignored, or worse, hated.

This represents a radical shift in your relationship with yourself.

You have now moved from a position of victimhood and avoidance to one of self-mentorship and attention.

You are no longer at the mercy of your feelings. You are now supporting the part/s of yourself who live/s in fear of these feelings. With your support, they can recognise that the feelings may be troubling but the feelings are not in control. **You are.** And now there are two of you on the same side. It's a formidable arrangement.

If all has gone to plan, at this point, you will now be experiencing some degree of emotional warmth surrounding those distressed feelings. This doesn't mean that the feelings themselves vanish or feel suddenly joyful, nor should we expect that. It means that the part of you who **suffers** as a result of the presence of those difficult feelings now has some sense that he or she has somebody on their side; is cared for, and therefore, safer.

When our vulnerable selves feel supported instead of abandoned, not only will they generate much less fear, but they are also much more likely to listen to what we have to tell them.

This is good because we do have some messages for ourselves. This is where we move to the reassurance step. You may have tried to reassure yourself many times before and had those reassurances make no meaningful difference. You may be asking why I think this will help now. I'll answer that.

When you attempt to self-reassure while you are in your everyday state of awareness or an anxious state, your subconscious beliefs are fiercely guarded. Your brain holds many ideas that may be irrational but your brain would rather hold onto those beliefs than live in uncertainty. Obsessions are, by definition, an attempt to control the uncontrollable aspects of reality. That means your guard thinks they are keepers even though we know they suck. Unless you open a meaningful felt conversation with the guard, whatever you say will fall on deaf ears.

With the practice suggested here, we have the guard's attention, and we have demonstrated friendly intentions. That's what makes the difference. That's why the guard will listen to the evidence and will be able to absorb the change in circumstances when you move into this state of peaceful communication with it.

Words have power. Words can harm and words can heal. Beyond words, we have tonality and body language. These must match the words we speak if we expect our recipient to trust what we are saying. Saying "sorry" with a scowl is not an apology and "I love you" without eye contact is questionable. Our deepest selves are not stupid. Our messages need to be delivered with compassion and sincerity or not at all.

The question is: "What does your vulnerable self most need to hear right now?"

Rule number one is that whatever you can offer, you must be able to say it with sincerity. At first glance, this may seem tricky but let me show you how to be honest in the presence of doubt, maintain your integrity, and still be soothing.

Let's take a selection from our earlier list and use them as examples: -

* "I feel like there's something wrong all the time and I don't know why."

It's a good idea to begin with a simple acknowledgement of the feeling. My preferred language is as follows: -

"I see/hear/get/understand/acknowledge that you are feeling like something is wrong all the time. I know that it's challenging to be feeling like that and I'm sorry that you've carried those feelings for so long now."

That's a deep acknowledgement. Not only does it communicate that I understand the feeling but it also communicates that it matters to me that you've suffered. It also emphasises that the feelings are culpable, not you.

We can go further. We can also give meaningful reassurance. That will sound something like this: -

"I want to help. If I could give you a 100% guarantee of safety in all things, I would give that to you in a heartbeat. Nobody can offer that though because the world is uncertain.

What I can do though is promise you that I will never knowingly expose you to harm. I will ask you to trust me to prove to you that this is a new arrangement that will make everything easier. I've got your back."

There's rather a lot going on here. We have the truth delivered with integrity. We are not mollycoddling our vulnerability. We are telling it as it is. There are no guarantees of safety. We state that. We are also communicating that we have pure intention alongside a "can-do" offer of solution which, one way or another, we are going to expect to follow through on with behaviour change.

Let's take another one from our list and work with it: -

* "I feel like I'm a danger to others."

The correct response is: -

"I see/hear/get/understand/acknowledge that you are **feeling anxiety** about **the idea** that you may do something terrible to harm yourself or somebody else. I know how incredibly scary and wearing it is to be **feeling** such awful **feelings**."

The language used here is quite important. Note the bolded words above. There are certain assumptions built into this statement. It reinforces that these are feelings and ideas, not facts.

We refer to our anxieties as feelings and ideas rather than facts and happenings.

If you didn't fully mentally download that last point, please take a moment to revisit it until it is firmly understood. Your feelings are not facts. You might **feel** like you may lose control but the facts do not reflect that possibility. This is a consideration when you formulate your self-talk.

Here's an example of the **wrong** way to formulate this deep acknowledgement statement: -

*"I see/hear/get/understand/acknowledge that **you might do** something terrible to harm yourself or somebody else. I know how incredibly scary and wearing it **is to have to stop yourself** from actually doing it or taking actions to make sure that **it can't be allowed to happen**."*

Do you see what's wrong with that statement?

It assumes that the feeling is a fact. It references needing to stop yourself from acting on your fear. That supposes that if you don't stop it from happening, then it will happen. That's a serious threat. It's also wholly inaccurate. That **validates** the perception that something is wrong in the real world. That's what OCD and anxious thoughts will have you believe. We need to refute the assertions that we are in real danger, at every available level of interaction with ourselves.

Don't worry. In the next few chapters, I'll provide you with some structure to make doing that much easier. At this point, you just need to be on board with the agenda, and that means that you must structure your self-talk statements with the language of **facts**, not feelings. There are some inner dialogues that you will refuse to entertain at all. More on this in the next chapter.

Moving on, we now want to provide some meaningful reassurance that it is safe for the fearful parts of you to relax. There's the possibility of confusion here because, in the next chapter, we will be looking at why continued reassurance will worsen anxiety. However, reassurance is correct when used as part of this meditational format.

With eyes closed, mind stilled, and an open channel of communication to your deeper self, you have initiated a healing space. In this quiet moment of reflection, a message of truthful reassurance has a chance of counting for something. We are subduing the Zealous Guard, demonstrating fearlessness in the presence of difficult feelings, and offering kind words of truth and reassurance to the understandably alarmed parts of ourselves who need to hear it. In this context, reassurance can help.

We are not discussing the content of our obsessions here. We are reassuring the vulnerable parts of ourselves that anxiety is telling us lies.

So... with eyes closed, feelings sat with - what does that part of you most need to hear?

I can't tell you exactly what that is but in the absence of anything specific coming to mind for you, here's my best general statement for tackling harming fears, as an example. This will follow from our last statement: -

"...*I know how incredibly scary and wearing it is to be **feeling** such **awful feelings**... BUT... I **promise you that you will never act on them** because they are part of an anxiety disorder. It is not in your nature to do terrible things to people and you have my unwavering word on that. Please relax. I've got this. You are safe and supported.*"

Ooh! That's a big promise, isn't it? How can you give that? How do you know?

As a sufferer of an anxiety disorder, you didn't suddenly lose your morals or your humanity.

There is no evidence whatsoever that you will lose control, only the feeling that you might, and an overblown imaginative scenario playing out in your head of what might happen if you did. That's not you. That's your brain getting itself into a pickle. The anxiety you feel is **because** of the thought, not despite it.

So, here, we can make a promise. It needs to be a promise too because let's not forget that obsessional difficulties are a doubting disease. If you leave the door open just a crack, you should expect that your obsessions will try to exploit that crack and blow the doors wide open again. This, in some ways, is probably where you've been falling along the way. You need to take a **fully committed** stance on these matters. When your resolve is 100% and that's a promise, then there are no cracks for your OCD or anxieties to exploit. Your position is that "I've got this." Well, have you, or haven't you? Your Zealous Guard will want to know one way or the other. Be bold, make it count, take a stand, and stick to it!

Finally, let's bring it all together into one smooth exercise. With repeated practice, this approach will take you a long way. In time, it can form the backbone of an **ever-present** sense of self-support.

When kindness towards yourself becomes your default response to anxiety in life, it can have the effect of silencing anxiety almost as quickly as it arises.

Oddly, anxiety itself can learn (be conditioned to know) that anxiety equals kindness. We arrive at that place by consistently practising kindness responses to anxious feelings. This is the trick that those Buddhist monks understand. They breathe in suffering and breathe out love. The brain links the two and love becomes the default response to suffering. When that equation is established as a default response within your mindset and neural wiring, anxiety often doesn't then bother manifesting without good reason.

The reassurance is present all the time, as a felt default state. That's the goal.

Summary

Do you remember I gave you this basic format at the beginning of this chapter? It's as follows: -

Still the mind - Sit willingly with difficult feelings - Self-soothe – Reassurance.

As promised then, here is the summarised version: -

1) *Still the mind - Sit or lie quietly. Close your eyes. Focus on your breath. Do nothing else. If your mind wanders, return to your breath gently. Stay with it for long enough to allow your whole system to settle. Five minutes minimum is recommended (while practising).*
2) *Sit with difficult feelings - Scan your body with your mind's eye. What feelings do you notice present in your body? Focus on the feelings and be deliberately close to them. Maintain your sense of*

calm, and be patient. Be present. Hold your nerve and pay attention to the results.

3) *Self-soothe – Be an ally to the parts of yourself who feel anxious or distressed by the presence of these thoughts and feelings. Speak to them (internally or out loud). Tell them that you understand what they are going through, that you are sorry that they have been having a tough time, and that you intend to make things better. Don't use pity. Pity looks down. It makes the receiver feel bad. Use empathy. That stands shoulder to shoulder. Make it count by speaking your (helpful) truth, from your heart.*

4) *Reassurance – Provide any evidence or genuine reassurance to your anxious self that the situation is safer than you currently believe. Don't try to "force" this counsel upon yourself. Deliver it and be patient. Your anxious self may need to hear it repeatedly before it sinks in. Make your point kindly but be authoritative and let your anxious self know that you have the situation under control. The clearer you are that you are speaking the truth, the quicker those protective habits will yield to your better judgment.*

Then, practice.

How will you know that it has worked? Wrong question. Sort of…

You're not fixing your car.

This method is about a one-eighty in your **approach** to dealing with anxiety, and for that matter, yourself. At this point, it is less about immediate results than it is about your approach toward anxiety and your belief in your power to build a sense of safety from within.

It is a commitment, alongside a method, which can build an effective sense of trust and self-support at the deepest level of your being, through repetition. Your primary reason for engaging with this practice is to form a strong foundation from which you can tackle your negative thought loops without feeling overwhelmed. Just register that it is not an Insta-fix. It is a necessary step towards a lifelong mastery over fear and the obsessional-compulsive difficulties that often come with that.

What you **can** expect, reasonably, is that you will learn how to handle anxiety in the moment. This tool should help with your immediate experience of that. Beyond that, it's a slow-burn but irreversible transformation. When you "know" how to do this and have the understanding that it helps, often enormously, then there'll be no going back to "helpless me".

So, back to the question, "How will you know when it has worked?"

Answer: When you have changed the way that you approach your anxiety, understood the benefits of calming your mind, learned to extend sincere empathy to yourself, and have become practised in the art of offering reassurance to the parts of you that need to hear it from someone trusted. In this case, that's you. And, it needs to be the right kind of reassurance.

Let's talk about that next.

Chapter Seventeen - Reassurance Is A Conversation For Never

I explained earlier that I would be presenting approaches that may appear to contradict each other but that they ultimately do different jobs depending on the context in which they're used. What I am about to say falls into this category. In the last chapter, I said that it is good to offer reassurance to the frightened parts of yourself. Now, I'm going to **appear** to say the complete opposite. Don't worry. I'll explain.

There's only one time that you are ever going to plan to be even remotely receptive to the <u>content</u> of your fears and obsessions. That's when you are practising the method you just learned in our last chapter – the heart bears witness.

That time of bearing witness is specifically put aside for listening. It is **limited** and hopefully, fruitful, unlike ruminating on intrusive negative thoughts which are infinite, circular, and draining. There is a difference.

The instruction wasn't actually to give your **obsessions** (or the content of your obsessions) plenty of listening time anyway. The instruction was to give the **parts of yourself who are distressed by those obsessions** plenty of listening time.

The same goes for reassurances. You can reassure the frightened **parts** of your being that they are in no danger. If you try to have that same conversation with the anxious **thoughts** themselves, you're going to come unstuck. The thoughts are junk.

Anxious thoughts will open a circular argument with you and will use the reassurances that you offer as a justification to continually demand more reassurances.

And that, right there, IS the obsessional problem. Don't do that. This is a monster that gets hungrier and larger every time you feed it. Do you remember at the beginning of the book, I said that it's time for you to turn your back and walk out on the thoughts? It's their turn to do the doubting. Well, that's now. No more food for the monster.

The part/s of you who is/are vulnerable to the effects of the presence of these thoughts is your treasure. Treasure receives reassurance and support. The junk is ignored.

The goal here is that we want you to stop giving your obsessions and/or compulsions energy. That means your attention and more importantly, your "buy-in", your belief. This includes discussing them repeatedly with yourself or others without a solution. You lose energy every time you get hooked by obsessive thoughts because they draw energy and attention from you. Now we are going to focus on the tools you'll need to unhook yourself and ensure that you remain unhooked.

As we move into the next section of the book, we are moving away from the acceptance and commitment approach for now and learning additional but not conflicting skills – it's different jobs in different contexts. The solution requires both head and heart. Now, let's understand the head part.

I can tell you from experience that many clients have wanted to have an in-depth discussion with me about the reasoning behind, and the validity of, their obsessional **content**. What they are looking for is continued reassurance that the horrors their anxious mind presents them with will not come to pass. They hope that I can say or do something that will suddenly make them certain of their safety, but we both already know that I am in no better position to promise such things than my clients themselves. What they want is unavailable. Anywhere. Still, the mind tries...

As I highlighted earlier, there are some cases where a discussion is necessary. Let's take contamination fears for example. Arguably, any anxieties one may have after a possible real-world contamination situation could have genuine validity. It could be considered entirely rational to seek further reassurances or even treatment in such a case and this is a conversation I'd be willing to have as a person's therapist. The same with health symptoms. Always get it checked.

Contrast this though, with the person who has obsessional health concerns about whatever happens to be on their mind for no good reason. Or, the person who has been repeatedly medically reassured by multiple physicians that they are healthy. There's every indication in these types of cases that the root of the problem lies not in a diseased body or an inherently threatening situation but in an obsessive, anxious mind.

The sufferer will be looking to me (as the therapist) for reassurance that they don't have cancer or whatever else their mind has decided to present them with as a possible illness. Quite apart from the fact that I **cannot** offer such reassurances, it's my job to hold a very clear line on any invitation from clients to discuss the content of such obsessions. There are plenty of other "what ifs" to keep us busy if cancer loses its shine.

We cannot afford to go there.

The non-obsessives among us just don't. Go there, I mean. We are aware of these matters. The threat of illness, death, or destitution is an ever-present discomfort but we live with the risks that are inherent in being engaged with the world because we know that we can't afford to quit, financially, energetically, or practically.

Human minds have to hold a staggering amount of information. Luckily, it seems, we can cope but I think we learn that there's not enough room in our lives for a life of such complexity **and** a full-time worry life. Only one of those lives will make it through this life intact. I think it's something we have to fight for sometimes.

The more I am willing to speak with you about your self-diagnosed (probably non-existent) illnesses, the more I am behaving in a way that **validates** the obsessive concern. My agreement to discuss it repeatedly sends an unspoken message that I also believe that it is something that needs to be spoken about, something that is worthy of energy expenditure. It isn't. You have no evidence that you are unwell but we do know that you have a mind that is prone to obsess and worry without evidence. The conversation would look something like this:

Client: "I had the thought that I might have cancer and not know about it and it's got me feeling worried now."

Therapist: "Are you feeling unwell? Do you have any specific reason to believe that you may have cancer?"

Client: "No. I'm fine. I just have the feeling that I might have cancer, all the time, and I can't get it out of my head."

Therapist: "Health concerns are extremely common and in anxious people, they can be very convincing even when the person is physically fit. You told me earlier that your doctor recently gave you a clean bill of health?"

Few obsessive minds would be satisfied and reassured by the therapist's response here. Most obsessive minds will want to argue.

Client: "Yes, she did, but I still can't be **sure** that I don't have cancer, can I? And, if I don't have it today, I could have it next month."

Now, right here, I could make a mistake. If I agree to take that question at face value and try to answer it, I will become complicit in my client's illness; an enabler even. This is known as "collusion" in therapy. We have to take great care not to become part of the continuation or worsening, however unwittingly, of our client's problems, and that translates to self-care too.

If I take the discussion on, then I have just fed the obsession monster. We will be speaking of cancer statistics, lifestyle factors, and such. These are not entirely irrelevant areas for us all to understand, but in this therapeutic model, we have provided no solutions and my client's Zealous Guard has me right where it wants me... discussing its favourite topic - cancer!

You see that, yes? We can't win that conversation. Even in therapy. There's no answer to it. The obsessive focus wants a solution but the only solution it will accept is impossible. It's asking for 24/7 365 knowledge of perfect health and safety at all times. You can't get that from a conversation. Actually, you can't get that.

The Zealous Guard believes that there is a threat and it's determined to protect its "truth" to the end. It's willing to argue. We need to be smarter than that. We need to refuse to get sucked into these conversations in the first place and then go on to **prove** our obsessive mind's anxieties are wrong, through action. We will go about our lives without bowing to the untruths and we will show the guard that nothing happens. Eventually, it will learn. Here, I've used health obsessions as an example. The same principle applies to all obsessional content.

My friend and colleague wisely once told me: -

"Either you hypnotise your client… or your client will hypnotise you."

It's my job (and now, it's yours) to avoid **colluding** with your obsessive illness by unskilfully giving the content of your obsessions unfettered discussion time. My job is to bring you back into the world of the well. That's me, hypnotising you. If I get repeatedly sucked into your world of unresolvable uncertainties, then you have hypnotised me.

Your job, as the person who will be bringing these obsessive worries to an end, is the same.

You'll need to stop entertaining an internal dialogue about the content of your obsessions.

That's your mind hypnotising you. Instead, use that brain power to start having a serious conversation about what needs to happen to beat the whole thing - all of it. We want the Hydra's immortal head and we want it firmly under control. The content is not the problem. An anxious/OCD brain is.

Let's go a little deeper.

What leverage do we have to ensure that we don't keep finding ourselves caught in these mind loops? Well, experience helps. How many times has your mind tortured you with one concern or another which has turned out to be entirely baseless?

You will argue, of course, that such episodes have been involuntary and I agree. They have been. Let's not omit the fact though, that they are also the result of a long-term pattern of buying into the obsessions that preceded them. At some point, we have to get a foot in the door and make a stand. Perhaps you are more ready now than you've ever been to put a halt to this nightmarish roundabout?

Something to be aware of is the potential for you to react with **shock** to your intrusive thoughts. We discussed this earlier. Now we're further along, we can ask, "Why are you shocked? Isn't this the same material you've witnessed over and over? You know what's coming." Remember we are more "suggestible" when we are in shock. This increases the likelihood of you believing things that are not true.

How do we avoid shock?

We anticipate.

Your job is to **anticipate** that the thoughts and feelings will come, and then **accept** their presence without reacting. These are the two A's - **Anticipate and Accept**. If you're expecting visitors, then you won't be surprised when they arrive.

Here's another typical real-world conversation that highlights the mercurial nature of these mind loops: -

Client: "I have these terrible thoughts that my mum is going to die suddenly. I know it's irrational but I find myself tortured by images of her funeral. I see myself looking ashamed, knowing that if I'd been there, I could have saved her."

Therapist: "So, how is your mum's health right now?"

Client: "Mostly, she's good. She did have a heart attack about five years ago but she had an artery stent fitted. She was given a clean bill of health and she's looking after herself much better these days. She's fitter than me now. I still worry though."

Therapist: "How much of your day do you spend feeling anxious about her health?"

Client: "Oh... it's all the time. It keeps me awake at night."

Therapist: "So... what kind of effect is that having on your life?"

Client: "Well, I call my mum at least three times a day to check on her. She's very good about it and always tries to reassure me but even after I put the phone down, I start worrying immediately. Plus, I feel bad for worrying her."

Therapist: "Do you think that the problem is your mum's health or your mind playing tricks on you?"

Client: "I'm not sure. I mean, nobody can say for sure that she won't die suddenly, can they?"

Therapist: "No. That's the uncertainty that we all live with. Let's talk about how we can settle your mind so that it doesn't bombard you with these awful worries and feelings all day long. We are going to learn how to self-soothe first and then I'll teach you how to handle these anxious thoughts so that they don't have so much power over you." (My client is lost deep in thought but not about the proposal I just offered. The obsession still has control.)

Client: "Do you think my mum could die suddenly though? You can't guarantee that she won't, can you?"

Therapist: "No. I can't guarantee that. Nobody can."

Client: "Well, how can I relax if I can't be sure that she's safe?"

Therapist: "Let's just suppose that I could give you a one hundred per cent guarantee that your mum will live happily to a ripe old age. Do you think your mind would be relaxed then?"

Client: "It would help a lot."

Therapist: "Have you always worried about your mum?"

Client: "I think it began after the heart attack."

Therapist: "Think back now. Before your mum had her heart attack, were you a very relaxed person?"

Client: "Er… no. Come to think of it, I used to worry about dying a lot then too. I thought about my sister and my dad and I often thought that I might die in my sleep. It stopped for years but came back recently."

Therapist: "What do you think that might tell us?"

Client: "Yeah… I suppose it's been going on for a while."

Therapist: "You were asking me a moment ago to try to give you some reassurance that your mum couldn't die suddenly. We know we can't get that and even if we had it, the mind would soon find something else to worry about because it's really all about anxiety, and that will find something to attach to. If it wasn't Mum, it would be something else.

Client: "I kind of know that. I just can't see how I'm ever going to relax?"

Therapist: We're getting to that…

Let's note that this client will need to stop calling Mum repeatedly for reassurance as her first task. That's where we will initially focus our attention. Those far-too-frequent reassurance calls are like oxygen to the anxiety-obsession fire.

If I had tried to talk to my client about the details of her mum's health, her statistical chances of dying suddenly, how she might cope if her mum did die suddenly, or any other version of talking about Mum's likelihood of dying, it would suppose that the conversation is valid and necessary. We would be talking about this as if it were a real and imminent threat. I'd be colluding with her anxiety. This is the same conversation that my client has been having with themselves for a long time. It's a stalemate. Nobody moves.

There is a time and a place for a rational analysis of any given obsessive concern but that should be a one-hit deal, written down, done. I'll be giving you that tool later. After that, further rumination on the matter is for rumination's sake and achieves nothing of value. Once you have analysed the situation logically, it should **then** become your agenda to discontinue giving your attention to the **content** of your obsessive thoughts. All of your brain power from this point forward should be focused on solutions. The monologue/dialogue where you seek constant reassurance that "X" might or might not happen is a conversation that has already been flogged to death and it will only lead you back to where you started.

With perhaps the odd exception (you decide... is it truly an emergency?) discussing the merits of the uncontrollable is a conversation for never. We, humans, can and do live comfortably alongside uncertainty every day. Some humans thrive in it. Risk is a drug to some. It is within our capacity, when calm, to tolerate uncertainty with excitement for what it may bring. We are quietly prepared for the worst but when we are calm, we are connected to the best version of ourselves, and we can thrive in the moment and ride the ups and downs of life more comfortably.

You are going to be policing how much time you spend in discussion with both yourself and others about the content of your OCD or anxious thoughts, going forwards. Make sure that you're not inadvertently working against your interests by keeping these conversations alive willingly or worse still, enthusiastically.

There is a world of difference between being kind to the parts of yourself who live in fear of what these obsessions might mean and being open to having endless discussions about the content of your obsessional thoughts and feelings. The question to focus on is not *How can I be sure that my mum won't drop dead suddenly?* It's *Am I being kind to the parts of myself who are feeling alarmed by these unnecessary and worrying thoughts?*

We know that these thoughts are intrusive, unwanted, and negative by definition. You're not to blame when they show up and demand attention but you do need to know that you can't afford to go there and get serious about refusing their demands upon your attention, consistently.

What To Do Instead

The advice is clear. Sit tight. Don't respond. Figure out what a normal life should look like for you and aim in that direction. Cultivate courage with small victories. Your obsessions will make doing that challenging but they'll show you where you still need to work. You will go towards that which your obsessions tell you to avoid and cease the safety behaviours too. Full defiance. At a measured pace.

Whatever directly challenges the obsession's unnecessarily fearful assumptions is exactly what you want to aim to be doing. Doing the polar opposite of what your obsessions tell you to do is the key to beating them. Once you get in your stride, you might even relish the challenge.

You have just learned how to "formally" sit with your discomfort or fear. The essence of the message that you will now have been sending to the anxious part/s of yourself is as follows: -

"I get that you feel afraid and I'm truly sorry that you are having a difficult time with these fears. I'm here for you and I want you to know that these feelings are not telling you the truth. You are safe because (plus *whatever your anxious part needs to hear right now*.) Trust me. I've/We've got this."

This statement is a huge departure from an endless conversation about whether your fears will be made manifest if you don't take corrective action.

Do you remember the go-kart racing earlier in the book? Do you remember how we looked at learning a new skill and how that skill eventually becomes automatic? And brain plasticity? This is that too. If you have been practising the format presented in *The Heart Bears Witness* chapter, your brain will have become familiar with that sequence of acknowledgement, witnessing, and compassionate reassurance.

As much as I made a big fuss about the importance of making time and space to formally practice this acceptance method of anxiety relief in a meditative format, what I didn't expand upon earlier is that once you have this sequence practised, it can actually be done in moments, anywhere at all. You don't need to have an undisturbed meditational space. You could be standing in the queue at the supermarket and run the sequence in your mind's eye. Yes, even with your eyes open. Nobody needs to even know that you're doing it. The idea is to bring that same practice into your everyday life, not just as a formal meditation but whenever you need to self-support.

Once you have an understanding of the basic format of going "to" your difficult feelings, as opposed to running away from them, then it is as simple as noticing that you're having a difficult thought or feeling and then bringing compassionate attention to that thought and/or feeling with an "I've got this!" message. Patiently. Repeatedly. Sincerely. You aim to feel it. You don't do this to make it go away. You do this to show yourself that you can tolerate the presence of a difficult anxious moment with calm and compassion.

You will not always be in a situation where you can take ten minutes out to sit yourself down and go through the process "formally". That's okay. I'm saying that once practised sufficiently, the formality becomes less important. In practice, you can just take a short moment to bring your attention to the obsessive thought with its accompanying anxiety and apply the quick version, "I get it. I'm sorry it feels scary. Trust me. I've got this..." message in seconds. It won't have the depth and engagement that you might expect from a formal meditation session but if you've practiced it for a while, you will have formed new neural pathways that will send the same message. Providing that your application is sincere, it should be sufficient to give you the clarity and purpose you need to refute your anxious thoughts and feelings in the moment. That's control.

When you look at it this way, we are talking about a few seconds of mindful attention. There's no promise that the feelings will magically vanish but we will be aiming for **tolerance** initially. Comfort will come later when you've won a few more battles.

The outcome of successfully implementing this strategy repeatedly and consistently is that it will begin to become second nature to you. Eventually, it becomes automatic. When that happens, fear itself becomes something that you are increasingly less afraid of and that's a huge part of the battle concluded. The brain ceases to generate anxiety about something it doesn't need to fear.

Chapter Eighteen – Morality - Don't Get Snagged!

Cognitive Behavioural Therapy (CBT) uses the helpful words, **adaptive and maladaptive,** to describe our patterns of thoughts and behaviours.

As human beings, we tend to feel that our experiences are either good or bad, right or wrong. That's called binary thinking. Black and white. But life is many shades of grey in between. The terms adaptive and maladaptive bypass this **moral** judgment and offer a way of studying our thoughts and behaviours more objectively, without blame or shame.

Asking whether a thought or behaviour is "adaptive" or not is another way of saying, "Does it help you?" That which hinders is labelled as "maladaptive." That which helps is labelled as "adaptive".

When a thought causes a feeling of moral judgment, it is immediately stress-provoking. If you find yourself judged by that thought (i.e. *I'm a bad or evil person for having these thoughts*), the chances are that you'll feel personal shame or anguish. If the thought judges something/someone else, then you may feel anger or hostility. Both are stress-related responses and the name of the game here is to reduce stress because it creates tension and anxiety in the brain and body and this will increase the power of obsessional content.

I was recently asked about Relationship OCD - a perfect example to use for this illustration.

In Relationship OCD, the sufferer will experience repetitive intrusive negative thoughts and feelings about their relationship/s. Most commonly, it will be a romantic partner. One very common theme here is the feeling of not being sure whether they (the sufferer) love their partner or will continue to love them.

Ordinarily, we could all feel this in a relationship. Feelings wax and wane, relationships go from hot to cool and back again in cycles and it's quite normal to have moments of questioning. This condition is different though. It's persistent, nagging, and filled with constant dread, usually without much reason.

All of the people I've worked with in this area have had nothing but glowing things to say about their partners, and there may well be a clue in that fact. Having met somebody so wonderful, the fear of losing them increases. On top of that, we have the old OCD favourite - *What if something I do or don't do causes a catastrophe?*

Then, there's the guilt. When this person feels like they "might" not love their partner, they can also feel like they must be a terrible person for thinking or feeling such things, especially when their partner is an angel in every respect. They may feel dishonest, fraudulent, and undeserving. At the same time, they will be terrified of being such a difficult partner, with their anxieties, that they may lose their partner as a result. Whichever way they frame it, they suspect that they will be the architect of a relational disaster, and all of these thoughts and feelings at once cause a sense of emotional overwhelm.

You see then, how there is a "moral" implication to the problem? There are "shoulds" involved. Poorly selected "shoulds" create anxiety.

Remember the helpful phrase, "Stop should-ing all over yourself."

The problem usually has little to do with whether this person loves their partner. It has everything to do with anxiety. It's partly about a fear of loss, abandonment, or failure. Were such a loss to occur, it would simply confirm that we were not good enough to be in our partner's life. Worry ensues because that outcome is too awful to contemplate and we therefore "must" avoid that happening. Then, what would normally be the relatively relaxed arrangement of allowing a relationship to have its normal ups and downs can suddenly feel like walking a tightrope and once that's happened, we have invoked "the law of reversed effort." The harder we consciously try to make something happen, the more difficult that action becomes.

When we apply this principle to "controlling" consciously those aspects of life that are usually taken care of unconsciously, we have hypervigilance, and here it is specifically about the relationship. That results in paranoia, second-guessing, reading too much into everyday interactions, and personal confusion. Real-life relationships are complicated and imperfect with occasions when we are the best and worst versions of ourselves. The last thing any of us should be doing is making long-term negative predictions based on momentary and passing upsets.

Enter… "Adaptive versus maladaptive". These two little words are here to save the day.

Anna (a fictional character) is to be married shortly to the man of her dreams. They are planning a baby too. She's ecstatically happy about it but as the days pass by she is feeling increasingly anxious and confused. This isn't just pre-wedding jitters. Her thoughts and feelings are a scrambled mess. She finds her mind ruminating on images of discovering that she and her partner hate each other after six months of marriage. She keeps imagining feeling nothing for him, even cheating on him. She keeps having the thought that she might not love the baby they might make together. She doesn't know what to believe. She has lost touch with what's real and what's anxiety at this point. These are called **maladaptive** perspectives. Mal is the Latin root word for bad. Maladaptive means that the current strategy is a bad adaptation to current circumstances.

The question we need to ask is this. "Are these thoughts and feelings **adaptive**?" Or, put another way: -

1) What is that you want? – Define it.
2) Does thinking/feeling this way help you to achieve that?

One could argue that Anna's problem is that she doesn't know what she wants. Anxiety will tell her that. That's a lie. She does know. She just has the ugly voice of anxiety whispering nastiness in her ear, causing her to doubt what she wants and doubt her ability to have and keep it. That's really what it's about.

We've established that this marriage **is** what she wants. Can we guarantee a happy ending? No. Nobody can. Life is risk. Nothing ventured, nothing gained. We can cope with that truth when we're not anxious.

If we know that she wants to make this marriage happen, then making it happen is the only relevant point.

The problem with problems is that our minds can get "snagged" on them. Snagged is the correct word. All of our focus goes to the problem, rather than the planned destination for the day.

What happens though if the "problem" is intangible? What if it's only thoughts and feelings that are holding us back? One of my colleagues once told me, "I always know what the right thing to do is. It's the exact opposite of what my fears tell me I shouldn't do." Granted, this could be a recipe for disaster if followed recklessly but I think the spirit of that position is admirable and useful. On the other side of the comfort zone lies a new world.

Problems of this mental/emotional nature can make us take our eyes off the ball. If we get snagged on one for long enough, it can become so all-consuming that we forget where we are going. This is what's happened to Anna. She has become so preoccupied with her problem that she now can't see clearly that she's marrying the man she loves.

The problem has not only managed to rob her of her joy, but it has also taken her certainty and convinced her that the marriage itself, or her trustworthiness, is the problem. It's not. The anxiety is the problem, not the marriage or her intentions. The anxiety is now so huge though that it's the only thing her mind is focusing upon.

Luckily, there's a way to remedy this. We just have to ask the right question in the right way. Here's what I'm going to ask Anna: -

"If you knew for sure that you love Steve with all your heart and that you intend to be with him, make a family, and stay together for the rest of your days, then how would you feel about this marriage?"

This is known as "removing the limiting assumption." Can you see how it works?

We are asking Anna to **imagine** what her situation would look and feel like if the problem **were removed** from the equation. Her imagination has gotten her into this mess. Now, we can use it to get her out.

Her mind may well fight us initially. She might say, "Yes... but ... I don't know that, do I?" It's this thought which has kept her locked in the battle. We persevere. We ask her to suspend judgment for a moment and just **imagine** the situation **without** the problem.

She takes the instruction, a deep breath, and closes her eyes. I can see that she is visualising it and her lips curl into a soft smile. "I'd be over the moon. I'd be looking forward to wearing my dress, celebrating with friends and family, a great honeymoon, and settling down with the man I love".

At that moment, Anna sees the situation. There is no tangible reason why that could not happen. There are doubts but nothing truly solid. We are reminding Anna of the destination. For a moment she can see **past** the snag. Yes, the doubt returns but even a glimpse is a start.

There is quite a lot going on here. It seems too simple to be helpful but if we understand the mechanics behind the exercise, we can find real value here.

Firstly, we have what we call a "re-frame". This "snagging" business demands our full attention, as explained. Our brains then literally do not see past that. It becomes all and everything. By removing the problem, **imaginatively**, we see the solution, **framing** the situation from a new perspective.

Sometimes, this is all we need to do. We simply need a glance at how things would look if everything turned out well. Anna has forgotten how to imagine things going well because the snag has become all-consuming. The paralysis is sustained by the lack of a definite direction. The mind can't work with that. That's why I keep saying, "Pick a side and stick to it."

In addition to this, we could go further. She's had a glance of what could happen "if the anxiety were no longer present". Now I'm asking her to flesh it out for me. I ask Anna to close her eyes and tell me the story of her non-anxious wedding in detail from start to finish. I want more than a snapshot. I want a video.

She begins…

"I can see myself arriving at the church in my beautiful dress. I have a few nerves but that's normal. It's a big day for anyone. I do maybe have the odd worry but this is my day and I won't let fear stand in my way. So, I relax. When I see Steve, he looks so handsome in his suit. I feel my heart skip a beat… in a good way though… and as I walk down the aisle, I'm feeling proud. We're doing this… I mean doing it. I made it. I'm here…

Laborious as it may seem, I prompt her to spend ten full minutes, with her eyes still closed, telling me the full story, the reception, the honeymoon, being pregnant, becoming a mum, living a long and happy married life with Steve. I know that as she relays her story, she must visualise it too.

Do we know for sure that it will all be happily ever after? No, of course not. We do know though that forecasting the future tends to amplify the possibility of a self-fulfilling prophecy so it's simple logic to aim for the best possible outcome. Anna might be doubtful. "What if" will arise, maybe repeatedly but we keep our focus on what will help rather than what we know definitely won't. Negatively forecasting the future is only going to make her anxious, so logically we focus on positively forecasting the future.

And that, right there, is what you call an **adaptive** thought pattern. It helps her to go where she **wants** to go or get what she wants to get. It does not guarantee an outcome but it does give us the best possible chance of achieving what we want to achieve.

Asking Anna to start at the beginning of the story and move all the way through to "happily ever after" is not only a good practice in the moment; it is also a form of mental re-programming. She has almost certainly not done this recently. The only images she has absorbed since her anxieties took hold have been those that focused on what could go wrong.

The simple act of a positive mental rehearsal (visualisation) of how things turn out when they go well overwrites the old images of disaster and reconnects her with positive feelings. Ideally, this process is practised in a safe place and a state of relaxation. When this positive mental rehearsal is repeated often, calmly, the brain learns to associate relaxation with that particular rehearsed event. This has the effect of desensitising the brain's fearful emotional response to the stimulus and also creating a positive expectation for the future. Both of these outcomes reduce anxiety and encourage better engagement with the world.

Right now, I just want to make the point that this **adaptive** approach to getting what you want is both effective and more importantly, sidesteps the potential pitfalls of approaching problems through the lens of morality.

If I'd asked Anna whether she thought it was **right or wrong** that she felt these feelings of doubt about Steve and their life together, I would only have muddied the waters further. The obsessive mind often looks for **moral perfection**. That's why we want to get away from labelling things as "good or bad, right or wrong." If we use the language of morality, we are placing ourselves at a disadvantage. It's easy for our fears to suck us into a conversation for never by using morality against us.

For example. If your obsessive thoughts tell you that your refusal to carry out an obsessive pattern or compulsive behaviour will result in somebody being harmed, then as a "good" person, you clearly must comply. Even risking such an outcome could be considered **immoral.**

In Anna's example, she considers herself to be recklessly risking Steve's well-being with the feeling that she may unwittingly betray him, and herself, at a later date. An "adaptive or maladaptive?" approach can bypass this problem instantly and painlessly. Helpful and adaptive are much better indicators of where we should be steering our thought processes and behaviours than right or wrong.

Will the marriage survive? Can Anna trust herself? We didn't go there. We avoided right and wrong, good, bad, and what-ifs. We asked instead whether her current thought patterns and behaviours were **helping** her to get what she wanted. Were those thoughts **adaptive**? No, they weren't. So, we provided a tool that helped her to "do" adaptive instead.

Will that be enough to completely solve her difficulty? Maybe. In practice, it's usually the case that other factors have contributed to the state of anxiety. In a perfect world, we'd address these too. We can be sure though that this simple shift in perspective, looking beyond the snags, will be at least a part of the overall solution. Adjust the principles to your needs. Use it formally, as part of your treatment plan, or informally in any moments of gloomy outlook. It will help.

Chapter Nineteen – Preparations

Back in the introduction to this third part of the book, I mentioned that some therapeutic textbooks are too complex to be user-friendly. I said, "Real-world therapy needs to be made simple for the recipient."

For the sake of thoroughness, I'm going to share with you the clinical terms that apply to our agenda. Then, I'm going to simplify the whole thing because too much clinical-speak may leave you feeling cold and excluded. We've come this far. I want to see you put everything you have learned into practice. That means keeping it simple enough that it's easy to remember and easy to apply, hopefully in just one read. Again, please don't be put off by the unfamiliar terms.

First, here's the clinical bit. Research will reveal to you that the main clinically recommended treatments for obsessive-compulsive difficulties are as follows: -

CBT – Cognitive Behavioural Therapy

Cognitive = How you perceive/think. (Recognise is to re-cognise... to know/perceive again).

Behavioural = How you behave in response to how you perceive/think.

Therapy = Learning how to use **adaptive** perspectives and behavioural change to challenge catastrophic thinking, decrease negative emotional arousal, and increase well-being.

ERP – Exposure And Response Prevention

Exposure = Willingly exposing yourself to material (usually feared) that you would normally avoid.

Response Prevention = Not doing (preventing) what you normally do when you feel afraid or threatened. That will mean either a) not "avoiding" feared situations (including inside your mind) and/or b) not "doing" a "safety behaviour" such as cleaning, checking, or ritualising.

These tools are both well-tested and occupy a similar field. They bring relief and control to many people. The main obstacle to making them work for you is **application**. If you don't use them, you won't see results, and if they seem complicated you may well not do them at all. I'm going to do my level best to help in this regard. Nonetheless, it will require some application on your part. I'm afraid that ultimately, even with a personal therapist, you'll still normally be advised that you have to do this part for yourself.

We'll open a fictional case study to illustrate how this will work in practice.

Nadia is a twenty-seven-year-old female. She has been troubled by intense unwanted intrusive thoughts since she was seventeen but she's never told anyone except her parents about the specific nature of her worries. They are "disgusting" - her words, not mine.

I ask her to tell me about them. She looks ashamed. This is a big deal for her.

"Probably the worst one…" she pauses, shaken, before starting again. "Probably the worst one… is the one where I hurt kids."

I wait.

"Like, if I see a kid coming towards me on the street, I have the thought that I might just push them into the road as they come by. Sometimes I imagine them being run over. Then I start thinking about how I'd go to prison and probably end up killing myself. I'd deserve it too. I couldn't live with that on my conscience."

She smiles, ironically, as she lowers her eyes, partly in embarrassment, partly in recognition of how it sounds when she says it out loud.

"And… have you ever acted upon one of these thoughts?" I ask, already knowing the answer.

"NO", she retorts loudly, her eyes suddenly upon me, before softening. "God, no. I couldn't imagine anything worse!"

*She doesn't realise how true and perceptive what she just said is. That's exactly the problem. Her OCD mind will use her **worst imaginings** against her,*

"So… how do you handle this in life?", I ask. "Do you have a strategy?"

"Well… if I see a young person walking or cycling towards me, I usually get my phone out and pretend to be looking at that. It helps me to distract until the kid has passed. On my worst days, I have turned around and headed home."

"Okay", I say, "and what other scary thoughts or themes do you experience?"

She looks serious. I can tell that she's unsure about sharing this.

"Well… sometimes I think about the fact that I have these violent thoughts about hurting kids and then I start wondering whether I have something against them. Then, my mind says that it's probably because I like kids… like sexually… and that I'm in denial about it, so I want to hurt them to deny my real feelings. If I'm hurting them, I can't be attracted to them, can I? Like, I'm not though… you know… a paedophile or anything. And I know I don't want to hurt anybody. I love kids but not like that. It still gets me though. Like, what if I am and I don't know it?"

…

Let's pause there. Based on what you've learned so far, how effective do you think it would be if I were to try to use pure logic to talk her out of the idea that she might secretly be a danger to children?

We know that Nadia cannot suppress her thoughts. These are automatic, involuntary, intrusive thoughts. She neither asked for them nor actively sought to retain them. Presently, it's fair to say that she is somewhat at the mercy of her obsessive-anxious brain. Suppression won't work.

We continue. I ask her for other examples of daily ruminations and we soon have a list of obsessive fears which play on repeat for Nadia at different times. The next step is to identify how these fears impact Nadia's daily life. What do these fears cause Nadia to avoid in life? What kind of safety behaviours (compulsions) does Nadia do to retain her sense of control?

We place them in order of severity and impact using a one to ten scale, with ten being the most challenging of her behaviours/avoidances to challenge. Here's what we end up with: -

10) Fear of carrying out a violent or abusive act upon a child. (The number one fear.)

Daily impact: Stops me from going anywhere there are likely to be children. I avoid children wherever possible. I take out my phone and look at it to pretend I'm busy. On a bad day, I might pretend I have forgotten something and turn around so that I don't have to pass them. I prefer to stay home whenever possible, especially outside of school hours. It's just easier that way.

9) Fear of going to prison for life.

Daily impact: I avoid opening official-looking post in case it's a court summons. Maybe I hurt a kid and forgot or suppressed the memory? Those brown envelopes bring me out in a cold sweat. I take this post to my mum's house and she screens it for me. I feel panic when I see a police car. I think, "This is it! They have come for me now. They know about my thoughts."

8) Fear of having a child of my own.

Daily impact: Regular feelings of loss and loneliness. I avoid romance. Nobody would want me to be a mother to their children. I couldn't trust myself around any child. I spend a lot of time ruminating about this.

7) Fear of accepting invitations.

Daily impact: I usually find an excuse to refuse an invitation. People have mostly stopped inviting me to things. I feel lonely and isolated.

6) Fear of movies, TV shows, radio presentations, or books that might involve children being harmed.

Daily impact: I have to read a review of a movie or show before I watch it. I usually read the spoilers too, just to make sure that there is a happy ending. If I can't be sure that the kids in the story or movie are safe, I just can't face it. In practice, I avoid most media, just in case.

5) Fear of ever speaking about children in case something awful slips out of my mouth. I often feel like I might say something that could make people think I want to harm children. Then I'd be "outed". I might even go to prison if they knew.

Daily impact: I never ask friends or family how their kids are doing. I change the subject quickly if they mention their kids. In practice, I end up putting off speaking to my friends and family, just in case. This one breaks my heart.

1-4) Various other thoughts and behaviours relating to child avoidance and guilt.

Daily impact: Minimal but wearing!

Using this model, we are going to classify the avoidance/behaviours within the 1-4 range as symptomatic spin-offs. We could work therapeutically on them but to do so might be considered tinkering around the edges. We will begin our work with those themes that cause real-life limitation and distress - those concerns rated five and above. When those are dealt with, these spin-offs will cease to operate. They are offshoots from the larger concerns.

For the avoidance of doubt, let's be clear that the chance of Nadia being a secret child-abusing sociopath who doesn't yet know it... is precisely, absolutely, indisputably... zero.

People who may be minded and willing to undertake such acts would have no reason to seek therapy and even less reason to share their intentions with a stranger. I will proceed with full confidence that Nadia's anxious mind is the problem here. She will be full of doubts about this as we begin our treatment. I will ask her to trust the process. The time for talk is over. We are moving into a place of **action** now.

With our completed list, we now have Nadia's top six obsession-related fears (5-10).

The next step is to identify the various ways in which Nadia is either avoiding or compensating, in response to these particular intrusive thoughts.

For clarity, we are going to categorise these as follows: -

Avoidance Behaviour = Any behaviour that seeks to avoid a confrontation with the feared object/theme (i.e. avoiding going out).

Safety Behaviour/Compulsion = Any behaviour undertaken to attempt to make the feared object/theme safe (i.e. excessive cleaning).

Pure "O" = Pure Obsession = Mental anguish and worry from repetitive intrusive thoughts.

With each of these categories, our basic plan is to aim to:

* Cease avoidance behaviours

* Cease safety/compulsive behaviours

* Desensitise our minds to the presence of frightening thoughts and ideas.

Here are the same categories, with the avoidance, compulsions and/or obsessions listed out so that we can see them.

10) Fear of carrying out a violent or abusive act upon a child.

Avoidance Behaviour: Avoiding anywhere with children present or subjects involving children, which often results in not going out at all.

Compulsion: Pretending to be distracted or lost. Carefully planning routes and times to avoid children.

Pure "O": A ruthless stream of fear and negative inner chatter when out in public.

9) Fear of going to prison for life.

Avoidance Behaviour: Avoiding opening mail. Avoiding police.

Compulsion: Having Mum open brown envelopes.

Pure "O": Fear of thoughts that contain ideas about going to prison.

8) Fear of having a child of my own.

Avoidance Behaviours: Avoiding any possibility of romantic relationships.

Compulsions: Dwelling on past relationships. Rehearsing terrible love outcomes in the mind.

Pure "O": Intrusive, upsetting thoughts and feelings of self-loathing and being a "bad person". Ongoing ruminations about having a restricted and lonely life experience.

7) Fear of accepting invitations.

Avoidance Behaviours: Withdrawal from social life. Deactivation of social media and chit-chat apps. Not answering communications.

Compulsions: Spending hours and hours drafting "appropriate" invitation refusal letters which are never sent because they never seem right.

Pure "O": Panicky feelings when receiving communications from anyone but her mum and dad. Racing thoughts about how to refuse invitations without severing friendships or people becoming suspicious. An ever-present feeling of guilt and concern about being "found out".

6) Fear of movies, TV shows, radio presentations, or books/articles that might involve children being harmed.

Avoidance Behaviours: Media avoidance.

Compulsions: Excessive checking of reviews and descriptions.

Pure "O": Anxious thoughts and feelings about what might happen next in the book, movie, or media which removes any pleasure from consuming media that might otherwise have been enjoyed.

5) Fear of ever speaking about children in case something awful slips out of my mouth. I often feel like I might say something that could make people think I want to harm children. Then I'd be "outed". I might even go to prison if they knew.

Avoidance Behaviours: Avoiding communications and invitations from friends/family who have children, in case the subject comes up.

Compulsions: Changing the subject quickly if the children are spoken about. Reading and re-reading all communications to determine whether there are any "hidden" meanings or veiled accusations of impropriety.

Pure "O": Feeling shame and guilt about even mentioning the name of a child. A sense of having done something terrible even though nothing has happened or will. Ongoing ruminations about what might happen if something inappropriate were to slip out.

Graded Exposure

There are two main ways in which human beings can desensitise from fear-invoking situations. The first of these is to have an epiphany. Whether it is by therapy, a life experience, or a grace, an epiphany is a moment in time when something that has seemed previously insoluble is suddenly understood from a much more helpful and illuminated perspective. When a message arrives that conclusively ends the reason for fear to be present (such as a new updated understanding), then it's quite natural for the Zealous Guard to scratch that item off the watch list. The result is that the fear around that object/situation vanishes. Poof! Gone.

The problem with this method is that it's not repeatable to order. It requires subconscious agreement and that is usually supported by a process of some kind. Logic alone cannot make this happen. It has to reach the Zealous Guard with enough evidence of its truth that the Zealous Guard **can** re-categorize the object as safe. That usually involves a fairly profound depth of understanding and often a new piece of information. We can create the conditions for such a thing to occur. Therapy attempts to do just that and succeeds often but eliciting instant epiphanies is not repeatable to order.

Desensitisation, however, **is** a science of sorts. It is repeatable. It is reliable. It doesn't require psychological gymnastics or deep and meaningful realisations to succeed. It is evidence-based.

It's a matter of spending enough time in the presence of an object or situation (without panic) that the brain is forced to re-classify that object's/situation's threat level downwards.

A lower threat level equals less anxiety. Less threat/anxiety means fewer and less intense obsessive ruminations.

We call this method **graded** exposure because it is not **random** exposure. We have already graded Nadia's fears from five to ten, with ten being the worst thing she could imagine being exposed to. Although she tells us that her obsessions focus on the fear of **harming** children, from a behavioural perspective, what is happening is that she is **avoiding** children and anything that involves children.

Now, we can begin to truly understand some of the earlier lessons in this book. Remember how I explained that there is a difference between the **content** of the obsessions and the real problem of anxiety? Well, that's what we are seeing here. To discuss the ins and outs of how likely it is that she'll lose control and harm a child is a conversation for never. We would be focusing on her fear of harming rather than her avoidance of normal life. That approach will be fruitless and circular.

What we want to focus on is how Nadia is going to do the things that she needs to do while tolerating the discomfort of the anxious sensations. One way or another, that's going to involve her deliberately challenging her mind's assumptions that she cannot be safely around children. As I said, the time for talk is over.

We can only achieve this with **action**. We are going to have to **prove** to Nadia's Zealous Guard that she can be around children safely, even with anxiety, with nothing untoward happening. We are going to do that by encouraging Nadia to face her fears directly and adjust her behaviours accordingly. That means deliberately placing herself in situations that involve children but we will build up to that in time. We must move gently if we are to succeed.

"Flooding" is a therapeutic term that proposes that the best way to get over a fear is to jump in at the deep end, that is, "flood" yourself with the object of your fears. If you fear snakes, just jump in a pit of them and stay there for an hour. Bingo! Your fear will disappear. Oddly enough, there's some truth in this but it's a terrible idea for most people. It's a method that will almost certainly result in our sufferer being completely overwhelmed, having an awful time, and feeling traumatised afterwards. Not the effect we were hoping for. Which is exactly why we don't do that.

Graded means "gentle". We don't start at ten. We start at the manageable but challenging levels, in this case at five, and we don't move on to the next fear until we have mastered each stage. If we threw Nadia in a ball pit with a bunch of kids on day one, she would struggle, to put it mildly. Instead, we commence at the bottom, with the least troubling of her fears, and set out to diligently begin the great pushback.

Chapter Twenty - The Great Pushback

You have been in retreat.

Every time that an obsession or compulsion has forced you to perform an avoidance or safety behaviour, you have lost ground. Your touchdown line is at the other end of the pitch. Think American football and you have your model. Your job is to get that ball to that touchline.

Just as with American football, you need pushback. Rarely does a player take the ball and run the whole length of the field with it. The ground is usually won in increments, sometimes just a few yards at a time.

An American football field is one hundred yards from end to end. You are beginning at the forty-yard line. You have sixty yards of ground to claim. It won't be a straight-line forward. You will lose the ball sometimes. You will lose ground on occasion. You will need to win it back and go again. Opponents aim to stop you.

Let's get back to Nadia. Her first task is to go from the forty-yard line to the fifty-yard line. Just ten yards. That's all.

If she expects to go to the eighty-yard line on her first run, she's going to be sorely disappointed, collapse in defeat and walk off the field. Small victories are how it's done. Every yard counts so count every yard.

Here, for easy access, is a reminder of the content of Nadia's first task to tackle: -

5) Fear of ever speaking about children in case something awful slips out of my mouth. I often feel like I might say something that could make people think I want to harm children. Then I'd be "outed". I might even go to prison if they knew.

Avoidance Behaviours: Avoiding friends/family who have children. Avoiding public spaces.

Compulsions/Safety Behaviours: Changing the subject quickly if children are spoken about. Reading and re-reading communications to determine whether there are any "hidden" meanings or veiled accusations of impropriety.

Intrusive Thoughts & Feelings: Feeling shame and guilt about even mentioning the name of a child. A sense of having done something terrible even though nothing has happened or will. Ongoing ruminations about what "might" happen if something inappropriate were to be said.

It would be easy to assume that we need to stop her negative thoughts before she can make progress with tackling her behaviours. That's incorrect. We know that it's the other way around. Make progress on the behaviours and the thoughts will have less fuel because her "belief" in the threat will be eroded by new evidence. So, for now, let's just put the thoughts to one side and concentrate solely on avoidance and compulsions.

The aim of our work is simple to understand: -

Everything that anxious thoughts and feelings tell you to avoid, you deliberately expose yourself to.

Everything that anxious thoughts and feelings tell you that you must do to remain safe, you stop doing.

Following that logic, and starting gently, here's our plan for Nadia.

1) Avoidance becomes an approach. Nadia's task now is to actively seek contact with her friends and family who have children and to ask them specifically how the kids are doing. (General chit-chat and reconnection are also welcome.)
2) Compulsion becomes a refusal to act on those urges. Nadia's task here is to refuse to act on her urge to silence herself. Her active work will now involve speaking up when she used to remain silent because she didn't trust what she'd say. That behaviour needs to go. It supports anxiety. In the simplest terms possible, Nadia is going to feel the fear and speak anyway.

Let's think about what Nadia has learned so far from this book and how she will use this understanding to complete this task.

1) Anxiety and/or a genetically wired worry brain is the true root of the problem.
2) She has recognised that her brain is sending her anxious signals which are in error. With an understanding of how and why this can happen to humans, she now feels more confident that she can challenge the obsessions safely. She has made a consciously-driven decision to stop feeding the anxiety monster with her "buy-in", with her "belief." She is now in a position to pursue treatment with a conscious recognition that avoidance and safety behaviours have nothing to do with harming children and everything to do with anxiety, despite what her immediate feelings or thoughts might tell her at any given moment.
3) She has accepted that a complete aversion to any risk is not a position that any human can hold comfortably in an inherently risky world. Living comes first. Living involves risk. She's gathered her strength. She is ready to take some risks. She understands that becoming more comfortable with reasonable risk is a primary factor in beating her obsessions, once and for all.
4) She understands that her anxious brain will be likely to respond initially with difficult thoughts and feelings when she refuses to do as her anxious intrusive thoughts demand. She is willing to tolerate this discomfort in pursuit of the greater goal of re-training her brain. It is through successful practice and repetition of

challenging the obsession's demands that she will see her anxious thoughts and feelings diminish through time.

5) She understands that ACTION is required to force her brain to make these new connections. With consistency, she will find that the new connections in her brain will become dominant and her old fears will eventually lose their power over her. Initially, she must take this on faith. Ultimately, she will know it as truth. She has agreed with herself that she will do what it takes. In short, she has committed to the treatment with a willingness to be patient and determined.

6) She has practised the steps she learned in "the heart bears witness" chapter and has learned that she can tolerate the discomfort of anxiety, reduce the intensity of her subjective experience of fear, and be extremely kind to herself in that process. She has already made progress in this regard. Where once, tolerating the anxiety would have seemed close to impossible, she now has a tool that works. She is ready...

We need two things.

The first of these is **consistent** application. Repetition creates new patterns. New patterns feel increasingly natural the longer they continue. Therefore, repetition creates ease and a new pattern becomes a natural pattern when it has been repeated consistently.

The second of these is proof. This will hold her steady when the mechanics of recall are putting a negative spin on things. We need an accurate record of her experience. Otherwise, she'll remember it through a filter of any fear she may be experiencing in the moment. In practice, this means that her brain will forget the positive and accentuate the negative aspects of her experience when recalled as a memory, sometime later. She can outsmart this inherent leaning towards negativity by keeping an accurate record of the outcome, as it happened.

Luckily, CBT has provided a common-sense tool just for this purpose. Please allow me to introduce the "Behavioural Experiment".

Behavioural Experiments

Did I mention that the word "experiment" is super-helpful in the context of anxiety-busting? An experiment doesn't imply success or failure. It simply says "Let's see what happens?" We will adjust our approach if the outcome isn't great. That tends to take the pressure off.

The Behavioural Experiment has three basic components: -

1) Record what you think will happen when you refuse to do an avoidance or safety behaviour. Use percentages of intensity to contrast the prediction versus the outcome.
2) Apply your new therapeutic learning/tools to enter the situation you would normally avoid or be compelled to do. Complete the task.
3) Record and contrast what happened against your fearful expectations.

Let's see Nadia's first behavioural experiment in action. We are beginning by setting her a task of telephoning her sister and asking how her sister's children are doing. This tackles both her obsessions and compulsions because in her case, speaking up is the polar opposite of her compulsion to silence herself. Making the call itself is a direct challenge to her avoidance.

Expectation	Strategy (Tools Used)	Outcome
Fear - 90% Cut the conversation short – 80% Blurt out something sordid or inappropriate – 90% Too afraid to ask about the kids – 80% Expects to feel upset and worried afterwards – 95% Expecting that people will think I'm behaving strangely if I get anxious – 70%	Risk assessment. What is the realistic likelihood of doing damage? Imagining what could go right (positive visualisation). Determination to complete the task successfully. Using acknowledge, self-soothe and reassure "parts" format before, during, and after the call. Planned questions to start the conversations.	Fear 60% Successful call completed. Asked about niece. Felt afraid and shaky but did it anyway - 70% fear. Did not say anything inappropriate. Did catch up – Relieved - 90% Felt good that she'd shown her sister and niece that she cares – 80% Feeling fraudulent and worried afterwards - 40%

Now contrast Nadia's expectations against the actual **outcome** when Nadia uses her new understanding and calming skills.

We see that the outcome is much better than she expected it to be. It's not perfect but we shouldn't expect it to be, especially at this early stage. The negative thoughts and feelings are still present but they are **less intense** (see the percentages) than she imagined they would be.

In addition, she now has two important positive feelings to include that she had not anticipated before completing the experiment. She has learned that by tolerating her fear, she gets to feel good about the elements of this interaction with her sister. She has also learned that she can speak with people without saying anything inappropriate. This has provided her with a somewhat "relieved" feeling. She records both of these positives and they, along with the reduced anxieties, now serve as **evidence** of competency and some inspiration to keep up the good work.

If we have the luxury of time, we'll suggest that Nadia repeats this experiment on multiple occasions, each time with a fresh sheet of paper (or digital record). In practice, Nadia's first success should set the foundation for subsequent experiments to elicit increasingly relaxed outcomes. With each phone call to her sister, she will gain her confidence and her brain will begin to adjust anxiety levels downwards. By perhaps the third or fourth call, Nadia will begin to feel like she has this under some measure of control. If all has gone well, she will expect to be recording some fairly major shifts in her perception of an activity that used to scare her half to death. By the tenth call, the whole "ask my sister how the kids are doing" should be a piece of cake.

Sounds great, right? Is it that easy?

Well, yes, no, and it depends. Mainly on who is doing it and how life is going on any particular day.

Firstly, we know that it's easier to not make the phone call than it is to make it. That means that Nadia might become fatigued from repeatedly asking herself to face her fears. We also know that Nadia has to deal with the fallout from each call. She will experience symptoms of feeling guilty or fraudulent after she makes the calls. Her doubts will probably continue, albeit reduced as she makes progress.

We can note that she recorded her fraudulent feelings at 40% after the experiment. That's okay. She can continue to use the acknowledge, soothe and reassure system. Her meditations could include messages directed towards her fearful self, such as…

"I get that making that call was difficult for you. I'm sorry it has left you feeling guilty and fraudulent but I promise you that you have absolutely nothing to be sorry about. These feelings are error signals in the brain generated by anxiety. Every time we hold our nerve, we are winning. This will get easier and easier over time. We can do this. I've got your back."

Can you sense how supportive that kind of atmosphere is for your inner obsessive? Not only is that a true and reassuring statement (this is the reassurance that's okay!), it's also great subconscious programming. Remember, these are not empty words. They require an emotional connection to have transformative power. Anything said often enough can influence our sense of truth. The Zealous Guard hears these statements too.

The other consideration here, with regards to it being "easy" is that every day is different. Some days are going to lend themselves to successful challenges better than others. We're going to look at this in more detail shortly but it needs noting here that we'll need days off from behavioural-challenging and we'll need some flexibility in our approach too. If you haven't got it in you to do your challenge on any given day, then cut yourself some slack and take the day off. Yes, we want some consistent pushback to gain ground that we will keep but that should never involve forcing yourself into overload. Nothing can be achieved if you are overloaded.

On this occasion, Nadia wins the battle. The war is not over but she's gained her first five yards. She counts it. She now has a **record** of it too.

This written record will protect her against the negative spin that her brain may present at a low point in the future.

Brains have a way of forgetting what's good in life when in a downward spiral. Her brain may tell her that she's not making progress on a bad day two weeks from now but her written evidence tells an accurate story. She **does** win some battles. If she plays wisely, she will win almost all of them. Keeping a written record (dated and chronologically ordered) of her small victories will make this an indisputable and verifiable fact, if or when her brain has a hopeless day and gets gremlins.

On bad days, it is difficult to remember or connect with your natural joyful feelings. I always factor that into my assessments of how to handle a difficult emotional time. That results in reminding ourselves that life can be joyful at times particularly when we can't feel it in that moment. We can still know it. Remembering that is important.

This is about consistency, not perfection.

William James, the Father of American psychology said the following about habits: -

"Put yourself assiduously in conditions that encourage the new way. Make engagements incompatible with the old; take a public pledge, if the case allows; in short, envelop your resolution with every aid you know. This will give your new beginning such a momentum that the temptation to break down will not occur as soon as it otherwise might; and every day during which a breakdown is postponed adds to the chances of its not occurring at all."

Nadia is going to need to keep this up for a while but as Mr James reminded us, the longer we can hold the ground we win, the less likely we are to find our efforts ultimately undermined. Every day that we enjoy a successful pushback is a win worth counting. It's not a waste of time. It just needs to be consistent for long enough for the new patterns to bed in firmly.

We have to be realistic. Nadia is not going to want to complete a formal behavioural experiment for every occasion she has to refuse a compulsion. That could be umpteen times a day, at first. It's a tool. She can use it when she wants to. Ideally, she might formally complete one of these once a day for the first week or so and then once or twice a week as she continues. It's a good way of setting any forward movement in stone and identifying any slides or stubborn resistances.

Positive Re-Focusing Activities

I deliberately omitted this important tool from any mentions until this point as I didn't want to confuse matters with additional information. Now that you can see behavioural experiments in use in Nadia's compulsion-busting plan, we are in a good place to elaborate on this.

In some ways, the whole "acknowledge, empathize, and reassure" system could be considered a re-focusing tool. Equally, any "mindfulness" techniques can serve a similar purpose. They are tools that encourage re-focusing the mind, positively.

For clarity, let's define a positive re-focusing technique as: -

"Any chosen positive activity, either physical or mental, that draws and holds your attention, away from your current negative focus."

We have a couple of problems here. The first of these is, "Didn't you say that we need to be meeting these fears and behaviours head-on? Now, we are distracting? Well, which is it?"

That's a fair question. It's all about URGENCY!!!

A positive mental distraction is an activity that you <u>choose</u>.

If you didn't choose your distraction activity, then you were driven to it, hence the saying, "driven to distraction". There is an urgency about that because you will be frantically attempting to stop the feelings, in the moment. A positive distraction activity is not primarily aimed at <u>stopping</u> the difficult feelings in the moment. It's an activity we use to help us learn to <u>tolerate</u> the difficult feelings of compulsion-challenging. This is **building** the neural pathways for easily switching mental tracks to another activity.

For clarity, tolerating these difficult feelings by using a **chosen** distraction activity **is** meeting the fears head-on.

When you choose the activity, you're in control. When your obsessions or compulsions choose the activity, they are in control.

In OCD sufferers, we consider that this function of automatically switching mental tracks is inhibited and must now be rewired through this brain re-training process.

In anxiety/obsession sufferers, we consider that the function of **automatic positive focus** has been temporarily suspended by high emotional arousal levels.

Again, this takes practice. It requires consistent repetition for new neural habits to form. The particular habit we are aiming to build here is the habit of recognising that there are error signals (anxieties) demanding that we do a compulsion, and then **doing** something differently instead. The very act of switching tracks, mentally and behaviourally, is something we are aiming to "oil". The gears in that particular transmission are sticky at best and seized up at worst. This is the language of Dr Schultz. He talks about gears and transmission in the brain. It's a useful metaphor.

Another useful metaphor is that of actors on a stage. Lines are rehearsed and for the last ten days, all the actors have delivered their lines as expected. On day eleven, one of the actors starts delivering different lines and the entire production quickly falls apart. Unless everybody does what they are expected to do, none of the other actors' roles make sense any more. When you consider that these obsessive processes run on autopilot, you can begin to see the value of doing something differently. You disrupt the entire production. In this case, that's good.

We need various types of distraction techniques that can be used according to the dictates of the situation.

Let's discuss longer-term versus immediate distraction tools.

The longer-term distraction techniques are activities that you can become involved in on an ongoing and existential basis. These are going to be best suited to those who have time on their hands, for whatever reason. It's also worth mentioning that having an activity that generates true passion and purpose is great anti-stress medicine. If it helps you stay fit too, that's even better. Having something to do, that we love doing, can give us many hours of absorption, away from the usual thought loops. Time out of the loop is healing time. I write and record music when I can afford the time and I can burn through a worrying number of happy hours in a musical haze. It's the only time I ever truly forget to eat. Finding a passion is heartily recommended.

Failing that, learning is also useful medicine here. It can open up new life paths. Learning has never been as easy as it is now. Type a request into an internet-connected device and resources flood our way. We can be making use of them.

You can do whatever helps you to re-focus. Just make sure that what you choose is not related to your existing difficulties. Don't, for instance, choose cleaning as your activity if cleanliness, germs, and order are the focal points of your obsessional content. (Hey OCD, that's cheating!) Then, find something completely unrelated to do.

If you need some ideas though, here are a few activities that could help: -

* Jigsaw Puzzles.

* Video Games.

* Writing for fun – a story, study, journal, or poetry. If it's great, maybe you can publish it? If not, call it fun.

* Learning to play a musical instrument. Some are very easy and there are endless songs you could play with just three chords. Ukuleles are great for newbies.

* Learn a different language or brush up on your existing skills. Join a foreign language forum and practice with others.

* Puzzles, Crosswords, Sudoku etc.

* Online and/or real-world games – Scrabble, Chess, etc.

* Learn to make art. The possibilities are endless and anyone can do it. There are many great free online tutorials.

* Read/Listen for fun – "how to" and "self-help" books have their place but a novel will entertain you... and it won't be about you or your problems.

* Meditate. This pretty much always helps. I'm telling you straight, the main obstacle to using meditation as a tool to calm the mind is making the time and getting your butt onto the meditation seat. Even ten minutes will make a difference. It won't fix your problems but it's a great distraction technique that focusses on nothing more than the breath and calms the brain.

* Exercise, sport, or table games – Everybody knows that exercise lifts mood, however passing this may be. Sports that involve competition and brain work are brilliant immersive forms of distraction. I recently discovered virtual reality (VR) headsets. The on-tap, palatable, dare I say, fun exercise is a new wonder. It has changed my life.

I already know that this rosy picture of happy-hobbies dispelling all of your worries forevermore won't be postcard-perfect in reality. I know that you've tried many activities and they haven't solved your problems. Why would now be any different?

These activities will not resolve obsessions in themselves. They are tools that are used to achieve greater victory, through time. Please do not make the mistake of saying, "I tried sewing for a week but I still had obsessions."

Were you using a considered and clinically-effective plan to break the obsessional habits at the time? Or were you just loosely hoping that a distraction should make it all go away? Hopefully, at this stage in the book, you will be clearer about the mechanics of the problem, the reasoning behind what to do in response, and how to apply it.

This time, you have a plan. This time, you will be using your chosen activity as an alternative behaviour to compulsions.

The main aim of distraction techniques is to get you through the next twenty minutes without doing the compulsive behaviour.

It's this series of refusing to perform the compulsive behaviours that improve your **control capital** over time. Every twenty-minute period in which you successfully re-focus your brain and refuse the compulsion is a small victory. Keep that on your radar. Don't ask what's different after a day or two. Not much, probably. Just keep pushing forward five yards at a time. At some point, you'll look back and see that you've covered some serious ground. Your obsessions and compulsions will begin to weaken.

So, let's draw a line under your past experiences with distractions. Start fresh with the intention of using your chosen distraction activities as a **tool** (not a cure) for tolerating the discomfort of refusing to do the compulsions. Treat it also as practice in the discipline of mentally switching tracks.

"In-The-Moment" Distractions.

What do you do when you're not in a position to sit down with a cup of tea and a jigsaw puzzle? Then, you'll need something instant that can help you to switch tracks. This requires a sensory and/or mental task.

One of the best and probably the most well-known of these is the "five things" tool. It's a mindfulness task but it's used in CBT too.

Five Things

The five things exercise follows a simple and easily remembered format. It's basically:

* Five things you can see.

* Five things you can hear.

* Five things you can feel.

This tool can be used as a formal meditational technique if you want to take some mental time out generally but it will also work when you are standing in the supermarket queue or walking down the street.

The basic idea is that it is a deliberate re-focusing of your attention onto simple real-world impressions and sensations.

You begin with five things you can see. Try it now as I explain it.

Look around you. Notice five things that you can **see,** at this very moment. Say them out loud or quietly in your head. Don't rush it. The idea is that it is a slowing down tool. Take the time to **notice** what is around you. Pick the five most interesting things you can see. Now, close your eyes and recall each one out loud.

Once you have done that, take a single deep breath followed by a long exhale. This breaks the rounds of "noticing" into distinct rounds but it also has a calming effect.

Now, we move onto the next one.

Notice five things you can **hear**. It's nice to close your eyes for this one if you can. If you can't, that's fine too. Using your ears, tune in to your environment and notice five different sounds. This will be easier in some environments than others. Don't stress about it if you can't find five but do be aware that you can count the sound of your breath or the sound of your clothes moving against your skin as noise, so that might help if you get stuck. Once you have five things that you can hear identified, name them, take another long deep breath and exhale a long exhale.

Finally, we have five things you can **feel**. In this instance, we are using physical sensations, not emotions. So, the breeze against your cheeks, the warmth from the sun on your shoulders, the sensation of fabric on your skin from your clothes etc. Once you have identified five sensations, name them, then take a long deep breath and exhale slowly.

That's round one completed. Next, you return to the beginning and go again, this time with just four things you can see, hear, and feel, remembering to take a deep breath between each completed item.

Ideally, if at all possible, try to identify a different set of objects, sounds, and sensations in each round. It's not a test. It's a focusing tool. If you can find new ones, great. If you can't, just make sure that you tune-in to the sight, sound, or sensation before you repeat it. This technique works by narrowly re-focusing attention, not remembering what you said last time. You re-engage with the act of focusing each time for best results.

Then, repeat the technique using rounds of three, two and finally one thing you can see, hear, and feel. Five-four-three-two and one. Done.

As monotonous as this exercise may be, it works. At the end of your five rounds of see, hear, and feel, you will have switched mental tracks. You will be feeling more centred, calmer, and quieter. It's a very simple tool that helps with anxiety reduction at multiple levels by re-focusing attention, encouraging a mindfulness mindset, and switching mental tracks. In addition, we have a skilful compounding effect which happens when we complete each round and take a nice deep long breath. Like completing a chapter when reading a book, the mind notes an end to a cycle and takes a quick pause and reset. Whether you are directly aware of it or not in the moment, each time you take that deep breath at the end of each round, this locks-in (anchors) the state of calm you've achieved so far. Each subsequent round should then compound that relaxation and you can do the whole thing without ever "trying" to relax, which bypasses the law of reversed effort we talked about earlier. "Trying" to relax doesn't usually work well. Doing something relaxing, does. It's a surprisingly effective tool and it belongs in your armoury, so practice it soon and use it often.

Sensory Distractions

You may well have heard about the rubber band around the wrist trick. The idea is that when experiencing an obsession or compulsion, you snap the rubber band sharply so that your mind registers a distracting physical sensation. Another famous one is holding an ice cube and noticing the sensations in your hand. You could do these. I've never recommended these tactics. They've always seemed slightly insulting to my client's intelligence, even when sold as a tool rather than a cure but they've helped some people so I'll leave those with you.

The principle, however, is solid. Sensory distraction can help. We have five main senses. Think about ways in which you can stimulate these senses in the moment, preferably privately when you are in public. The idea is that the sensation should be something that can dominate your sensual awareness strongly enough to encourage your brain to switch tracks from thinking/obsessing to noticing sensory experiences. Here are some ideas: -

Taste – Try a sour/spicy/unusual flavour candy or a piece of gum. As you suck or chew, pay attention to what is happening in your mouth. Notice the texture, the flavour, and the feel of the object on your tongue. Is your mouth watering? Could you describe the flavour to somebody else? Notice the nuance. Likewise, when you are eating a meal, pay careful attention to the entire experience.

Smell – A handkerchief or a sleeve can be doused with a scent that you love. Preferably, make it a scent that brings warm memories and associations with it - your partner's perfume, a food flavouring (test for colourfastness first) or your favourite essential oil. A small discrete drop should be enough, so you can take this one out into public areas discreetly too. Take a sniff and allow your mind to linger on that smell. Close your eyes if you can. Give the smell your full attention. If it's a perfume, can you identify what flowers, incenses, or spices might be in it? How does it make you feel? If it's a good feeling, can you tune in to that more deeply?

Touch – Our sense of touch is on all the time. Play a game with your toes in your shoes. See if you can make them do a Mexican wave. Put your hands in your pockets. Notice the feel of the fabric. Is it woven or silky? If there is a textured surface nearby, pay attention to the sensations it produces when you touch it. Set yourself a different challenge each day to notice the variety of sensations you can experience in different settings. Fabrics, walls, plastics, woods. Plants are particularly tactile. If you find a tactile sensation that you love, find a way to replicate that and take it out with you each day. Fidget gadgets are available to buy. They'll serve the same purpose.

Sight – Eye-spy, anyone? It sounds ridiculous but that's the basic idea. Name the objects you see in your environment and for an extra twist, see if you can pick ten objects and then remember them and list them in alphabetical order. That should keep your brain busy for a few minutes. Repeat if necessary.

The other way we can use sight as a sensory distraction is the old favourite of closing your eyes and imagining yourself somewhere that you can feel all of the joys of your existence. Beaches come to mind for me but it's your daydream.

Sound – Well, thanks to the advent of earbuds and music players that fit in your pocket, music is now available anywhere, anytime and the variety is practically endless. Uplifting music is the best drug in the world, all things considered. We know that it has a rousing effect on positive brain chemistry. It has been used to mobilise entire nations. It can make you have goosebumps all over your body. It can speak to you, figuratively and literally. It costs barely anything to use. It doesn't run out. It's an addiction worth having. It isn't dangerous. It doesn't take a single thing from you and it is guaranteed to be hangover-free. If you choose music that has a positive meaning for you, that counts as positive programming too. It is unique in this regard.

Beyond music, you have podcasts, talk radio, educational listening etc. Use what you want to use. As long as it has the intended effect of distraction without urgency, it's a win.

Nature makes pretty noises sometimes too. Tuning into the sound of rain, wind, birdsong, running water, tree leaves or even silence when you're close to nature is a sure bet for switching up both your attention and your mood.

Mental Distractions

I'd prefer to call these games or puzzles. This might feel a bit like going back to school. This stuff is supposed to stretch our brains. If it looks complicated, it's supposed to be. You want something that requires concentration and focus but not something that will frazzle your brain, so set it to the difficulty you are most comfortable with.

Let's begin with an easy one: Apples, Berries, Cherries, Dates, Elderberries. F…

Pick a subject. Any subject. Now use the alphabet to make an A-Z list. The list above is fruits.

We could do animals: Aardvark, Bear, Cat, Dog, Elephant, F...

Too easy?

Here's one that you can tweak to your preference.

In your mind's eye, choose a number from between two and five.

Beginning at Z, mentally move backwards through the alphabet using your chosen number to collect the letters which are at those intervals. If you chose four for your intervals, you'd have **Z**, y, x, **W**, v, u, t, **S**, r, q, p... Note that W and S are our letters. Counting on your fingers might help.

The next one would be? If you got "O", you've understood the game correctly.

See if you can mentally put your letters to one side until you have enough of them to make a word. You can use as many letters or as few as you wish to make your word. Vowels are free to use in any way you see fit to complete your words.

Example: Using our four intervals above, we end up with the following letters - W, S, O, K, G, C. Using these letters to make a word using any vowels (AEIOU), we could make the following words: -

Sow, Wok, Oak, Was, Saw, Sew, Sack, Wake, Wise, Sock, Weak, Woke, Soak, Sake, Awake, Siege, Wicks etc.

See if you can make different words from the same letters using different vowels. Challenge yourself to make longer words as you practice. Vary it by changing the interval number you choose or starting with a different letter. Then, if you want to go further, see if you can join your words together in any order to form a coherent sentence. Plenty here to keep your mind busy!

Please... don't make these games something to be stressed about. Nobody is marking your work or scrutinizing your words. This is a tricky game to hold inside your head, especially if you are shooting for long words or have a lot of letters to remember. If it's too complex, just begin with three letters and then move on to more as you become more practised. It's supposed to be tricky. It's designed to demand all of your attention and concentration. This game is to be picked up when needed, used to fill a gap and then discarded without a trace. Its main function is as a mental distraction. There is no "wrong", It's just there to tie your brain up with something other than the usual for a short time. No stressing, okay?

The same can be done with numbers. Starting at a hundred, count backwards in intervals of seven; 100, 93, 86... etc. Again, change the start place and/or intervals to vary the exercise. If you want to increase the difficulty, try adding or subtracting the numbers you identify at the intervals.

I'm acutely aware of a piece of conflicting information here. Earlier, we discussed the obstacle of mental rituals with the Pure O form of OCD. If you anticipate that these distraction activities may end up being just another form of mental ritual for you, then give them a miss. Choose something sensory or physical instead.

Otherwise, these games alone offer plenty of time-filling, brain-teasing distraction that can be engaged with in the shopping line, on the train, or at your workplace, privately.

Tongue Twisters and Soul Searchers

She sells sea shells on the sea shore…

Peter Piper picked a peck of pickled peppers…

You get the idea. Google some tongue twisters and learn them from start to finish. Practice saying them mentally or out loud (in private). No urgency, please. If you're reciting tongue twisters at seven words per second, that's hardly relaxing. Keep it light, be playful and aim to become brilliant at reciting them with ease. It's not profound as a therapeutic tool but it keeps a brain busy when you need it to.

As for soul-searchers, why not take the same principle and make it meaningful at the same time, preferably with an anti-anxiety message? A favourite poem or inspirational passage will do the job. How about Desiderata?[10] "Go placidly amid the noise and the haste…" Not only will learning every word of such a piece be an enjoyable challenge but you'll also be highly cultured at party recitals! Seriously though, inspirational quotes are a great tool for mental distraction and positive programming all in one. Use what speaks to you.

Or, if you're motivated, write a positive poem or an inspirational passage for yourself and memorise it for use in tricky moments. Here's my try: -

I'm making time for me today. I'll notice what goes right.

I'll be kicking out the scary stuff and staying in the light.

I'm taking back my life today, a little at a time.

And just to make that message clear, I've made this quirky rhyme.

I won't do that or this or that or anything you say,

It's my life, my thoughts, my choice, we're doing it my way.

I've seen you here before my friend but you're no friend of mine.

Just save your breath today ol' chap, I'm wise to all your lies.

You once said jump and I complied but that was back before.

When I still feared your spiteful words. They hurt me to my core.

But things are changing fast 'round here, I've got your number now.

And nothing that you say to me can take my spirit down.

---

[10] https://en.wikipedia.org/wiki/Desiderata

Because you are just a ghost to me. You moan and wail and cry.

You speak of great catastrophe where all I love will die.

But I will show you life, Dear Fear, I will show you fun.

I'll heal your hurts and bring you home, in truth, we are but one.

Be involved with your healing. If you feel it strongly, it will count for something.

Chapter Twenty-One - The Next Ten Yards

It has been a week since Nadia made her first call to her sister and started asking about the children, and Nadia is beginning to **believe** that asking how her niece is doing does not make her a heinous predatory criminal, even secretly. We are making progress.

We are going to need to keep it up though. Victory is not assured. The opposition team hasn't gone for a cup of coffee. They are eyeing up different attack lines. Nadia could be hit by an unexpected play and find her gains wiped out. We want to harness Nadia's hard-earned momentum, dig in, and win that next ten yards.

It would be over-explaining if I were to illustrate every step in Nadia's five to ten steps in detail. One step is the same as the next in terms of structure. To be sure that the process is clear though, we'll just take a look at Nadia's next ten-yard play as an example. Here's a reminder of the next of Nadia's graded challenges: -

6) Fear of movies, TV shows, radio presentations, or books/articles that might involve children being harmed.

Avoidance Behaviours: Media avoidance.

Compulsions: Excessive checking of reviews and descriptions.

Pure "O": Anxious thoughts and feelings about what might happen next in the book, movie, or media which removes any pleasure from consuming media that might otherwise have been enjoyed.

We'll move this one along more quickly now that you have the basic idea.

Nadia needs to start doing what she is avoiding and stop doing what she's compelled to do by her anxieties. We build our next behavioural experiments using these criteria. We'll begin with her avoidance of media. With Nadia's agreement, the new behavioural experiment sets out the following task: -

Spend a minimum of thirty minutes each day engaging with different forms of media <u>without checking</u> reviews and descriptions for content.

Expectation	Strategy (Tools Used)	Outcome
Fear – 90% See or hear something (child-related) which causes obsessional upset – 90% Expects to feel disturbed and worried afterwards – 60% Won't be able to do it – 80%	Ten-minutes of meditation or relaxation to calm the mind. Imagining what could go right (positive visualisation). A revised and determined understanding of what to do and why it needs to be done. Using acknowledge, self-soothe and reassure "parts" format before, during and after the media engagement. Belief change. What is easier than your mind told you it would be? Keep notes! Positive Mental Distraction Tools.	Watched a 30-minute news programme on TV (Monday) – Fear – 70% - Reduced to 40% with acceptance and reassurance. Listened to talk radio for an hour. (Tuesday) – Fear 60% Read some news articles online (Wednesday) – Panicky – 80% Thursday – No challenge accepted – rest day. Watched a comedy show on TV (Friday) – Nerves – 40% Laughs – 35% **Feelings/Thoughts** Won't be able to do it – 20% Still some uncertainty but slowly gaining confidence. – 65% Felt disturbed and worried afterwards – 10%

Here, we see some notable points. With the application of the correct therapeutic tools, Nadia was able to reduce her emotional disturbance across the board. In addition, she was also able to enjoy some laughs when she watched a comedy. Her pre-experiment assessment suggested that enjoyment would not be part of this exercise.

You'll also note that she took a day off on Thursday and didn't engage with any media at all. Is that okay? Nadia needed a rest. She took one. She didn't slide backwards. She just stood still. More on this shortly.

Nadia reports only 10% upset after her media engagements. We can assume that this is because she didn't run into any strongly triggering material. If she had done so, she would almost certainly be reporting more significant emotional disturbance in her outcome column. Would that be a failure? Let's call it feedback. Hopefully, we would still have seen an improvement.

An axe requires a stone to sharpen itself against. If your obsession and/or compulsion challenges are not challenging, then you're not sharpening your edge.

Nadia's job here is to learn to welcome these challenges, not fear them. Her first instinct will be to decide that this therapy business is too upsetting and quit the work. That would be a mistake.

Where she has been triggered is precisely where she needs to work most consistently.

She just needs to recognise that in this instance, at this particular moment in her process, she's been deeply challenged and that the spike in her anxiety and obsessive-mind activity is entirely to be expected. Nothing is wrong.

Victory was never going to be achieved without being challenged.

Now is the time to dig deep. The showdown has arrived. If she stops engaging with media at this point, she is unlikely to make progress. She will do what she has always done and she will get what she always got.

The idea is to let the fear cool down, give the mind a little time to settle, and then go again.

Let's not forget that before doing this work, Nadia's default response would have been to hunker into fear and become even more vehemently invested in her position that she must avoid media. All she needs to do right now is to be **defiant**. For all of the years of back and forth with this stuff, the unending worry, the nausea of anxiety, the prison that her life has become, it's all about THIS moment. What are we going to do, Nadia? Come out fighting? Or go back to square one?

Rise, Nadia. Now is your moment!

What I want you to take on faith right now is that your mind will adjust when you repeatedly expose yourself to the challenges of either not doing a compulsion or moving towards that which you fear. I'm not suggesting that everyone always succeeds. I'm saying that human brains can and do desensitise when given the correct conditions. I have seen it happen with many clients and I've worked through and fully resolved my own phobic responses with sheer bloody-mindedness and defiance. We may all be different but our brains desensitise in the same way. It just requires steely resolve and skilful handling.

We could if we wanted to, go through the formality of creating a separate behavioural experiment for Nadia's compulsion to check reviews and descriptions before consuming media. Some people may prefer to micro-manage the plan in this way but in real-world application, she's probably just going to progress with the plan with the inherent understanding that checking is off the menu. If refusing to check descriptions and reviews causes her any significant obstacles, then she might want to formalise it with a detailed behavioural experiment but in the interests of streamlining the process, she can save herself some work and just engage with the media without checks. I'm confident to give you this advice because that's how it so often pans out in the real world.

We have two scenarios outlined here. In the first, she makes good progress. In the second, she hits a stumbling block. Either are possible outcomes. In a way, the second outcome is preferable because we've hit the area where she will grow the most when she successfully challenges her default responses. At some stage, she will be challenged. If it wasn't here, it would come later. These are also the areas where she will make the greatest progress in re-claiming her life.

If she's ready to move on to the next challenge, that's great. If not, the advice is to stay with the current experiment until she has mastered it.

Without wishing to complicate things, it's worth understanding that she may get stuck on a challenge. Maybe, when we made our list from five to ten, she'd underestimated how challenging one aspect of her experiment would be. If it is too difficult, she has the option to shelve it and move on for now or change the parameters of the experiment to make it more manageable. Perhaps she'll find that she can master the next challenge more easily, despite it being a more difficult challenge on paper. That's all good. It's quite likely that if she makes good progress with another challenge, she will be able to return to consuming media without checking descriptions and find that it's easier than she remembered. That would be a nice sign of real-world progress.

We need some flexibility in our approach to this work to avoid burnout or over-trying. You have permission to shape and re-shape your plan according to your own needs. The system shouldn't be seen as rigid. It's a **framework** that we are using to clarify, formalise, and **contain** the recovery.

Adjustments are okay as long as they are not being used as an avoidance tool.

Chapter Twenty-Two - The Road To Victory

Victory is not as difficult as you may think it is. The mind adjusts quite quickly when it senses that determination is present. Here's the psychology of it: -

One of my therapeutic trainers explained that the subconscious is a lazy and childish mind. His point was that it prefers to be unbothered by change, however necessary, and it is prone to tantrums when it doesn't get what it wants.

When you ask an average child to do a task, what response do you expect? Do they go graciously and tidy their rooms? Er... no. The problem is, you asked nicely. You thought that reason and virtue would prevail. What you get when you do that is trouble. More accurately, you get resistance.

I'm all for treating children with the same dignity and respect that any adult deserves, more even, but let's not sugar-coat it. They need guidance, and that guidance needs to be **authoritative** because they do not yet possess the mental and emotional resources to manage their lives in their own best interests. We have to train them in healthy habits and patterns. They won't like this but we know that it's a case of being mildly cruel to be kind. Those same patterns will save them untold grief later in life. Brush your teeth kids. Dentists are expensive. So, how do you get a child to do what they **need** to do?

Answer: You make sure that they know that you are the boss and that no means no and do it means do it. No arguments. Penalties are pending. This message needs to be watertight. If the child senses even the slightest weakness in your resolve, expect that weakness to be exploited. They know how to wear you down. Until you deliver **that** tone, and then the whining stops. Having boundaries is not a withdrawal of love. It's a demonstration of control. When you have clear red lines, compliance follows. Even without complaint.

When it is understood that tantrums will not deliver an excuse or a reprieve, your taking control of the situation does everybody a favour. They know precisely where they stand and no further mental energy needs to be wasted. This matters enough that you'll fight for it. You have your eye on those dentist bills. It becomes the working assumption that no means no and teeth must be brushed. Our minds work in the same way.

If this all sounds a bit too nineteen-seventies, there is a way to soften it. The idea is that you give the illusion of choice. Instead of "You WILL clean your room today", you ask, "Would you like to clean your room first, or play on your Xbox first?" It's softer but the command to clean the room remains unshakeable. You can happily make similar requests of yourself. Right now, we're looking at how to manage the child-like whims of the lazy side of our minds. You'll have to use what works for your personality type. Scheduling a healthy reward for the completion of an undesired task is effective. It's called delaying gratification. Chores first, pleasure after. That's good mental hygiene. Just make sure that the task is attended to before delivering the reward because if the reward comes first, the task will probably not get done. That's a bad message to send oneself.

Believe it or not, discipline makes children feel secure. When you tell them to brush their teeth, they do it. It's easier than having a scene every day. There are exceptions but this will be the rule. Now, apply that same understanding to the programme you are engaging with here. Can you see how your mindset is going to affect the outcome? If you are half-hearted or short on resolve, expect a tantrum. That means regular tests upon your resolve, otherwise known as a hard time.

Conversely though, when you do put your foot down, you can expect that the task/s will be completed much more easily with far less fuss. The line is drawn. We have created a sense of certainty that we will do this and that in itself is a formidable force.

With the programme you've learned here, we've included compassionate attention for your inner child. Being authoritative doesn't imply being mean, uncaring, or unsupportive. It means "I love you and that's why we have to get this done." It's showing up for oneself in a time of importance when the grown-ups are called for. Kids know the difference between the withdrawal of love and love applied fiercely. Make sure your approach is the latter.

With any "change" task, usually, the most difficult part of the process is arriving at the place where we are committed enough to exchange pain for gain. It's rarely a can't. Mostly, it's a won't. Won't is fine too but when you are serious about something, you'll have authority.

As does Nadia.

Remember I said that it would be dull of me to work through all of Nadia's steps using the behavioural experiments? Instead, I'm going to tell you what happened to her.

Eight weeks after Nadia began her treatment, she finally faced her number one fear. She had worked, methodically, with each of her five to ten steps, gaining confidence incrementally.

We catch up with Nadia in week four. Her next challenge, following the experiments we've already detailed here, focused on accepting invitations.

As it happened, she'd been so out of the loop with friends and family that there were no longer regular invitations forthcoming. We tweaked the plan to kickstart things. She called her sister and fished an invite to dinner during the week. Her sister was delighted. She decided before going that she would include hugs with her niece as part of her plan. This was a huge challenge for Nadia and it wasn't without some anxious moments. She reasoned with herself - *the obsessions or my family?* That's what it boiled down to. She said of this: -

"Sure, I was scared. I knew it would feel all wrong to be hugging my niece but, in the end, I knew that these worries had to be ridiculous. I mean she's my niece for goodness' sake! I did my compassion exercises and spent some time imagining what could go right. That all helped. Then, I just stepped up and did it, and even though it was scary, we ended up having a great time. I committed then. I don't care what these fears tell me, I'm never avoiding my family or refusing to hug my niece again."

It wasn't a straight-line recovery though. At week five, shortly after her commitment epiphany, she was hit by what she called a "disastrous week". She was convinced that she had fallen right back to square one. The unreasonable fear returned and she couldn't bring herself to even attempt to call her sister and ask about her niece. Her mind was running overtime and she was besieged by doubts and guilt. Intrusive thoughts rushed in. She felt angry, frustrated, anxious, and disappointed in herself. She wanted to quit the stupid treatment plan. She was going nowhere.

She was quite shaken by her anxiety. This didn't surprise us. When the limbic system hits that highly aroused state and locks that in, it pretty much always takes some time to settle down again. We should be aware of this. Days to weeks are normal.

Sometimes, it's the right thing to do to step back for a bit and let the dust settle.

Of course, when people are experiencing repeated or terrifying frights, as they may do with obsessional worries, overwhelm remains an important possibility to monitor.

Little will be achieved in overwhelm. If I'd pushed her to push herself too hard at this point, we may have done more harm than good. If she'd thrown the towel in completely, then it would be much time before she'd come around to trying again. Better to wait for the anxiety to calm down and then push ahead when the conditions are more favourable.

We have to walk a fine line between meeting our anxiety with courage versus pushing on when the conditions aren't right for success.

We agreed then that she'd take a break from trying to push forward at this moment in time and that she would do so with her blessing.

We discussed that it's not a failure if you choose it. Then, we call it a rest, a recharge.

She went back to hiding in her house and not calling anyone. The break did her good though and she also had time to reflect. I reminded her to continue with her exercises of acceptance, acknowledgement, self-soothing, and daily relaxation sessions. I also counselled her to contemplate her behavioural experiments. Did they suggest that nothing could be or had been achieved? Perhaps she wasn't up to the behavioural experiments right now but maybe she could just start with tiny changes and mini victories. Her anxieties settled a little more each day and as her energy returned, so too did her fighting spirit. Week five had been bad but she reminded herself that she'd been kicking obsessional butt in the first four weeks. That wasn't nothing, was it?

She mentally re-grouped, beginning week six with a resolute call to her sister and niece (which went fine) and by Wednesday of week six she was celebrating a massive win. She had signed up with a dating agency in week four (just before she'd had her blip) and in a moment of renewed determination and defiance she went ahead and arranged a date with Miles. She was scared but she'd learned that a little bit of daring can pay dividends. She knew that she wasn't quite there yet. Arranging a date had seemed like madness but she knew that the messages that she sent to herself now would be more important than ever before. She'd had a serious blip but once things calmed down again, she could see clearly. She might have been down but she was definitely not out. When you've come that far...

At the beginning of week seven, Nadia went for the Monday night dinner date with Miles. It went better than she expected. (She completed her behavioural experiment for this event). There were notable moments where she felt like a "normal" person, living a "normal" life. The food was delicious and Miles was a gentleman.

She remained anxious about the "one day being a mum" part. Was it dishonest to consider a relationship with the possibility that she might be too afraid to have kids one day? *Woooah! Slow down there, Nadia. It's the first date.* Plus... what does she know about these thoughts and feelings? Are they the truth? Where might she be in a year from now? When she focused on what could go right, it looked and felt so much more hopeful. A big win. It was becoming easier.

Nadia made her touchdown at the hundred-yard line in week eight. She was busy with life at the time. She now had weekly dinner dates booked with her sister and her niece and even though the negative thoughts still came, she went anyway. When her sister suggested that they go to the park for a picnic at the weekend, she recognised a great opportunity. She said yes, immediately. Then, she regretted it. A flood of worries came at her in waves of discomfort. *What if? What if?*

To remind you, this was Nadia's worst fear.

10) Fear of carrying out a violent or abusive act upon a child. (The number one fear.)

Daily impact: It stops me from going anywhere there are likely to be children. I avoid children wherever possible. I take out my phone and look at it to pretend I'm busy. On a bad day, I might pretend I have forgotten something and turn around so that I don't have to pass them. I prefer to stay home whenever possible. It's just easier that way.

But... she was not the same Nadia who had embarked upon this committed and determined recovery journey just two short months ago. She was wise to the lies now. She had also perfected the art of holding her nerve. The outcome? Normal life. No deaths. No prison cells. No accusations. No accidents. Nobody harmed. Nothing happened. Other than gaining a sister, a niece, a very nice guy to date, and more hope than she'd experienced in a long time.

...

The warmth of the sun on Nadia's face brought a smile to her lips. Her nostrils drew in deep breaths as she savoured the sweet fragrance of summer in the park. Her sister and niece walked with her on the wide path leading to the playground.

A child, about six years old, approached from the distance on a small bike with stabilisers, her mother trailing behind her. A pang of horror jangled its way through Nadia's nervous system as the young girl rolled ominously towards her. The familiar electrical jolt of the Zealous Guard raising its defensive weaponry made her chest wind tightly like a spring, stealing her breath. An image flashed through her mind. She imagined her hand, escaping her control as it lashed out and pushed the girl violently to the floor. Instinctively, she held her right arm with her left as if to restrain it. For a moment, she had to remember to breathe. For a moment, she wished she had stayed home.

Fear and love. The two opposites. Meeting. Finally. Here in the park. The outside; where Nadia could at any moment lose control of herself. Except she won't and she knows it. She breathes deeply again; this time with authority. Authority… and something else. With love. There would be no loss of control. These images were lies. They meant nothing.

"I get that this is challenging, Nadia", she said quietly to herself. "I'm sorry that you feel afraid right now… but you are safe. We've got this. Together."

And with the next few breaths, the tightened spring in her chest responded. With each breath, more love. Pride. Where once, there would have been only fear and paralysis, now, Nadia saw opportunity. Each challenge, a moment to love more deeply, to defy more proudly, and to support unconditionally. No. She was not the bad guy. The monsters in her mind were the bad guys and now she knew it. This was a test. She could beat it.

She steadied her nerve, breathed deeply with love, let her arms swing freely, held her head high, and smiled at the young girl on the bike as she peddled past.

And then, it was over.

Chapter Twenty-Three - What Does Recovery Look Like?

Suppose that I am in the lifelong habit of eating a poor diet. My brain is a creature of habit. It craves what it knows. If I think about choosing a salad, I am averse. My brain tells me to go for the fast food instead. *Much tastier. Salad is work - bland, boring, and unsatisfying.* I choose the fast food.

Three weeks after I upgrade to healthy eating, after much resistance to the new "regime", my brain begins to support my decision to choose the salad repeatedly. I start to **want** the salad. Why?

Well, my behaviour changed. Then, my brain had to create a narrative to explain to itself why the convenience food stopped coming. It adapted because that's what human brains do when conditions change. I gave it the information about salad being the superior choice, including why, and I kept choosing salad even though my feelings initially urged me to opt for convenience food.

Now, the previous feelings of aversion begin to wire themselves differently. The narrative now supports salads as the **desired** choice because my brain is telling me a different story about what salad is. Instead of "bland, boring, and unsatisfying", it is now seen as "healthy, nutritious, medicine." Not only do my thoughts adapt to support the new behaviour, but my taste buds change too. In the absence of high-taste foods, my brain tells my tastebuds to be a little more excited by salad. I become aware of a deeper depth of flavour that I've never tasted before; a surprising bonus. I focus on new feelings of satiety that good nutrition provides. I start to like that feeling. Eventually, I like it even more than I like the lure of pizza or fries. I'll feel trashy when eating those. I feel good after nutrition. My brain has re-wired itself. I gave it the direction and held my focus, and it adapted. I showed it a better way. Now, it **wants** the good stuff and avoids the fast foods. I can still choose the latter but now it's a choice, not an imperative. There is resistance at first but support follows later. This is not a direct comparison to the challenges of anxiety or OCD but it is a working analogy for how brains adjust to long-term change generally.

Here, I have some good news for you. I'm cautious not to present unrealistic expectations but over the years I have noticed a very interesting pattern when observing OCD recoveries in action.

My client and I would come up with a list of behaviours (compulsions) that we were going to tackle. Typically, we'd agree on a preliminary five-step plan to cease just one OCD-related behaviour per session. We would begin with the least challenging behaviour first, tailoring each session to prepare for the week or two ahead. With the tools learned in that session, my client would aim to have reduced or ceased that behaviour by our next appointment. Then, by agreement, we'd scratch it off the list and move on to the next, slightly more challenging item.

That was always the plan. Here's what sometimes happened: -

Me to client: "So, how did you do this week? Did you manage to walk away from the front door after checking it was locked only once?"

Client: "Yes, I had a bit of a breakthrough this week. It was tough but I was determined and it wasn't as bad as I thought it would be."

Me: "That's great. Well done! So, are we ready to move on to the next item?"

Client: "I've already done it."

Me: "Pardon?"

Client: "Yeah... I already did the whole list."

Me: "What? All of it?"

Client: "Yep. Actually, I've booked a trip to Europe in a couple of months."

Me: 😲 Oh!

These were best-case scenarios but I saw this happen as a noteworthy pattern. It would usually occur around the third behaviour that we were successful in challenging.

That's interesting, isn't it? What could it possibly mean? Are they cured?

I was once taught that "how you do something is how you do everything". That's rather a cryptic statement but it applies here in the modified form of "how you overcome one compulsion is how you overcome them all". It's tough at the beginning to make progress but it becomes easier. Confidence builds. We have small successes, and at some point, the whole obsessive-compulsive pattern is undermined. This isn't wishful thinking. I'm reporting what happened many times, in practice. It surprised me repeatedly.

This will be down to three main factors: -

1) Mastery of the tools and understanding needed to challenge the behaviours.
2) Anxiety reduction as a result of doing fewer compulsions.
3) An increase in self-confidence and "control".

If this sounds rather too rosy an expectation - it might be. Not every OCD sufferer can push through a few challenges and see their woes vanish. We also must allow for the possibility of relapse later. I am reporting to you with hand on heart though that I saw this too many times for it to be a mere freak happening.

We have to be careful with our expectations. What I've described above shouldn't be translated as meaning that my client's OCD ended at that point. It didn't. What ended was the unbearable loops and mental overload that they were stuck in. The OCD was still present. They had just learned that they could slowly master the condition to the point of a good life. Think of it more as the beginning of their long-term recovery rather than the end of their OCD.

There's more good news too. I was discussing this book with my wife this morning and she asked me, "Did you ever see anybody have a 100% complete recovery from OCD?" My answer was immediate. "No. I never did." That's good news?

We'd often arrive at a point where the client was well enough to get back on with their lives quite happily and they would end their active therapeutic work on their OCD. When I asked why they wanted to quit now, the usual answer in one form or another was "I'm used to my OCD. It's part of who I am. I actually wouldn't **want** to be without it. I just don't want it running or ruining my life."

I respected that. They knew the drill now. Another teaching from the front line. The counsel to keep an eye on it and continue managing their stress levels obviously followed.

If you are an OCD sufferer, you may have extra work to do, and your relief may not be as complete as it may be for the average worrier or acutely anxious person. Just know that OCD can be routinely improved to the point of a happy life with the right understanding, some determination, and a bucketful of courage. Sometimes, it's easier than you thought it would be. Not always but sometimes.

PART THREE – TOOLS, TIPS, AND ESSENTIALS

This third section of the book is devoted to three chapters - pep talks for the road, common difficulties, and a section for family and carers. While not every category will apply specifically to your situation, I'd recommend reading it all anyway. It will give you more reference points to understand how we approach various aspects of different anxieties and compulsions. The principles can be transposed to your needs.

Chapter Twenty-Four - Pep Talks For The Road

The Limbic System

Here's what to expect from an anxious and negatively aroused Zealous Guard. This is crucially important.

The guard can bounce back quickly from small, isolated shocks. In non-anxious life, it does so routinely. You realise that you haven't paid your car tax. It expires tomorrow. Emotionally, this sends an anxious feeling through your nervous system. There's a threat here. Forget to do it and you'll be in trouble with the government next time you drive. The anxiety continues until it's paid. Then, once it is paid, the anxiety evaporates.

That's not what happens when you've been deeply disturbed. When you feel existentially threatened, in trouble, heartbroken, betrayed, afraid, or unsafe, the wounding is deeper. When we are under threat for a longer time, the anxiety becomes chronic. That type of anxiety does not evaporate in an hour or a day. Even, theoretically, if you made everything perfect in your life today, the anxiety would continue for some time. Why?

Well, anxiety has momentum. It has energy that must be allowed to **dissipate** - the aftershocks, and that typically takes days to weeks to happen fully. Remember, it's an animal brain that has become chronically aroused. It's in emergency mode. That doesn't switch off immediately. It slowly de-arouses, ever cautious to be sure that the danger has passed. Watch a cat or a dog after they've had a big scare and you'll see them being jumpy and anxious for days to weeks afterwards. Any small subsequent scare will cause an overreaction. That's the limbic system. We've got one too. It has its own rules.

In practice, this is problematic because it obscures the correct understanding of cause and effect. We are used to taking a headache pill and having the pain go away. If we extend that logic to anxiety, it should mean that if we halt whatever is making us anxious, then the anxiety should stop too. It will. It just won't do so immediately. First, the anxiety must burn its remaining fuel. Our first job is to stop adding fuel to the fire.

If you're applying therapeutic tools and finding that they don't appear to be helping, there's a good possibility that your overall level of emotional arousal (stress, anxiety, panic, worry) is too high to feel the benefits immediately. That does **not** mean that you're doing the wrong thing. It just means that you'll need to be patient with the outcome because your brain, when anxious, can take days to weeks to fully calm down. It's like a balloon slowly emptying of pressure. Do not make the mistake of trying a couple of exercises and concluding that they don't work. You simply cannot make a reasonable assessment of progress in such a short space of time.

If we are depressed, for instance, also a limbic system response, it will take time to lift. We will need to do what is known to help long before we feel the benefits of that. In the depths of a depression, we force ourselves out of the door for our daily exercise. Everybody tells us that this is one of the keys to beating depression but the exercise is still miserable because we are. We must do it anyway. It is the cumulative effect of doing the right thing over and over that brings notable change. Just as doing the wrong thing brought us notable misery. That also took time to develop into a crisis.

Be sure to note this point carefully. When the limbic system is chronically or severely aroused, it needs time and stillness to settle. We want to avoid agitating the mind further. Remember that muddy water analogy we used earlier? It's that again in a different context. We must find a safe space to rest and be still, mentally and emotionally. That doesn't mean avoiding activity. It means cultivating a sense of inner quiet.

Expect that even when you are doing all the right things, it will take time. An anxious brain is a threatened brain. It doesn't let its guard down easily. It needs to be convinced that safety is once again available. That may mean that you've only taken care of a part of what's troubling you or that the bag of anxiety is still emptying. Keep going!

I speak personally and with authority on this. Just because I'm a therapist, I don't get a free pass on stress and catastrophe. I've had plenty recently, and sometimes other people bring it to our door. That's not something that we have much control over. I know what to do. Don't stir the pot. Be kind to myself. Attend to the needs of my wounds. Extend compassion, and most importantly, wait it out. It will pass. It always passes quicker when I bring acceptance, patience, and compassion to the unpleasantness of the time. It's an important lesson for all of us and you'll need to remind yourself of this as you begin your journey back to health. Patience is a virtue. Anxiety takes time to settle. Remember this and trust the process.

Experiment Design

Designing your behavioural experiments might require a little creativity and lateral thinking. This will be especially relevant for the Pure O people who don't have real-world compulsions but are troubled by doom-laden themes that continue to create a strong fear response. The variations on themes and concerns are too numerous to cover comprehensively. I've covered a few of them in more detail in the "common concerns" chapter towards the end of the book. Hopefully, the principles are now clear enough that you can tailor the experiments to your specific needs.

Here are some ideas for exposure and response prevention experiments according to common obsessive themes: -

Perfectionism: -

* Leave some of your work imperfect or incomplete. Don't go back to correct it.

* Deliberately make a minor mistake in a task. Leave it there.

* Delegate a task to someone else and don't check on their process or finished work.

* Do something your perfectionist would never do. (Keep it safe, legal, and honourable.)

* Don't apologise for something trivial.

* Say no to someone else's expectation of you when you would usually say yes. Tolerate the guilt!

Health: -

* Expose yourself to illness-related information, discussion, and media. (If you are averse. Stay away from it if you are compulsively reading it.)

* Refuse to ask for repeated reassurances on the same concerns from loved ones or doctors.

* Visit a doctor, hospital, or other medical environment. (If you are averse).

* Where hygiene is central, reduce hand-washing/cleaning/checking.

* Stop over-checking and monitoring the body.

Contamination: -

* Touch something yucky like a toilet or a grubby corner. Wait as long as you can before washing your hands. See if you can beat your record each time.

* Eat food that is close to the expiry date or that someone else cooked or prepared.

* Deliberately go somewhere public that you perceive as unclean. Spend increasing amounts of time there. Touch the surfaces, door handles, and seating. Delay washing your hands (but do it later before your hands touch your mouth or food.)

* Wear clothes and shoes that are suspected as contaminated.

* Reduce cleaning routines to a minimum time. Set a timer. Keep to it. Do not clean frantically, just normally. Stop when the time is up. Refuse to return to it that day.

Security Checking: -

* Leave a door unlocked for a short time in a controlled way.

* Spend time away from home.

* Refuse to check any security features more than once.

* Refuse to carry out any compulsions (external or internal) relating to security.

* Refuse to repeatedly check plug sockets etc.

Morality And Blasphemy: -

* Cease all shame-supporting behaviours such as apologising, begging, regretting, confessing, or repenting. Mean business with this. If you're always apologising for taking up space, your first task is to stop that, spread out a bit, and hold your nerve. You've as much right as anybody to be here and to be treated with respect and warmth.

* Engage with media and conversations that cover theological, philosophical, and moral discussion.

* Say something controversial and don't apologise or backtrack for what you said.

* Visit a holy place and/or attend a religious service. Tolerate your discomforts and negative thoughts with compassion.

* Tell a deliberate but largely inconsequential lie.

* Read a holy text. Don't react. Just read.

Harm/Self-Harm: -

* Expose yourself to fear-inducing situations such as handling knives, driving a car, looking after a child, or sitting for someone's pet.

* Refuse to carry out reassurance and safety behaviours such as hiding knives, asking someone else to cut the vegetables, returning to the scene to check for harm, or asking others to confirm that no harm has been done.

* Engaging with media that contains harm and violence without seeking reassurance.

* Visit public places where you fear that you may harm someone. Stay there for as long as you can. Next time, stay longer.

* Hold a weapon in your hands. Spend time getting used to it.

Be aware that you'll probably find specialised forums on each theme, including your own on many of the social media platforms. I recommend joining these groups. You'll pick up plenty of positive stories and learn from others' mistakes and successes. The message repetitions also help galvanise understanding and intent. Most importantly though, that community wisdom will float your boat when you need a lift.

Do also be aware that forums could contain triggering themes for people in high anxiety or severe OCD states. There is a level of anxiety where you don't need anything stimulating at all right now. Do listen to that. We do what we can when we can. You're the boss. This is your recovery. You do it your way and if you find that forum use is fuelling your anxiety or obsessive behaviours (overuse and checking), then ditch it for now. I'm highlighting the benefits for some but forums won't be good for all.

It should now be understood that when undertaking any of these or similar challenges, you don't do so without reason or preparation. That would only lead to you having a bad time but making no progress. Remember when reading these alarming suggestions that with the application of what you've learned here, as uncomfortable as day one may be, you're going to find growth and freedom in this process. It will get easier. I can't prove that to you before you've done it. You must discover it for yourself through your experiments.

If it is too difficult to do it in the real world immediately, then one way to take the difficulty level down a notch or two is by first running the experiment in your imagination only. This also happens to be the tool that those with Pure O will use.

Tips for "Pure O"

Pure O presents us with a bit of a problem. Since there are no external behaviours to cease, we need some other way to have the brain be in the presence of what is feared. For example, how might I expose myself to death-related themes without actually risking death? Or a fear of harming someone without them being present?

You will remember, right back at the beginning of the book, that we discussed how the brain will respond similarly to threats, be they real or **imagined**. The counsel there was to recognise that imagined horrors also generate anxiety and we should therefore work to reduce or cease negative rumination in the mind's eye.

We can also use the imaginative mechanism to action behavioural challenges. While an imaginary challenge is not quite the same as a real-world challenge, it can serve as an important stepping stone to completing the challenge in real life because when the mind is confident, real-world action follows more easily.

A person with a fear of spiders might not move straight to holding one. Interim steps could include imagining a spider first, then seeing a picture of a spider, followed by holding a realistic fake spider and giving the brain time to acclimatise to its shape and feel. It's safe but it still triggers the Pavlovian anxiety response. This "virtual" experience in the imagination provides an opportunity to safely desensitise the fearful material while also being **guaranteed** real-world safe. Nifty, huh?

Imaginal Exposure – I might imagine myself at my own or someone else's funeral. I could imagine sitting with a dying person, stranger or known. I could imagine my deathbed.

In Real Life – I could read books about death, watch movies about death, or visit a cemetery or other death-related place and spend time there.

With imaginal exposure, the experiment will proceed as it might in real life. For instance, suppose you want to go somewhere but you avoid it because your fear tells you that something awful will occur. Then, your imaginal exposure experiment will run the inner movie of you arriving at the place you would like to go, doing the things that you want to do, and completing the event safely, just as you would aim to do if you went in person.

When your mind starts to throw up obstacles in the form of negative thoughts, doubts, or fears, your job, just like your OCD compulsion-busting counterparts, is to continue to remain in your imaginal experiment while holding your nerve and self-soothing where necessary.

This is where you get to do your work. The idea is to stay present in that visualisation. Hold your ground. **Freeze** the movie if you need to take a break. Attend to the parts of yourself experiencing fear, compassionately, with self-soothing, and then run your movie again. You should find that the point at which your mind threw up a fearful moment is now smoothed over and you get further along in your movie before your mind throws up another objection or anxiety. Repeat this until you have attended to all of the snag points and can watch your movie without it snagging on anxieties. That's a good indication that your mind is accepting that life can be done without all of the attendant fear. Any subsequent real-world experiments should then be significantly less challenging.

You could take imaginal exposure one step further too. Instead of merely tolerating the negative imagery, which is perfectly correct as part of your behavioural experiment, you could then go on to re-imagine the same event from a helpful and adaptive perspective. For instance, what might a peaceful and fulfilled death experience look like? How might we feel about it all then? Adapt this principle to your anxious themes.

Thought Exposure

This tool will be of particular relevance for those with Pure O OCD.

Negative thought patterns that are usually feared and fought against can be greatly weakened when we stop fearing them. Our fear sustains their intensity and we demonstrate our fear through safety behaviours and avoidance. What is the polar opposite of avoidance? That is approach.

How do we prove that we no longer fear a certain thought? We approach it. Deliberately. Our calm presence alongside that thought, teaches the brain to stop fearing it. Now, we can make that thought manifest. Most of us have a phone or device that can record our voice. If you have compatible headphones, for directness and privacy, that's better still.

Choose a negative thought that repeats for you, causing a disturbance. Then record it into your phone, just as you usually hear it in your mind. Leave some space at the beginning and end of the recording so that when you loop it, it isn't back-to-back words but sentence, space, sentence, space, etc. Say the thought calmly and slowly. Then, play it on a loop and apply the methods you've learned here for sitting tight despite the difficult feelings, focusing on self-soothing and correct reassurances (we've got this). Hold this space until the anxiety diminishes or vanishes. Then, record another negative intrusive thought, and repeat. As I'm sure you can see, this is another form of desensitisation.

Asking For Help

Intrusive thoughts and feelings are on a spectrum. Severe OCD is considered to be a serious mental health difficulty. More commonly, many people are irritated by troublesome thoughts but are otherwise fit people. One size will not fit all here. Some people won't need outside help to make progress with the tools in this book. That's great. Others will need more support. That's not a failure on anyone's part. Needs vary.

Good therapy can be worth its weight in gold. Nearly all public health services are stretched when it comes to mental health. If you need it and have the means to make private therapy happen, please give it some serious consideration, and don't forget that therapy can be short-term. It needn't cost the Earth. It should be considered a valuable investment in oneself rather than a regrettable expense. Even a little help might go a long way. Others can often see what we cannot, especially professionals. The right tools for the job can save a lot of unnecessary floundering.

If private therapy is beyond your means, then depending on the healthcare available in your location, your doctor may be able to offer you various types of support, sometimes including social support, CBT, medication, online resources, help with diet, group support, etc. Find out what help is out there for you locally. Charities too are a great starting point. They can signpost you according to your needs and some offer therapeutic support too. Find your way to your people. Having group support is helpful, and there's a world of help online these days.

I get that fear is also a serious obstacle to asking for help. It is not always a matter of quaking in terror that it will be an awful or unaffordable experience either. We fear change because the familiar is more certain. It just seems uncomfortable. It's an effort to find a therapist, attend, and pay. At least we know where we are and roughly where we will be soon and that feels safer than not knowing. What if we make things worse? What if it's a failure? A waste of money? What if it hurts?

These fears don't need to be horrors to be obstructive. They can be quite minor in the scheme of things but they can still be enough to delay action; the affront to our autonomy, the discomfort of leaning on someone else, the stigma, the cost, the uncertainty, sharing our intimate being with a "stranger", and making the first call. These are obstacles. Each consideration brings the promise of some discomfort. It seems easier to do nothing. For a while, it probably is. When we're being battered by emotional storms, we are already overwhelmed. The mind will tell us that therapy is a complication.

Fear won't remind you of the benefits.

Things do change both emotionally and practically when you get moving, with determination. Your sense of inclusion, support, community, growth, learning, and achievement all receive a boost from stepping outside the front door, metaphorically and literally.

The thing to know is that moving beyond the comfort zone, while initially uncomfortable, usually brings unexpected positives. Life, with or without OCD, asks us to step forward, to engage. We can ignore the call but we will stay where we are. Freedom demands courage and courage is a great teacher. It almost always brings improvements. And lessons. There are always lessons.

So, when, one day, you decide that you have had enough, whatever the pain and cost of enlisting help, it becomes untenable to do nothing. Finally, you push through your mind's objections, swiftly recognizing how much they've been limiting you. It's the first sign that you are going outside of your comfort zone for yourself. That's a good message. It signals that you are ready to do what it takes, and ultimately, that you are ready to win.

When you enlist external support, it creates something **real** in the world. The "problem" is not just in your head anymore. Now, you are interacting with other real human beings, hopefully, that you like and respect and your whole being responds to that action. Their knowledge condenses many years of experience for your immediate consumption, providing safety and certainty.

The message incoming is, "I care. I'm doing something about it. I'm no longer alone with this problem. I have help now." This alone doesn't guarantee success but it signals movement and if you're on the road to somewhere else, then you aren't stuck where you were. You can always switch paths if something isn't working out as you'd hoped.

Summoning the courage to act decisively can be summed up by Susan Jeffers's famous quote, "Feel the fear and do it anyway." I think we are wise to learn that delaying what **must** be done, usually extends our pain. What can be done is optional. Asking for help, if necessary, might feel like a leap of faith but once it has some determined energy behind it, the process unfolds with unstoppable momentum and is rarely regretted later. Getting started is the hardest part.

Friends And Family Support

Should they help? Yes. If they wish to. Within limits and with provisos. The advice is: -

Never let a family member or a close friend act as a "therapist" for you.

Why?

Loved ones aren't trained for the job, first of all. Then, when the work is over, you remain connected. Even an accidental harsh word, insensitivity, or over-sharing from a loved one during this unusual power dynamic could hurt the relationship. Privacy concerns and more could also be messy.

With all of that said, if you live with people and interact with them closely, including your loved ones and significant others, they're already involved with you and your patterns regularly. They also might want to help and be perfectly placed to support you in all the right ways.

If you have suitable support around you, it's fine to enlist their help as long as everybody is clear about what's expected, permitted, and encouraged by both parties. They also need to know what you're doing.

At the end of this book, I have written an explanation for your loved one/s of what you have learned here, what your plan is (loosely), and how they can best help you to succeed with it. I have explained the reasoning and mechanics of the treatment, and with your prior agreement, they promise to: -

* Refuse to discuss the **content** of your obsessions/intrusive thoughts with you.

You: "No... but do you think I might have cancer though?"

Loved One: "Sorry, Bill. I have orders! I can't discuss that with you, remember?"

That means not discussing whether it's rational or real, imminent or otherwise. These are **your** rules. They are not being horrible. They are doing what you asked them to do.

* Refuse to give repeated **reassurance** about the same thing. You are giving them advance permission to say, "I can't discuss that with you."

* Help with distraction activities (if all agree and it's practical.)

* Accompany you during your challenges (if you both wish.)

* Be patient with the process and know that it will take time. They are not to push you to complete challenges unless you ask them to. YOU set the pace and challenge level.

* Graciously retire their role with no hard feelings if either party feels the arrangement isn't working well.

To be clear then, they can be involved a little or a lot. You can discuss where you are most comfortable and make your own agreements on how involved they will be. Make sure there won't be any hard feelings if either of you chooses to discontinue for any reason. Calibrate as you go.

The main point is that if they've been making huge concessions for your anxiety, they have unwittingly, been enabling it. You can see that now, yes? Their responses have been part of your problem, albeit unwittingly.

If your loved ones don't wish to be involved, this doesn't change the rules. You agree not to ask them for continued reassurance or discussion of the content of your intrusive thoughts. Going it alone has benefits. It sends a stronger message of "I've got this!" back to the Zealous Guard, so all is not lost if you find yourself going solo. Do it anyway and be extra proud that you're doing it for yourself.

You'll find the chapter for your supporting loved ones at the end of the book. Have your supporter/s read it.

Digging In

Our success depends on numerous factors. These include: -

1) What we expect from ourselves.
2) What others expect from us.
3) What others demonstrate as possible.

Sir Roger Bannister was the first recorded human to have run a mile in under four minutes. The record was set in 1954. Since then, over sixteen hundred people have repeated the feat. It's become normalised as a standard for professional runners. As of the time of writing, the fastest mile run stands at 3:43:17 - almost seventeen seconds faster. This is how we operate. Something seems impossible until we see somebody else do it. Then, not so much. Limits move.

Action is concrete. Undeniable. It creates hope and it makes a statement.

I'VE HEARD IT ALL BEFORE

While much is made here of being gentle with yourself and approaching your solution incrementally, there is one pattern that you want to avoid. That is repeatedly quitting your behavioural experiments before you have given them your best shot. That creates "suggestion fatigue".

When you renege on a deal that you made with yourself without real effort, you send a message to yourself that your promises and intentions aren't to be taken seriously.

You're all bark but no bite. Thus, your goals are not supported at the subconscious level. As a child will run rings around a pushover parent, so too our resistance to change will exploit any weakness in our intentions and boundaries.

Our sense of "control" is weakened by repeated half-hearted action attempts because the brain has heard it all before, so it is "fatigued" by repeated suggestions for action that are never delivered. Please don't do this. It's not only soul-destroying but you are doing all of the work without ever quite reaching the benefits, and weakening your resolve with every attempt. You may be close to a breakthrough right before you send yourself back to the beginning.

Rest first. Prepare until you are ready, wait for the right time, and then go all in. If you fail, that's fine. Re-group. Adjust. Go again when you are ready. Just don't be half-hearted. Success is in sight.

WHAT'S THE WORST THAT COULD HAPPEN?

*** Conflict Alert***

Repeatedly imagining worst-case scenarios without a solution is, by definition, catastrophizing. Discussing such outcomes with yourself or someone else repeatedly is a negative thought loop and a conversation for never. "What's the worst that could happen?" could be seen as an invitation to create endless horrors in the mind. That's not the idea. Don't do that.

Here, the invitation is to use this question as a CBT tool. That's a different angle altogether.

Analysing a situation as objectively as possible while framing potential solutions, should the worst occur, is contingency planning. That's what you're invited to do here.

Anxious minds are often filled with swirling half-formed worries. We rarely get as far as the end of the mind's anxiety movies because we get **snagged** on a pain point, and that's the loop that plays on repeat, creating the obsession. Our mind drops us into the imagined horror and that's where we remain, emotionally absorbing the message that we are done for. Rarely do we push past the snag to see how we'll solve the problem or how life will look when it's all over. That's not a recipe for hopefulness.

One way to disarm the endless "what-ifs" is by answering that question, specifically. *Okay then. What if?*

Here's the format: -

*   Define the "vague" worry. What exactly do you perceive might happen? What is the worst that could happen?

*   Realistically, what is the likelihood of this occurring? (Use a percentage i.e. 40% likely)

*   What other more positive outcomes might or could occur? (Define the percentage of likelihood of each outcome).

*   Are there any steps you can take right now or soon that will decrease the likelihood of the worst-case scenario occurring? How will you implement these? Create an action plan.

*   Are there any steps you can take right now or soon that will alter positively the likelihood of the best-case scenario occurring? How will you implement these? Create an action plan.

*   If the worst-case scenario were to occur, what options would be available to you to move through to a solution? *Define your options clearly. Do not list only comfortable options. Define ALL of your options.*

*   Will the situation eventually be resolved? If so, how, and when? One can ask, "And then what... and then what?" Follow it through to the solution.

If you choose to use this exercise, please make sure that you write this information down. Don't assume that doing it in your head is enough. It isn't nearly as effective. Once written, you can come back to it on another day for reference. Hopefully, once completed, you'll be able to recognize that you have many more options available to you than you'd previously considered.

Do Your Worst

Some OCD people champion going one step further than exposure. This is the "do your worst" approach. Frankly, it's tempting fate but when fate is just superstition, it can pay to do that.

A memorable therapeutic story I learned during training was about a person who was terrified to travel because they thought that they might lose control of their bladder, as a passenger. The driver, a loved one, stopped the car and confronted his passenger.

"If you can pee in the car in the next thirty seconds, I will give you five hundred dollars. You have my permission to pee in my car."

They couldn't do it.

It was a renegade move, not recommended, but some people favour an approach that has this spirit of confrontational challenge to OCD.

"Go on then. Do your worst! Make my Mum drop dead, right now!"

Of course, it never happens. And if, by some outside fluke it does, well that's a correlation, not causation.

One courageous socially anxious client told me that they'd recently completed a fairly extreme anxiety challenge after reading a book on exposure techniques. Being the centre of attention was their idea of a bad time with anxiety so they stood by the doors inside a London underground train and bravely called out each station on the entire line loudly to their fellow travellers as the train pulled into each stop. I was impressed. I asked what people's reaction was. They said it was mixed - some smiles, some sour faces too, but they were delighted when multiple sets of tourists thanked them for the service! That gave me a smile too. Was it helpful for them? They said it was but I remember them being proud of themselves above all things.

This is defiance with bells on. It's a consideration.

Naming The Voices

If you have intrusive thoughts that haunt the corridors of your mind, wailing like ghosts about how awful everything is, we might call that mental voice, "Wailing Walter".

Thoughts about catastrophe, you might call "Doomsday Dan."

The voice that repeatedly tells you how wrong you are might be delivered by "Judgie Julian."

Carl Gustav Jung proposed that the human mind is governed by two forces. One of these is visible. That's the conscious mind. The second force is largely invisible and unknown hence it is called the unconscious mind. The name of the game in personal growth, according to Jung, is to make the contents of the unconscious mind, conscious. Why? Because that which remains unconscious has far more power to affect our lives in unwanted ways **because** it remains hidden. An assailant in the shadows is more dangerous than one out in the light.

Jung reminds us that as we make aspects of the unconscious conscious, we embody our wholeness more fully and free up the energy wasted on subconscious defensive patterns for better use on fruitful pursuits. The majority of problems in human psychology have their origins at the unconscious level of awareness, and we, at the receiving end, often receive little more than conflicted thoughts and feelings as a result. We remain confused.

Naming the voices is one form of antidote for this.

If the anxious mind tells us that we are useless or awful, it's an attack, but where is it from? Is that **my** voice? Do I **believe** that I am useless? Should I give this greater consideration?

If I call that same doubt, "Judgie Julian", then it's no longer hidden. It's doubt, but it's not mine. It belongs to Judgie Julian, the judging component of my human psyche. Judgie Julian is a protective brain subroutine but I can give him form and drag him from the shadows of my being into the light of awareness... where I can keep an eye on him!

Judgie Julian is the voice of all of the judgments I've received or believed. He thinks he's keeping me safe.

"If you're better, then you'll be loveable, good enough, accepted.

It's hogwash. That's a fantasy. You'll feel accepted when you accept yourself, complete with the understanding that life is complex and asking for perfection is a road to pain. Is constant harsh self-criticism an "adaptive" routine? Will it help us to get where we want to go? No. So, let's not entertain any conversation with him either. The same goes for Wailing Walter, Doomsday Dan, and any other characters you identify as the voices of obsession.

I can now tell Judgie Julian, "Thanks for your thoughts, Julian. I know you think you're trying to do me a favour, but I'm very clear that you're in error. It's not up for debate. I'll prove that it's safe. You'll need to adjust."

No further discussion should be had. It won't make the feelings go away immediately but it places you in a position of power. "I see you, Judgie Julian." It's a felt position that you aim to hold.

Jack Kornfield called these repeat visitors, "The top ten tunes". He likened the obsessive mind's anxious themes to tunes on a jukebox. These are the loops that play on repeat. Each tune has a theme. By naming them all, tunes and voices, we have a mental framework that **compartmentalises** the offending material and allows us to relate to it as "another" - not us, not as our world. It's a useful tool.

Balloons, Leaves, And Rubber Stamps

There are various visualisation techniques that you might find helpful.

One of the central learnings of this work is that we are not our thoughts. This is a tricky concept to embrace but since the subconscious mind speaks in imagery and metaphor, one way to communicate this position to the anxious mind is through the use of meditative visualisation techniques.

If you want to get straight to the point, try the "void" stamp!

When an intrusive thought pops up, imagine slapping it down with your red ink void stamp. Plaster big void stamps all over that thought. Add in the game-show wrong answer sound too. "*Uh-er!*" It's a mental-visual representation of your intention to ignore anxiety's lies, one that you can be gleeful about even, and still be very clear about what your position is.

For a softer visualisation, if you've learned to use the basic meditative relaxation method, then, once settled, you can imagine that you are blowing up party balloons. Visualise blowing the intrusive thought and the fear that comes with it into the balloon. Put some intention into it. When it's full, tie it off and let it go. Watch it float away into the distance. Rest for a moment. Feel into your body again. Does anything feel different now? If not, maybe a lesser worry will respond more definitely. Blow up and release as many balloons as you wish. See how you feel at the end of a ten-minute session. This probably won't be a fix but it may be a useful tool in supporting your well-being and will almost certainly help you to feel rested and calmer afterwards. If you want to play some soothing music when you do this, that can help to create a calmer atmosphere for your visualisation, especially if the music moves you positively. It can bring a shine to the mind's eye.

Finally, one well-known mindfulness technique is the "leaves on a stream" meditation.

You close your eyes and take some nice deep breaths to announce to your body that you intend to have quiet time. Then, you begin by focusing on the breath and allowing that to find its own natural, steady rhythm. When you're feeling focused, you visualise sitting by a beautiful autumn stream. Leaves have fallen from the trees into the stream and you watch as they float slowly on by.

Sounds good, right? But what happens when you close your eyes intending to settle down into calm and you are assailed by busy or intrusive thoughts?

That's why leaves are floating down the stream.

As each jostling thought arrives in your mind, imagine plucking it from your mind and placing it on any one of the passing leaves as they float on by. Watch the thought float way into the distance and then return to focusing on your breath. Naturally, other thoughts will arise. One at a time, send each thought downstream on a leaf. If the same thoughts return, that's fine. Again, place them on a leaf and watch them float downstream. Repeat and relax. The goal is not to stop the thoughts coming but to practice handling them skilfully. Be aware that these exercises are forging new habits and positive associations in your brain's architecture.

Gratitude

We average around twenty-eight thousand days alive. The day you or a loved one has something terrible happen is only one of them. And yet worry might ruin the rest, given the opportunity. Each day is a day that has the potential to be a day to be grateful for. We must use logic to decide what continues to receive our attention.

At some point, acceptance of uncertainty is the position that offers the greatest existential peace and that's not something we can automatically generate on demand. It takes focus, intention, and regular practice, and one way that we can practice this is to have the intention to notice what is going right for us today. Slow down. Notice the sunlight mottling on the ground through the trees. Listen to the birdsong. Feel the warm sun on your arms, a gentle breeze, a moment of magic. And then remember that these are the simplest but most profound elements of all life. Touch. Light. Sound. Nature. Love. These are good places to find simple things to be grateful for.

Gratitude for the moment is a good strategy for managing the existential anxiety of impermanence.

I'll concede that it's difficult to feel gratitude when you're under the weather. When you get a window of opportunity though, pay attention, don't waste time, and recognize the magic in the small precious moments. Be kind when you can. Choose to listen more. Build something helpful. Notice when you are comfortable. Permit yourself to feel joy. Refuse habitual negativity. Be nice to yourself. See the best in people. Forgive when you can. Pay it forward. Be grateful for the blessings and the days that you do have and those you've enjoyed to date. This is repeated wisdom wherever you look. The same rules apply. Gratitude, like courage, strengthens with use. But…

To know gratitude, you must first know need.

Fear can be a terrible enemy but it can also be a teacher of humility, gratitude, and acceptance. To have empathy, it helps to have known suffering. You learn what you do want by experiencing what you don't want. Illnesses provide that lesson and personal suffering can make better people of us. When we have suffered, we know that reducing suffering matters, both in our lives and in the world. When expressed healthily, that means that we aim not to be the cause of it for ourselves or others. Some go further and enter the world of actively reducing the suffering of others.

There is a form of Tibetan Buddhist meditation called Tonglen, where the visualised focus is on breathing in the pain of the world and breathing out compassion. This teaches the mind how to transform pain into compassion. I think of this training as neural plasticity, done right.

Studies have shown changes in the emotional regulation of brain structures in experienced meditators affording them an increase in tolerance to pain and negativity. They could also view negative images without significant negative emotional responses. Non-meditators will see their Zealous Guard jump into action with those visceral responses, like disgust. This disgust is the "aversion" of Buddhist teaching. What disgusts us generates fear. Quell your disgust and you quell your fear. Get okay with what's uncomfortable. That, it would seem, is what advanced meditators can do.

Resilience to negative stimuli then, is something that we build, like a muscle, with use. The mental training that Tonglen provides also includes learning to forgive oneself and others, and to see our struggles, as those of our enemies, with compassion. We aim to meet courageously the reality that all suffer, that all is eventually dust, and to cultivate acceptance of life on its own terms. There is no light without darkness, no achievement without failure, no growth without challenge. Gratitude aims to account for all of that in its final assessment.

NEW SCIENCE

Researchers are recognizing that there is a causal link between low GABA levels in the hippocampus and intrusive fear-based content in the brain. Valium and other benzodiazepines are known to reduce anxiety. Their action for doing so is that they increase GABA levels in the brain.

GABA is an inhibitory (as opposed to excitatory) neurotransmitter that **calms** brain excitation and has a soothing effect on the central nervous system. By enhancing GABA's fear-inhibitory actions, Valium can help reduce anxiety, improve relaxation, and create sedation. Unfortunately, benzodiazepines like Valium are highly addictive and rarely prescribed, for that reason. We can see though that when GABA is increased, anxiety decreases. Conversely, when GABA is in short supply, the negative thought suppression system is compromised. This is seen in OCD, PTSD, and anxiety disorders.

This is newer science. Researchers are still working on it. The hope, of course, will be that our researchers will find the medical means to end unnecessary anxiety for everyone. In the meantime, we have to make do with half of the completed science. That means that we aim to reduce adrenaline and cortisol (the stress hormones) and increase GABA, the calming neurotransmitters.

The good news is that everything in this book aims to do exactly that, naturally.

The research suggests that increasing GABA activity within the hippocampus may help people reduce or even stop unwanted and intrusive thoughts. The following recommendations for naturally increasing GABA levels in the brain include: -

Regular exercise, mindfulness and meditation, stress management, good sleep, nutritious foods that are rich in glutamate, magnesium, and vitamin B6, stress reduction, and probiotics.

No. I Can't Do It!

Okay. There are almost certainly going to be times when no matter what we do, the wins won't come. There are many possible reasons. Here are a few: -

* You have additional stress in your life (recognised or unrecognised.) - If at all possible, begin your plan when things are as settled as they are

likely to be. If your stress levels are too high generally, you may want to consider some anxiety relief tools to be used before or alongside your intrusive-thoughts-busting plan.

* You bit off too much at once. If a level five challenge is too difficult, try a four or a three first (yes, even though the plan suggests starting with five and above). Start with what you can cope with and only move up a level when you have some wins under your belt. If you underestimated the challenge level of an item, feel free to re-rate it and try a different one at a lower level first.

* It's a bad mindset day. They happen. Sometimes for little good reason. A bad dream that's been forgotten? Hungry? Overly-tired? Stressed by something else? Body and mind at a low point in your cycle? Try again tomorrow or another day. Leave it longer if you need to. The challenge and the win may be inexplicably easier then.

* You lost your nerve and fear won. – These are "challenges". By definition, therefore, failure is a possibility. But failure is not final. It is a stepping stone on the way to success; a necessity for mastery. Black is not white but failure can be successful. Go home, sit for a short meditation, acknowledge your feelings, and self-soothe the parts of yourself that carry these feelings. Your inner dialogue here should sound something like this: - "I get that you felt too much anxiety to do this today and now feel feelings of disappointment, failure or helplessness but you are a champ for giving it a go, and thank you!"

Set a date to try again or try a different-level challenge. Self-support no matter what.

* Do your "therapy skills" need a little more practice? Did you under-prepare? Have you formally prepared your plan with paperwork? If not, please include this. It's part of the process. Remember, you can also take time to visualise it going right at home first. You can also spend some time developing your ability to self-soothe so that your inner sense of safety and self-support is more robust when you come to do your challenge/s in the real world.

* Did you go into your challenge with white knuckles and an *If this doesn't work, I'm screwed!* mindset? That's too much pressure. You have a whole lifetime to nail this. The situation is that you have some new understanding, some new tools, and a clearer idea of how to make things better. Remove the tension. Your challenges are supposed to be behavioural experiments, not ordeals, and nobody ever successfully rushed therapy. Remember, you're a garden, not a mechanical appliance.

*   Perhaps you need additional assistance? This is only a single book - a small thing in a large world. It has limitations. It can't compare to one-to-one therapeutic assistance, and it's only one angle on knowledge and treatment, albeit the "official" one of ERP. Try some more books. They may say something that I haven't that lights you up. The knowledge of multiple helpers' experience will only clarify and reinforce the key points of the others. Please don't think in pass/fail terms. The learning in this book is not a pass-or-fail situation. It's complementary. Take what resonates and discard what doesn't. I put it to you that if this book didn't bring you a full solution, then it educated you to know more about your condition. That's not wasted time. It's a stepping stone. Keep doing that with different information sources and eventually, a picture that you will call your own will emerge, and that, almost certainly, will be how you crack this. Don't give up, eh?

Chapter Twenty-Five – Common Concerns

Though it isn't practical to cover all possible permutations of worries here, I want to offer some additional information regarding some of the most common obsessive and compulsive themes that I have helped people with along the way.

Pure O

"Pure O" is shorthand for "pure obsession" and this has been the term used to describe OCD which is obsessional but doesn't include any compulsive safety behaviours like cleaning, arranging, checking, or remedying (perceived) dangers.

OCD-UK, a leading OCD charity is now publicly advising that the Pure O label is a bit of a misnomer. They say: -

"It's (the Pure O label) unhelpful because a person suffering from OCD might fail to recognise their symptoms (compulsions), hindering their recovery."

They also explain that as far as treatment is concerned, the approach remains the same for Pure O as it does for full OCD. This keeps things simple.

Ordinarily, the primary approach for the treatment of OCD is to tackle the compulsive behaviours and avoidances **first**. If a person's obsessions focus on contamination, then our first goal is to eliminate compulsive cleaning and any other avoidance responses that centre around the themes of contamination.

If you have a "pure O" diagnosis, that causes a problem in terms of approaching treatment because how can you eliminate a compulsion that (apparently) doesn't exist? Thus, our Pure O sufferers can believe that their difficulty is an anomaly and that the "cease your compulsive behaviours" rules don't apply to them. Worse still, they may think they are untreatable.

There are compulsions present and when these compulsions are refused expression, recovery will happen in the same way that it will with full OCD. It is more accurate to say, therefore, that Pure O sufferers do experience and respond to compulsive cues but they don't always recognise that they would be considered compulsions. Some behaviours are less obvious than hours of cleaning or checking routines.

The most prevalent of all unrecognised Pure O compulsions is the need for reassurance. This can take a couple of obvious forms. The first of these is reaching out to something or someone in the external world to ask for reassurance. Often, this will be a search for reassurance that the obsession isn't real and/or the peril imminent. That could take the form of discussing the obsession repeatedly with a family member, a friend, a professional, or in online forums.

The second is the search for reassurance inside one's own thoughts. For the majority of sufferers, this is rarely fruitful because the anxious brain will find something to focus negatively upon. If you manage to out-argue your obsession, it will just move along to the next fear or doubt point and you'll need to start all over again. This internal argument also belongs in the "conversation for never" category. Seeking reassurance is a form of checking. The need to action that urge is a compulsion. Every time you do it, you inadvertently reinforce the hold that your obsessions have upon your life for all of the reasons explained. Yes, even when it's inside your head.

Avoidance is another compulsion that you probably do but which you may not call a compulsion. Arguably, an avoidance is a compulsion of sorts. You are compelled to avoid. There may be certain situations that you know are likely to trigger spikes in your intrusive thoughts. It's quite natural to want to avoid being in those situations. Avoidance refusal is just as important as compulsion refusal if we are to send the correct messages back to the Zealous Guard. We'll do more than just avoid those situations. We'll make a point of being in them regularly, as we move forward with the treatment.

Finally, we have rituals. While some OCD sufferers will have behavioural rituals that they will action in the external world, for the Pure O sufferer those rituals can be purely mental. These can include intricate mental efforts to order, count, control, neutralize, check, or replace content.

Dealing with rituals, including mental rituals, follows the same rules as all the other treatments. Do more of what you fear and stop doing what you are compelled to do. When you are compelled to do a mental ritual, explain to yourself why the need to ritualise is happening (signal error). Refuse to do the ritual. Self-soothe when your refusal to do it creates anxiety. Give correct reassurances (you are safe) to the frightened parts of yourself. Re-direct your attention to an **external** real-world focus. Repeat.

One sentiment to remember as useful when your thoughts are bombarding you with catastrophic or nasty material: -

"I'm not God! I cannot cause things to happen just by thinking about them."

Instead, let them be. The thoughts can come. Your job is to remind yourself that they are meaningless, no matter how convincing they seem.

FALSE MEMORIES

A person who presents for therapeutic help with anxiety and depression believes that their distress may have stemmed from being the survivor of ritual group sexual abuse at a very early age. There is just one hitch. They suspect that their memories may be rooted in a series of childhood nightmares.

With hypnosis, excavating the truth of a case like this would be off the menu because of the possibility of **false memory syndrome**.

It's something that every therapist must be aware of, hypno-assisted or otherwise because memory is famously inaccurate and unreliable. Hypnotically retrieved memory is not permissible in a court of law for this reason but hypnosis is not the sole culprit for the mnemonic inaccuracy – the brain is.

Let me explain.

When you think about an event in the future, your mind builds a rudimentary picture of how you expect that event to be. The very act of making a mental image creates an impression in the mind. That impression is more than just a picture. It also carries a feeling, a mood, the nature of which depends on whether your mind predicts doom or delight in your forecast. This is also drawn from your historical interaction with that subject.

Whatever the mind predicts, it will take the feeling that was present at the last recall and build upon that with each subsequent recall. Over time, we can have a "pass it on in whispers" effect - a copy of a copy of a copy. One person tells another and so on, with each re-telling adding and omitting elements. By the time the last person gets the message, it's unrecognisably altered. Memories can do that too. We can feel convinced that the memory is accurate… and be wrong. Composite memories are also a thing: real memories that are jumbled up in the wrong order with other memories that seem entirely real and complete.

This advice then is double-edged. Misused, it could lead one to conclude that everything should be doubted. That's not the outcome we're after. The real message here is that if you suffer from OCD-style doubt, then this is a vulnerable area for you. If you are spending time questioning your memories of multiple events against your OCD doubts, then you already have your answer. Non-OCD brains are not spending their time in repeated questioning of the reality of their memories.

Keep this simple. We'll borrow Dr Schwartz's line, and tweak it: -

If it feels like it <u>might</u> be a false memory, then it <u>is</u> a false memory.

Is that a guarantee? No. It's a position. This one follows the same rules as all of the other lies. Pick a side. Stick to it.

Don't go there. It never happened.

How do we know that? **Because** there is doubt.

Where there's doubt, throw it out.

Treat it with the same disparagement as every other negative intrusive thought. While there is an outside possibility of an important memory being mistaken as false when it's real, that's rare. Experts in these areas tell us that as many as fifty per cent of our memories are somewhat unreliable. True repressed memories are extremely rare - too rare by far to account for a long list of questioned memories. If you've seventy-eight traumatic memories that you're not sure about, that's obsession's doing and needs handling as such.

DWELLING ON THE PAST

It is human to dwell on the past. Grief and loss are companions for life. Regret is unavoidable. *What could have been* is painfully poignant. These are normal feelings that may arrive in our low moments but are otherwise mercifully quiet.

Anxiety, depression, and OCD can all supercharge negative ruminations about the past. Then, we are driven more by feelings than logic. Feelings drive thoughts that drive more feelings that drive more thoughts...

An obsessional focus on the past can be a complex mix of concerns over embarrassing moments, perceived life failures, missed warnings and opportunities, broken relationships, poor choices, and foolish actions. Yes, there's plenty to be upset about in the past, and wishing things had been different is a painful feeling to tolerate, shared by nearly everyone at some time.

This one requires a bit of discipline. The past may be enticing for many reasons.

We can remain locked in our "story" - the narrative that we tell ourselves that contains who we are and why we are what we are. A story is defining. It's safe because it's familiar. It's certain, unshakeable, undeniable. The story is a rock. It provides a sense of identity and continuation and it's a necessary component of a developing and functioning ego. We know who to be today because of our yesterdays.

The problem is that to grow into the next version of ourselves, we must continuously let go of our old beliefs because beliefs create patterns of behaviour, and our old behaviours eventually become incongruent with who we are working to become.

Our beliefs don't like being challenged though. They are among our most prized treasures in life. We earned them, fought for them, and until now, we have lived by them. We are invested in them. Replacing them with something more nuanced is a humbling step into the vulnerability of the unknown, as a beginner, once again. There is a payoff though. The beginner's mind is curious, open, and unbiased. Jaded rigidity dissolves. The beginner's mind receives new wonder and perspectives. Alternative paths are recognized, transforming life into something richer. When the student is ready, the teacher will appear.

If we recognise that psychological growth is challenging territory then, we can empathise with the human instinct to avoid it. One method that the human mind can use to avoid the need to grow into the demands of today is to remain tethered to the past - an identity, a wound, or even a golden age. If we believe that all of our problems today are **because** of our past, we will make victims of ourselves because who can change the past? The solution isn't here and now. It's seen as unreachable. *If only things had been different... or stayed the same... then I could...*

There is truth in this for some. We can be damaged by our experiences and we've covered that in detail already but our narrative will contain elements that we built to keep us safe at the time, that have now become prisons. Later, when life has moved away from the awful circumstances that called for an internal lockdown, we must work to shed the stories of powerlessness when they no longer serve us.

The memories we'd rather forget are lessons, not life sentences.

Everybody has a box of such memories. Nobody lives a perfect life with no regrets. And you should remember that nobody but you are thinking about your less-than-brilliant moments. Do you spend your time trawling your memories for other people's imperfect moments? Others care less about your imperfections than you do. We are, after all, our own harshest critics, and most people are self-focused anyway.

Action on dwelling on the past takes the same format as the other difficulties addressed in this book. The narrative that is heard about the past, and its apparent importance in the present is unhelpful. That brings it into the "maladaptive" thought category. 'Does it matter what it has to say? Are those things helping? No? What will?

Recognise that it's an erroneous signal/focus because it's not helpful. Dis-identify with it. Yes, it's your story so far but the rest of your life begins today. Most of us could do something today that will change our world tomorrow. That is not dependent on the past.

If you think of repeated negative focus on the past as a form of intrusive and unwanted material, then you can separate yourself from seeing it as a hugely relevant and even welcomed part of today's life. No. It's a form of rumination. I have seen people ruin their lives with this. Concluding powerlessness today based on the past is unhelpful.

Like most intrusive content, it will argue its case. And, maybe it has one? Maybe you were a jerk that day? Perhaps you were never the same after that event? That's not the point. The point is, going over and over it is achieving nothing practical but it's making you feel horrible feelings about your past, which are stirring up emotional arousal in your brain **today**. If there was a real point to that, perhaps it would be encouraged but it offers nothing of therapeutic value. It's simply negative rumination on the past, without a solution - as sure a cause of depressed and anxious feelings as any. Therefore, it's unwanted, intrusive, unhelpful, and now, unwelcome.

Follow the same plan here. Call it an anxiety error. Refuse to go there. Sit with the discomfort of refusing to respond fearfully. Self-soothe and support. Re-focus. And here, particular attention will be welcomed on the re-focus stage. It means not only re-focusing momentary attention on a distracting activity but also re-aligning life meaningfully in the present. We get over the past partly by going into our rightful future. Prove to your mind that there is more ahead than behind you by building a future in which you can live comfortably, or better still, joyfully. It will take time but it begins with you setting your intention and that position will be galvanised by actions that support that agenda.

CONTAMINATION AND CLEANING

As you now know, your intention needs to be tack-sharp and your game plan crystal-clear, thus avoiding that weak resolve that I explained earlier will be exploited by your mind's natural resistance to change, given the chance. I know that compulsive cleaners have often lost their perspective on what's "normal". Here, we set the rules.

We are looking at the contamination and cleaning theme.

Set a **reasonable** cleaning schedule. Have a non-obsessive person help you with assessing what is "reasonable" for you if they know your living circumstances. Otherwise, as a rule of thumb, one hour a day, as a **maximum** is more than enough for general cleaning unless you are actively dirtying that space (i.e. preparing food). Aim to shorten your cleaning time as you progress.

Once a week is probably about right for a deep clean of two to three hours in one session.

You allow yourself to clean in "normal" (allotted) cleaning time **only**. Outside of that, you agree with yourself that the agenda is to **stop all excessive or compulsive cleaning.** You can mop up a spill but nothing needs to be cleaned more than one time in a single day.

You've cleaned the toilet with disinfectant. That's done. The kitchen counters have had a wipe over with a clean cloth and soap and water or kitchen spray. That's done. And a wipe means a wipe. No more than one minute to clean those counters, and keep your clean times short for everything else too. Unless you go for a full bleach decontamination of every nook and cranny, there will still be germs present after you've cleaned. If they are not there ten minutes after you cleaned, then they will be a few hours later. Germs are not the problem. Anxiety is. Confronting this directly, with courage and kindness toward the scared parts of yourself is how you will overcome this.

Deal with your discomfort as a symptom of anxiety rather than an indication that you or your environment is dangerous.

No amount of cleaning will ever satisfy. You know this. Those terrible feelings that everything is contaminated exist as a result of you behaving **as if** everything is contaminated. Germs are everywhere. They are meant to be. Without them, life wouldn't function. We use basic hygiene measures to minimise our exposure to germ farms in areas where we eat and live but that's as far as it goes. Medical sterility is for hospitals, where people are unusually vulnerable to infection.

Cleaned once is clean enough. Anything else is obsession and anxiety.

With regards to avoidances, there may be plenty of them. The whole outside world may appear to be a contamination threat. The same rules apply here. Figure out what you avoid. Start moving towards that. Gently. In the graded format that you've learned here.

This is a general guide. If you have severe contamination anxiety, you may need or wish to grade your anxieties and tackle your cleaning routines in manageable chunks. Instead of cleaning five hours a day, you'll aim to do it, perhaps, in four hours for the first day and then keep reducing cleaning times each day. You can distribute your timings as you see fit. I'd aim for something ambitious though. Remember, you want it to be challenging or it won't be as effective.

Health Anxiety

Once called hypochondriasis, health anxiety is now known as IAD – Illness Anxiety Disorder. It's the pervasive anxiety that a serious, possibly terminal health issue is present, likely, or imminent. Generalised anxiety or an OCD focus can become hypervigilant to the presence of every physical irregularity, amplified by fear. Catastrophic imaginings unfold, creating further anxiety. Points of frequent concern include the organs, brain, digestion, cancer, and mental and sexual health.

One of the problems with anxiety is that it can make us feel physically awful. When the fight or flight system is activated, the body is running with the accelerator to the floor. Adrenaline and cortisol, while fun for some on a roller coaster, are draining and wearing when in your system constantly. There are the churning guts, the fluttery heart, the hot and cold flushes, sweating palms, the metallic taste, nausea, jangled nerves, fatigue, fear, and despair. These responses are designed to give us a jolt of readiness but being constantly amped takes a toll on the body. Throw a symptom or two into the mix and you have the ingredients for endless rumination about possible illnesses that feels highly convincing. People with health anxiety often mistake this malaise as an indication that they are on their last legs, which is mostly far from the truth.

Is my headache a brain tumour? Is my nausea stomach cancer?

Here's an example of how anxiety can take the smallest thing and turn it into a crisis. Beginning at the bottom of the hierarchy, we have three thoughts that could trigger a person with "health anxiety". Any of them arrive at cancer as a conclusion. As you'd expect, health anxiety is extremely common.

These are the cogs of the machinery.

1) What's that blemish on my skin?
2) I've heard that negative thinking can cause cancer.
3) I got sunburned. That will probably turn into cancer.

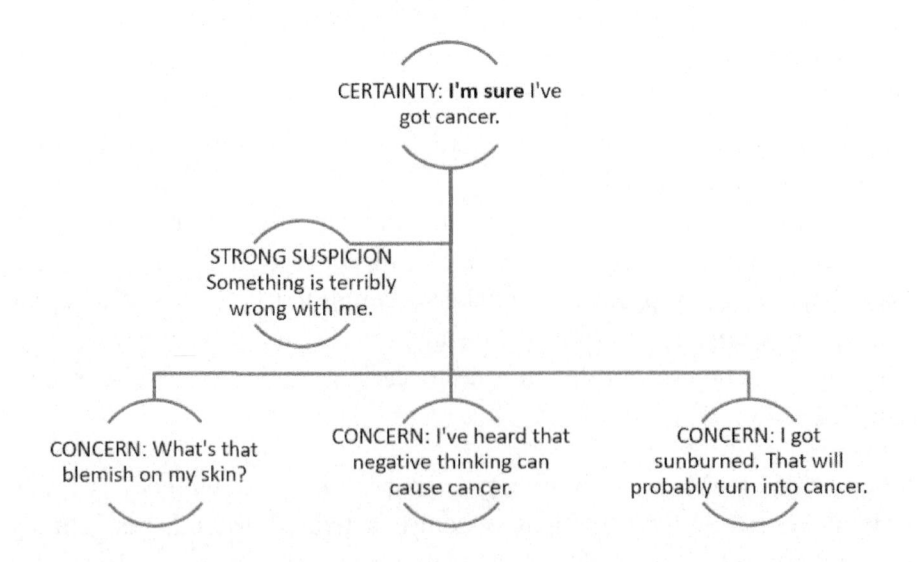

CERTAINTY: **I'm sure** I've got cancer.

STRONG SUSPICION
Something is terribly wrong with me.

CONCERN: What's that blemish on my skin?

CONCERN: I've heard that negative thinking can cause cancer.

CONCERN: I got sunburned. That will probably turn into cancer.

In the second tier, our example subject is having a bad anxiety day and they have a strong feeling that "something is wrong with me" because "wrong" is what anxiety feels like.

Then the mind pins it on something.

The mind joins the dots. The anxious thoughts and the anxious feelings form a partnership and the outcome, at the top of the tree, is a conviction that *I'm sure I've got cancer*.

Beliefs drive feelings.

This is a mind that moves from minor concern to suspicion to catastrophic certainty. Then, anxiety can take up longer-term residency and become a self-perpetuating cycle of negative thoughts and anxiety. We discussed beliefs earlier. They're tough to shift.

The theme of health anxiety is not entirely irrational. Our negative thoughts have us at a disadvantage because we know that the statistical probability of developing cancer at some point in life is approximately two to one, which makes this kind of worry extremely common and difficult to refute. Plus, the themes that we are most likely to be troubled by personally will relate to the experiences of our own lives. If you've been around a lot of illness or death, naturally, you'll be more attuned than most to the attendant concerns.

While we noted that repeated discussion and reassurance-seeking are off the menu, again, that rule can be suspended for CBT work. We need to create a clear and factual understanding of exactly what the truth of our position is. We touched on this earlier when we looked at the "what's the worst that could happen?" questions. Similarly, here, we want to start moving past the anxiety snags and imagine ourselves with a long life and good health. If you've had thousands of days of worrying about your health and no major health crisis to date, you've already got proof that the worry is a liar. Thousands of days of worry? For what? Are you any healthier or safer for all that worry? No. So, begin there.

Health isn't the problem. Anxiety is.

Until it's not. Then, hopefully, you'll catch it early enough to get treatment and survive. Vigilance is fine. Anxiety is not required. For sure, we should all be aware of the possible signs of illness and have anything suspicious checked out as soon as possible by a doctor. Regular wellness checks are a good idea too. Intrusive negative thoughts though, will, by their very nature, assume the worst. The mistake here is **belief without evidence**.

Cancer is just one theme among a potentially endless list of possible medical worries that an anxious mind could seize upon. Many of these worries will be underpinned by a genuinely rational concern, maybe even a symptom, but at the extreme end of obsessional difficulties, we can also find strange ideas taking hold, including magical thinking. If you have medically benign symptoms, it can still generate the fear of serious illness. Health worries are universal and occasional health crises are very much a part of normal life. Avoidance is not an option. Preparation is advised.

I'll cut to the chase on what you can do to help yourself on this. Consider all of the following points: -

> *1) Learn basic CBT. This book has taken just a few concepts and worked with them. CBT is user-friendly and free to learn online with many resources given generously.*
> *2) Join a forum or support group. While you and they are tackling these problems, you are each other's people. Be with your people. You'll find answers there. And support.*
> *3) Try relaxation, hypnotherapy, mindfulness or meditation. They won't be for everybody but they each offer tangible benefits if you can make a practice of them.*
> *4) See a therapist about any unresolved phobias or traumas. They are likely to be contributing to the overload. Don't assume that life can't get better unless you do. It can. Just do it if it's a possibility for you. You'll almost certainly benefit.*
> *5) Keep a journal or diary of the repetitive intrusive thoughts and feelings and make a habit of challenging those themes with rational counter-perspectives. Call it fast CBT. It's something to engage with that's less formal than the behavioural experiments.*
> *6) You have health anxiety, so clearly that will be exacerbated if you are not looking after yourself physically because it makes becoming ill more likely and both you and your subconscious mind know that. Anxiety ensues. Healthier food and exercise choices translate to an increase in resilience and well-being.*

Health anxiety can also benefit from some belief restructuring. There may be misunderstandings about risk and human fragility, or what's normal and what isn't. Here are a few Socratic-style questions to get you started.

Cognitive re-structuring questions: -

1) What is the evidence that you have a serious illness?
2) Are there any other explanations for your symptom/s?
3) How common is the disease or condition you're worried about? Do you have ALL the symptoms?
4) If you did become seriously ill, how would you move through it?
5) What do you do to support your health? Do you see signs of strength and resilience in yourself? Should they be counted?
6) Have you recovered from ill health before? What can you learn from that?
7) When you are not feeling so anxious, then how do you perceive your health?

The idea here is to actively challenge your faulty belief systems by demanding robust evidence and logic. Remember, limitations that are fought for will be retained. Your job here is to be a lawyer putting those faulty beliefs on the stand. Now, they have to explain themselves. If they can't, then there has to be a better way of framing the situation. What would that look like?

Evidence **against** the health obsession might look like this: -

1) I have been ill many times and recovered to full health.
2) I have seen many other people be affected by sometimes serious illnesses, who, with medicine, have gone on to live long and happy lives.
3) Most forms of cancer are now more survivable than ever. We know more than ever about how to minimise the risks.
4) I exercise regularly and take care of my body. That's where my level of control begins and ends.
5) My blood test and physicals are all "normal". My doctor assures me that there are no signs of serious illness.

6) I'm actively working on anti-stress exercises and can expect these worries to diminish as I feel better generally.
7) I know that my mind has a propensity towards health catastrophising. Might this be a case of that?
8) I have experienced periods spanning years where I have felt healthy and vigorous. Would this be happening if I had a long-term chronic hidden illness?
9) I have achieved and enjoyed much, despite my worries.
10) I have worried about many health concerns that have turned out to be baseless.

Once you have your detailed list of reasons to dispute the health anxiety thoughts, then you aim to keep drilling the messages home to yourself. We all know that if you hear something often enough, it becomes believed. The same principle applies here. Adjust those negative thoughts with better logic and aim to feel the power of your corrections. Eventually, your mind will agree with you. Behave accordingly too. This one follows the same rules for behavioural adjustment. Cease avoidance and compulsive actions. Approach that which is feared. Hold the fearful parts of yourself compassionately while they adjust and acclimatise. Refocus your attention positively elsewhere.

V(OMIT)

It's a rough word, isn't it? It belongs with moist, phlegm, foetus, and smear.

I know that if you suffer from this difficulty, you probably hate seeing the V word. Consider reading this page as your first exposure and response prevention exercise. If the V word triggers you, pause, employ the self-soothing techniques you've learned already here, and create a little calm. Then, read a little more. If you are still triggered by the words and content, soothe again. Repeat until your anxiety responses diminish or disappear. It's a good place to begin. No harm will come to you. These are just words on a page. Even the V word, which, alongside the S word, will be on proud display for the rest of this article. If you don't want to read it now, mark it as a challenge for later.

I must make clear that feeling sick could indicate a medical problem not related to anxiety. Please do see a doctor if you're feeling unwell or being regularly sick. Assume that what follows is the information that I would share with someone medically diagnosed with OCD or emetophobia (fear of vomit) and confirmed otherwise medically fit. Emetophobia can be considered to be a phobia as well as an obsession.

The core survival instructions for human beings are to shelter, eat, protect, and procreate. Poisoning and infection belong to the "protect" instruction. Vomiting is the main strategy a human body uses to eject ingested poisons and viral and bacterial invaders. It's not something that we have a great deal of wilful control over. If your body decides it needs to vomit, it will do so, with or without your blessing. That's another tick in the "uncontrollable" column – any obsession's favourite leverage point.

Vomiting has connections to fatality for several reasons. Having vomiting people around has always been a threat to survival. It could mean that there is a poison in the food source or an infection that might strike the entire group down. We are programmed to be wary of vomit.

Whether it's ourselves or someone else who is vomiting, it's not considered good news by the Zealous Guard. People can involuntarily vomit in the presence of someone else vomiting; further illustration of the evolutionary roots of the vomit aversion. This "sympathetic" vomiting is the body's way of erring on the side of caution. If Bill is vomiting, I may have eaten the same food. I don't feel ill but my brain can make the association with Bill's sickness and my stomach will provide the vomit response, just in case.

Next up, the act of vomiting itself is unpleasant. When vomiting is forceful, it can feel quite frightening because it can be difficult to catch a breath between expulsions. In practice, this doesn't tend to last very long and breathing ease soon resumes. If the person panics though, the experience can still be enough of a fright for the Zealous Guard to register vomiting as a potentially life-threatening event, thus, forming a phobic imprint. As we know, once the limbic system holds a negative belief about something being threatening, it will gladly generate oodles of anxiety to ensure that we avoid that possibility, going forward. Thus, an obsession is born, complete with endless worry, intrusive thoughts, and crushing avoidances.

How do we avoid vomit? Well... it's not easy to give yourself any guarantees. People are vomiting on TV, in books, and in real life. And then there are the germs, the food additives, and the intolerances. The emetophobic brain sees potential danger everywhere and sufferers can experience obsessive attention to food hygiene and diet with all of the knock-on effects that has on a person's life.

Emetophobia sufferers usually avoid or strictly limit their alcohol intake. There's the possibility of being sick. They'll also often avoid places where people are likely to be drunk... and then sick. Schools, public transport, and community venues are often suspected of being hubs for bug transmission. As a therapist, I always knew quickly when Norovirus was doing the rounds. My clients with kids would tell me a week or two before it hit the headlines, with schools usually being the first hit.

Excepting a city centre's drinking district, it is rare to come into contact with vomit in public spaces in daylight hours but it's not unheard of. This possibility makes the whole public world a potential threat. This can lead to the complication of withdrawal from the world. The technical term for the fear of going outside is agoraphobia; literally, "fear of crowds" but it's often used to mean that people fear leaving the home. Panic becomes the default response to going outside.

Do people ever vomit from the effects of anxiety? Yes, it does happen. Some people experience regular vomiting with anxiety but it's unusual. Nausea, however, is frequently present with anxiety.

Here's the way it works. Chronic anxiety is a physically toxic state. Cortisol and adrenaline, the chemicals released into the bloodstream during fight or flight, the anxiety response, are Nature's rocket fuel – high-energy boosts evolved to be reserved only for emergencies. In small doses, these are performance-enhancing hormones. In continuous high doses though, they become toxic. In the same way that you wouldn't want to drive your car with your foot on the floor all the time, you don't want your body full of performance-enhancing hormones all the time either. When we go into long-term anxiety, we are burning fuel hard and it's not welcomed by the rest of the body or the brain. Cortisol overload, in the long term, is known to be neurotoxic.

Then, there's the sense of feeling physically poisoned - itchy skin, metallic mouth, exhaustion, insomnia, and nausea – the scooped-out-guts feeling. My periods of stress have always included a nauseous component. It's not true for everyone but you should know that feeling nauseous can be a central symptom of anxiety and/or depression. This is a key piece of understanding to have to hand if you are an emetophobia sufferer. We have a negative feedback loop.

Nauseous feelings create anxiety and anxiety creates nauseous feelings.

As troubling as this is, the belief that you are about to be physically sick is almost certainly inaccurate. Nausea lends that lie credibility. Feeling nauseous is not the same thing as vomit imminence. They just happen to share the symptoms of nausea.

In keeping with the rest of the approach explained in this book, ultimately, you will beat this difficulty by challenging your avoidances and withdrawing from compulsive safety behaviours.

In summary, you are going to need to redefine what that nauseous feeling is. It's anxiety, not sickness.

You will need to disagree with the guard's assessment of imminent danger. The guard will tell you that all the fear that you feel is about vomit, infection, harm, or death. It's not. It's anxiety that has vomiting as its focal point because you happen to have a psychological template or vulnerability in that area. If your anxiety wasn't focused on vomit, it would be focused on something else. Vomit is not your problem. Anxiety is. Anxiety is what makes you feel nauseous.

The procedure here is the same as it is for all other obsessive difficulties. Just know that this added complication of feeling sick is a misattribution. Your mind has labelled it as something it is not. Treat it as a symptom of anxiety. It's a highly tedious and discomforting symptom but be clear that it is not proof of doom or imminent harm. As stress levels reduce, things should improve.

Sex On The Brain

Sexual obsessions are the torment of many sufferers. Here, we're talking about mental sexual thoughts, ideas and images that are unwanted, intrusive, upsetting, and/or out of character. Doubts about gender and sexual orientation as well as sexual health are also common.

This particular vulnerability sometimes arrives with an extra complication. It can include unwanted physical sexual arousal and this can masquerade as "proof" that we are indeed depraved perverts of the lowest order. This is a complete lie by the way, but you'll need to understand how and why such a thing can occur. In OCD communities it's called "groinal response."

It's worth knowing that activity in the genital area can be non-sexual. For instance, males have penile erections during the rapid eye movement dreaming period of sleep. These do not relate to sexual dreams or erotic desires.

Touch or pressure can create sexual arousal <u>without desire</u>, as can attention.

Our skin, the largest organ in the human body, is extremely sensitive to sensation. Our genitals, many times more so. When our attention is hypervigilant to the presence of physical sensations, normal sensations in the genital area can easily be mistaken for arousal, or imagined into arousal. When that causes anxiety, blood pumps faster and it mimics the physical aspects of sexual arousal. Then, our moral compass and the automatic arousal system conflict with each other. Morally, we have no wish to give consent to this arousal but the body suggests a different intention and the OCD mind gets snagged right there.

Human Beings have four main survival instructions: shelter, eat, protect, and procreate. The urge to have sex is one of these primary biological impulses. When activated, sexual arousal will make itself felt whether we want it to do so or not. Many are the jokes about genitals having a mind of their own.

In physical sexual arousal, the heart rate increases and the breath quickens. The same thing happens in a state of anxiety.

In the 1970s, two researchers, Donald Dutton and Arthur Aron, employed an attractive woman to stop, interview, flirt a little, and then share her phone number with several random men who had just walked across the Capilano Suspension Bridge in British Colombia. The Capilano Bridge is no ordinary bridge. It's a 137-metre wood and cable walkway suspended seventy metres above a rushing river. It wobbles. Reportedly, though safe, it requires some courage to negotiate it.

They then repeated the same experiment at a wide solid concrete bridge and waited for the "let's set up a date" calls to come in from the propositioned men.

The follow-up revealed that only two out of eighteen men called the flirty interviewer from the solid concrete bridge while nine of the eighteen called from the wobbly Capilano bridge, that's nine per cent versus fifty per cent. They also noted that there was more "sexual content" in the interviews taken with the guys from the Capilano Bridge.

Further similar studies using roller coasters and other pulse-racers have confirmed similar results. The research concludes that attraction, sexual arousal, and fear are very similar experiences. In fact, they are physiologically so alike that many people have difficulty correctly distinguishing between the two states. It is the mind that flavours the arousal towards excitement or anxiety.

The concrete bridge guys who were propositioned in non-aroused states of awareness showed less interest in a romantic proposal because they were, literally, **less aroused** at the time of the invitation. Conversely, those who just traversed the bridge of fear, thought, perhaps oddly, that a date might be just what they needed.

Anxiety and excitement are two sides of the same physiological coin. Both are the result of limbic system arousal, both involve the release of adrenaline and cortisol into the bloodstream, and both make our blood pump harder. These studies highlight that anxiety and attraction or sexual arousal can be confused with each other because the body is doing roughly the same thing in terms of chemistry and response. Both anxiety and excitement can make our hearts thump hard and steal our breath. One can feel like a nightmare while the other is a thrill.

This is great news for those who suffer from obsessions and fears that involve attraction or sexual arousal of some kind. The fact that you have fears and obsessions confirms the presence of excessive anxiety within you. It shouldn't surprise us too much then, that if we throw the mention of something sexual into the mix, then there is the possibility of confusion about whether you are feeling sexual attraction, arousal or just plain old anxiety. Am I anxious or attracted? It may be tougher than you think to tell. There's a doubt that you **can** use.

Dutton and Aron call this, "The Misattribution Of Arousal".

How often might attraction or arousal be wrongly assumed when the feelings are, in fact, the result of anxiety?

> **Does he or she make your pulse race with desire... or is that anxiety?**

Things are potentially more complicated still.

Sexual arousal itself is not always predictable. It's a Pavlovian response and that means that the automatic responses of your body are not subject to your will. You salivate when you are hungry in the presence of food. You can't say to your body, "I don't want to be hungry" and have your body not salivate. The smell of delicious food wins. Likewise, if sexual arousal is triggered, you can't say, "I don't want to be aroused" and expect your body to suddenly withdraw its automatic response. It's an animal body programmed to reproduce.

You can, however, divert your attention elsewhere and then the response will fade. What you cannot do is "will" the response to disappear. As you may know, the opposite is usually true. Fighting these responses strengthens them.

> **The harder you try not to think about a thought, the more you will think about it because the subconscious mind doesn't "do" negatives.**

The subconscious mind hears "don't be anxious" as "be anxious" because the focus of the whole sentence is the word "anxious". We are keeping the "anxiety" theme in view. It's a loop. The solution lies in stepping outside of it.

If we want to get the subconscious mind to help us out, we need to use positively phrased language. "No, please don't get an erection" contains the words "get an erection." It's a brain loop. Don't use that.

Don't say what you don't want to be, say what you do want to be.

Instead of "don't be anxious", we need to use the words "do be relaxed". Instead of "I'm not a pervert", try instead "I am a kind and loving human with honourable intentions and behaviours." Even if you have questions, this is preferable. Aim to deliver your statements with sincerity. Amend your statements to fit your situation. Feel the truth of your statements.

What causes any individual to feel sexually aroused depends on countless variables. If you are aged between late teenage years and thirty, please remember to factor in that your body is producing "have sex" hormones in abundance. At a physical level, sex may be very much at the front and centre of your attention during those years particularly. Sex is also something that promises to give us pleasure. When the mind is healthy on the matter, we like to think about it, fantasise about it, and ultimately do it too.

This is all happening whether we have anxious obsessions or not.

Giggles at a funeral. Our bodies can get the better of us in the most inappropriate circumstances. Giggling at a funeral is only intensified by the fact that it is inappropriate. The more we tell ourselves that we shouldn't be giggling, the more we collapse into a loss of control on the issue. It is wrongness being funny and we invoke the law of reversed effort. The harder we try to stop laughing, the less we succeed. The giggles have nothing to do with the death. Sometimes, the seeming wrongness of something just makes it happen more.

An anxious mind is locked into a similar dynamic. The wrongness of a certain thought evokes extreme effort to shut it down, resulting in the opposite; an escalation of the focus and intensity of the resisted material.

With this in mind, if you are experiencing anxious obsessions about sex, you are naturally highly attuned to the presence of **anything** that might be considered even remotely sexual. More than a non-obsessive brain would be. There are too many permutations to mention. This is what we call hypervigilance. In this case, sexual hypervigilance. The mind is overly sensitive here and will be looking for even the tiniest hint of something sexual. In some instances, if there is nothing sexual to focus on, the brain will provide something. Add anxiety and perhaps a vivid imagination into this mix and you have a potential recipe for some badly crossed wires.

This hypervigilance, ironically, keeps SEX at the forefront of the mind. The capital letters here are deliberate. SEX, SEX, SEX! "Yes, thank you, Brain."

You're going to notice it. This isn't your fault.

In this context, it's the product of the anxious brain but it still means that you'll have sex on your mind more than is helpful considering the obsessive circumstances. It only takes the smallest doubt about whether such sexual feelings are appropriate in any given context to start focusing on the genital area to test whether there is a sexual response. And, let's not mince words here. We are talking about the possibility of triggering physical sexual arousal – erection, lubrication, stolen breath, and sometimes in the most inappropriate "giggles at a funeral" way. Do be clear, if you are already a sexually charged individual, with or without obsessions, these responses might not take much in the way of suggestion to activate. Instead of thinking that such arousal could only occur with your agreement, **understand that arousal can be triggered without your consent.**

When this does happen, it can be distressing to the sufferer, who will then try to make sense of this event. That's a mistake, right there. On the face of it, there's only one explanation. *I must be sexually corrupt.* By extension, *I may be a danger to myself and others,* and worse still, *I'm an awful and worthless human being.* We are missing a crucial piece of information here though.

Sexual arousal can occur in the presence of ANY sexual thought.

Think about this carefully.

We don't have any immediate control over **which** thoughts arrive in our minds. A sexual thought arrives. It may be inappropriate, abusive, blasphemous or debauched. Remember our Tourette's comparison? It is uninvited, intrusive, unwanted, and has nothing to do with who we know ourselves to be. Nonetheless, it is a **sexual** thought. It may cause an **automatic** arousal.

The wording the experts use is, "arousal does not equal consent".

Or, put another way, arousal is possible without desire, and for the record, desire does not automatically equal consent either.

Feeling aroused is not an indication of a desire to act on that arousal.

A trick that sufferers can use therefore for these situations is: -

So-what!?

Flippant, eh?

Another form of this is the, *maybe I am, maybe I'm not* approach. The idea with this one is that we sit with the discomfort of not knowing, and by implication, care less.

We must remember that sexual feelings belong to the animal body. Lust, though included as one of the biblical seven sins, is a natural part of human sexuality. Whether lust is necessarily a positive force is up for debate but it's part of us and it's not always wanted or welcome.

Why then, would you treat a sexual intrusive thought with any more validity than any other intrusive thought? If your intrusive thought tells you that you might be about to inadvertently kill your mother, you shut that thought down. You call it out as junk. If your intrusive thought tells you that you're ripe to commit a rape, you shut that down too.

Suppose you walk past a stranger in the street and their fragrance triggers sexual arousal. Your brain delivers a sexual response. You feel your heart beat a little faster, there's a twitch in your pants. You panic. *What? Am I a rapist now?* This is what I mean by **any** sexual thought or feeling potentially delivering unwanted arousal and then quickly developing into a problem. It was the perfume or aftershave that excited the brain, perhaps by some association with another memory. It is not evidence that you are a sexual predator intent on harming anyone. A thought could have the same effect as a sniff of perfume because the most powerful sexual organ in the body is the brain. Erotica is primarily in the mind.

Where you find yourself snagged on that arousal, others can brush it off. Non-obsessive people can also have these experiences. They just don't get snagged on them. That's not to blame you. It's just to highlight that these thoughts can arrive and pass without doing any damage when anxiety is removed from the mix. When we don't attach to them with urgency, they become less important and eventually lose their power altogether.

Non-anxious individuals will generally recognise such unwanted arousal for what it is, write it off as a quirk of owning a human brain connected to genitals, and move on. I think I can speak for most people in saying that we have all had those moments and we've all been through the, *am I a pervert for having that thought?* experience. *Nope. I'm a human being and human brains and bodies are busy generating all kinds of thoughts, feelings and arousals that we then have to make sense of.*

"So-what!?" encapsulates this understanding in an instant. It says "I know myself."

Your second mistake therefore, was having the "conversation for never" with your own brain. You **doubted yourself**. *What if I actually wanted to touch him/her inappropriately though? Like, what if I would have actually liked it? What if I really liked it when his/her hand brushed past me?*

Shrug your shoulders when you say it. "So-what!?" It only carries the meaning you attach to it. "So-what!?" is a statement of power in this context. Say it like you mean it. It tells the Zealous Guard that we are not playing ball.

I know that this is not an easy bind to break. I have watched many clients struggle with this even after clear explanations and encouragement, especially those who have experienced physical sexual arousal alongside their anxieties. It is a cruel twist. A more ironic nemesis there has rarely been. They have required more reassurance than most of their good nature.

Sex is always going to be a problem area when it comes to obsessions. We must remember that the obsessive brain will focus on the themes that appear to threaten to undermine our lives most powerfully because that's what fear does. It looks for likely problems and the worst of them will be found, and then worried about, first. With themes such as rape, abuse, and paedophilia being among the most widely reviled behaviours, it is hardly surprising that anxious obsessions form in this area. The physical arousal thing is a huge complication in the middle of it all. Life is full of complications. We just have to engineer around this one too.

So, there you have it. In the final analysis, sexual obsessions are subject to the same rules as any other obsessions. Yes, they are trickier than most obsessions because of the physical component but you're going to need to understand that these responses say nothing about who you are or what you choose your life to be. You know in your heart that you have no wish to harm anyone or behave inappropriately. Please trust that. It's how you will get out of this. Everything else is unwellness and you need to approach it as such.

Sleep

There are many reasons that sleep can be disturbed, so a medical diagnosis and assistance is advised.

One of the main causes of sleep disturbance though is anxiety. This is a tricky one. I covered sleep in detail in *Anxiety Relief*, and there's a fair bit to know but here's a quick synopsis: -

Picture a bucket. This is your stress container.

When you sleep, you cycle between deep sleep and REM (Rapid Eye Movement) sleep. In the deep sleep phases, the brain is at rest. The body and brain are being repaired for fresh energy the next day.

REM sleep is an active brain state. It is less restful than the deep sleep phase. We dream in the REM sleep phase and it is through the process of dreaming that the brain discharges the stress in the bucket. When the bucket is overloaded with stress, dreams intensify, sometimes creating nightmares or terrors as the discharging system works harder as it attempts to process the overload. The REM dreaming period also extends as the brain has more to process. In practice, this means that when stressed, the brain is working harder at night to balance things for the next day but it has limits. Consequently, you wake up in the morning feeling exhausted and anxious because your bucket hasn't emptied. You've had neither the rest nor the peace that extended deep sleep brings.

Now, with creeping fatigue, the mind begins to fixate on sleep, how you'll get enough, and what will happen if you don't. The negative thoughts of a sleep-deprived future become ruminations.

This anxious focus on sleep is noted by the Zealous Guard. So, what does it do? It marks sleep up as a threat. Is it safe to sleep when there is a threat in the environment? No. So, we'd better stay awake then. The brain refuses to shut off. Sleep is considered too dangerous. If that wasn't bad enough, you've got responsibilities. You are acutely aware of the exhaustion and you start to worry about how you will manage if sleep doesn't improve. Bedtime becomes an ordeal. Nine a.m. becomes a frightful deadline. Daily thoughts are consumed by what will happen tonight. For some, rituals and safety behaviours are the go-to strategies for securing some shut-eye.

This is another area where we see the law of reversed effort in action. **Trying** to sleep is becoming consciously involved in a process that would otherwise be unconscious. Sleep is not the sole problem. Anxiety is.

In addition to anxiety reduction, there are specifics. For instance, you might have the thought "I have to get eight hours of sleep or I'll be a wreck." This kind of thinking is known as "inflexible" thinking. It is rigid. It sets a boundary and implicit is the instruction that something is wrong if we don't get the expected eight hours. That's setting the brain up to become anxious when the rule is broken and that will offer less sleep, not more.

CBT offers a whole field of therapy on this. It's listed under CBT-I. This is a treatment that aims to re-train the brain to sleep at set hours. I'm keeping this one short and sweet here but if sleep is a problem for you, that's where to focus to work on it.

Chapter Twenty-Six - Family And Carers

Family/Carers Support Information

This chapter is offered for your loved ones, carers, guardians, or housemates. If they want to help with your recovery, and you're happy to let them, hand them this chapter to read.

...

Carers, Guardians, Friends, Family, Loved Ones. Hello!

I hope this information will help you to help your loved one in their recovery. For ease of reading, I'm going to call your loved one "they" and "them".

You want to help them but you don't always know what the best approach is. You may feel like you've tried tough-love, reassurance, logic, and on occasion, exasperation. You have probably advised them to do exactly what this book is advising them to do. You may be frustrated from previous attempts to help. I must ask you to draw a line under all that has gone before. This will be a fresh start from a wiser, clearer, and more committed position. Your support, properly targeted, will never have been more powerful than it is about to be – should you accept the position?

Your role will be to remind them, by prior agreement, of the rules of treatment.

We'll clarify this in a moment.

First, a few words about the position your loved one, as a sufferer of anxious intrusive thoughts or OCD, is in right now.

They experience an ongoing sense of threat and anxiety that creates a high level of security vigilance, meaning their brain is currently over-estimating threats and possibly perceiving threats where there are none. They are, broadly speaking, aware that these perceptions are distorted but the feelings remain challenging nonetheless.

The anxious or OCD mind will produce fearful and upsetting thoughts in response to any perceived threat, alongside feelings of fear and disturbance that are difficult to tolerate. Both can take up long-term residence. You've had similar feelings yourself in moments of crisis. The problem is, your loved one has those repeatedly and intrusively, often without good reason. They're not choosing it. Their brain is locked in an anxiety loop and specific actions are required to pull out of that loop.

The message they receive from these anxious thoughts and feelings is that if they don't make concessions to anxiety's demands, then the anxiety may cause them a great deal more suffering. For some, anxiety threatens to overwhelm them completely. Understandably, they live in fear of that outcome. We call this "fear of the fear". It's sometimes called a secondary disturbance. It's an added complication.

To an outsider, these worries and fears may appear to be infuriatingly irrational. Logically, they are, and they are aware of that but panic is extremely unpleasant and they are doing their best to avoid being overwhelmed. That's why they worry and that is why they do compulsions and avoidance.

The problem is that they are being blackmailed by their feelings. It's bad when they do the avoidance and safety behaviours but it's worse when they don't. The options aren't great. They are not dramatizing their distress. They are the inheritors of an anxious or obsessive brain, possibly with a different configuration to the one that you live with. Possibly, recent stress overload has kicked the anxiety up to a crisis level. You're not expected to know what their experience of this is like but do please believe them when they say they feel illogically afraid. Your acceptance will help. It is not a "just snap out of it" or "be logical" scenario. When stress increases, these conditions worsen too, so anything you can do to help them with their stress levels is also a bonus.

OCD is considered a psychiatric/medical condition and it is recognized as having a neurological component, namely, a poorly functioning "anxiety/action-off" switch in the brain. This doesn't function correctly in OCD-affected people.

When you feel worried about something, you take action to make it safe and then you go back about your business and the feeling of concern dissipates. In anxious/OCD people, the concern remains after they've made it safe, and the whole cycle loops, with each action taken (compulsions) reinforcing the validity of the (unnecessary) concern. The more the anxiety is appeased, the bigger it gets.

They need to manually compensate for the faulty signal that tells them that something is wrong.

In practice, that means that they are asked to recognise that the anxious thoughts and feelings are in error and proceed according to logic, **despite** their anxious feelings. That's why it's a tough challenge. Doing so, initially, goes against instinct itself.

The human brain is protective. Anxiety is Nature's mechanism for alerting a person to the presence of threat and danger. Anxiety is a restless, fragile and uncomfortable state of mind, insisting that we take action to deal with the perceived threat. You've probably heard of the term used to describe this? **Fight or flight**. Stand and defend, or flee.

If you've ever had a toothache, then you'll know that an upset tooth nerve is sensitive to hot, cold, or pressure. Sufficiently jangled, it can radiate pain throughout the head, neck and jaw. Anxiety is similar. It's self-perpetuating, with one raw nerve irritating the next. The more sensitive the system becomes, the more it irritates itself and that is how human minds get locked into anxiety ruts. It's brutal when it happens. The sufferer might see this happening but feel powerless to stop it which only increases their sense of helplessness.

When any person feels anxious, it is difficult to feel safe. Intrusive thoughts and anxiety are entwined. Comfort and normality feel out of reach. The feeling that something is "wrong" is persistent and the desire to make it right is urgent. This urgency worsens the condition. It's accompanied often by physical symptoms of shakiness, breathlessness, nausea and fear. Courage is in short supply. Thoughts race. The future appears questionable. Doubts flourish.

For this book, we've called this anxiety-generating part of the brain, the **Zealous Guard** – the brain's security system. Clinically, this area of the brain is called the **limbic system**. It's the part of the brain that generates fear and other strong emotions. It is an **emotional** brain as opposed to a logical one. It is all about survival. Logic is taken care of by another part of the brain. When stress is dominating, the emotional brain overrides logic.

That's a quick overview of where they are at.

What's The Plan?

Here's what we want to achieve.

They have been instructed to make a list of their top six obsessions/worries/fears and place them in order of severity, with the scariest thing of all at the top-rated ten. That will be their last hurdle. Then, the next most worrying thing at nine, the next at eight, seven, six and five. Five is the least unsettling of their hierarchy of worries so we will begin our work there because we want them to be **challenged but not overwhelmed**.

The process presented here involves brain re-training through repetition.

That is, learning to regulate the anxiety response downwards in the presence of challenging stimuli. It will take time. It will be a process. Their brain will need to learn a new response. Progress will sometimes appear to take a step backwards because the change comes with successful repetition of new actions and some days will go better than others. If you know this ahead of time, you can prepare for it accordingly.

You should also know what to expect in terms of recovery times. There isn't likely to be a sudden flash of insight that "cures" the condition. In practice, repetition of new habits of behaviour and thought will change the person's inner world and help them to reclaim control of their lives, incrementally. Slow and steady is best. Smaller changes don't trip the brain's alarm system. When the anxious mind isn't on red alert, then the new habits have time to establish themselves fully, without undue resistance, becoming eventually automatic. Think in weeks and months, not hours or days, but with wins along the way, slowly transforming their courage, resilience, engagement, and freedom levels.

People do recover from these difficulties using these methods and the slow and steady route is how most people achieve long-term relief. Therefore, do celebrate small victories with your loved one. They should note them. Small improvements are just fine. Keep going.

The basic premise of the therapy presented in this book follows the medically-recognised primary treatment for obsessive, anxious intrusive thoughts and compulsions. It's called Exposure (and) Response Prevention (ERP), and it is as it sounds. The participant agrees to deliberately expose themselves to the triggering material and hold their nerve (prevent the usual response of avoidance and compulsion) while they are doing it.

It is a mental conditioning and desensitising process based on the principle that by confronting the fear head-on, with tolerance and kindness, we are reinforcing personal safety while obliging the anxious mind to re-assess the situation. By spending time in the presence of what we fear, as we hold our nerve and refuse to bow to the anxiety's demands, the mind learns to adjust its anxiety responses downwards.

If you have already been trying to help your loved one with these difficulties, you may be saying, "… but we've tried that before."

I'm sure you have. Together, even.

What's different this time is that there is a plan. In addition to the plan, they now also have some new tools and information that should inspire them to know how and why to hold their nerve like never before. We hope that they will have far less doubt about what to do, why to do it, and how to succeed. The compassionate attention format offered here will also be a potential game-changer for them. This time can be different.

As a supporter, you should understand that initially, it will feel to them that they have a gun to their head. They are taking on a bully. Their feelings will tell them that there will be negative consequences to their actions. The anxiety will be unpleasant and they will feel like it will always be this way. It won't. What's tough today will be easy in a month from now. The therapy involves them holding their nerve despite these feelings. If you can be sympathetic to their experience in this regard, it will help you to feel more patient with the process and your loved one's challenges. Your support will mean a lot.

We're going to ask them to keep confronting their avoidance and compulsions, preferably daily, each time learning that nothing untoward results from their defiance. Only a repetition of consequence-free action will bring lasting relief. Their brain needs to see it, repeatedly, to believe it.

Feelings are the most difficult part of this process to move through. This book provides a powerful method for tolerating these difficult feelings while these adjustments are being practised.

This takes the form of "acceptance" exercises which ask the sufferer to separate themselves from the intrusive thoughts and compulsions and focus their compassionate attention toward the parts of themselves that are frightened by the intrusive thoughts. By focusing on self-soothing, instead of engaging with the worry content, the sufferer can experience that it is "just anxiety" without being overwhelmed by their feelings. With repetition, they can learn that none of anxiety's threats come to pass as a result of their defiance and they slowly gain confidence in seeing through anxiety's lies and claiming their chosen life.

They begin with the least-challenging behaviour-change experiments and then move up to the next challenges as they master the last. For this, they will be using behavioural experiment worksheets.

This tool asks the patient to design an experiment where they can test their ability to tolerate the situation without giving into fear. They first identify and write down what they expect to happen, then how they can handle the situation differently. Then, they either resist a compulsion or enter a formerly avoided situation. The outcome is recorded and compared with their initial forecasts, often revealing evidence of a brain that is over-estimating threat. This "evidence" becomes a cumulative record of anxiety's lies that can be relied upon when taking on tougher challenges. Nothing bad happened last time. It won't this time. Even when anxiety says it will.

WHAT CAN YOU DO TO HELP?

This is day one. You should both be clear that your agreement to assist doesn't form a therapist/patient relationship. Stay **friends**. Your role is as a supportive friend, witness cheerleader, and referee. Keep it light.

Friend – Be nice. Have a little patience. Want the best for them.

Witness – Having someone loving around at a scary time can help. Having someone else see you be brave can count for something. It's official then!

Cheerleader – "Yay. Go, Flo! You're doing it!"

Referee – "That question is disallowed." (Blows whistle! Shows yellow card.)

Before you agree to take the role, have a quick read of what's expected. If you can't hold this dynamic comfortably with your loved one, can someone else help? If not, they're on their own. That's not always a bad thing, so only agree to be an assistant if you're **happy** and **able** to fulfil that role. No assistance is better than bad assistance. Your loved one has their instructions. It's not all on you.

Here's the essence of what you need to know to be a helpful experiment buddy: -

1) *The anxious feeling that they are feeling that tells them that something is terribly wrong or that they must do a certain (unnecessary) behaviour is a false signal. Every time that they do as the anxiety demands, their difficulty is reinforced because they are tacitly agreeing with anxiety's assumptions which is like saying, "More anxiety next time too please."*
2) *They may believe that these thoughts, feelings, or urges say something about their core intentions or self, causing crippling self-doubt. Often, this can take the form of worrying about hurting others or being harmed. Those feelings are caused by an erroneous signal due to anxiety/OCD. In treatment, they need to be regarded as the errors that they are, despite the feelings that insist otherwise. You can remind them of this if they run into doubt.*
3) *By exposing oneself to avoided situations, we are sending a message back to the anxious brain that says "I'm not adjusting. It's you (the anxiety/OCD) that has it wrong. There is no threat. I know that it is a false signal and I will prove that by not avoiding the world or giving in to compulsions." Over time, this forces the anxiety to adjust and revise over-zealous danger assessments. With repetition, the brain will form new connections and habits that will supersede the avoidance and compulsions.*
4) *This will initially make them uncomfortable. Remind them that learning to tolerate the discomfort of not doing the behaviour is an act of power that will pay off. No lectures, please. Encourage them to see their experiments through. If they want your physical presence for support, can you offer that? If so, great. Just having someone there for moral support may make the necessary difference. If not, that's fine too.*
5) *Remind them that with time and repetition, the brain will learn that there is no threat. Remind them that if they can do it this time, they'll be less anxious next time. Remind them that they are to use the self-soothing method to remain calm. Remind them to turn their attention to something other than their thoughts or urges. If they can re-focus on doing something positive or interesting for five to fifteen minutes, the anxious feelings will subside and they will have a small victory.*
6) *When you see them have a victory, encourage them to write it down in their diary so that they won't forget it or talk*

themselves out of it later. Note what has been learned. A high five maybe too?

7) Do not force your loved one to challenge a behaviour. Your role should be encouraging and cooperative, not coercive. On days when they don't feel up to it, allow them to make their own choice. It's their recovery and they will do it in their own time and their way. Have faith in them.

8) *Refuse to offer reassurance on obsessive fears.*

The last point is central. In an earlier chapter entitled, "Reassurance Is A Conversation For Never", we took a look at the insatiable need for reassurance that often plagues anxiety/OCD sufferers. Here's where it becomes confusing for helpers.

What kind of a monster won't give their loved one reassurance when they are suffering?

It's tough love on this one. Though the kindness in your heart wants to offer safety, to do so is counter-productive. The rule is that discussing the **content** of intrusive worries and thoughts is a conversation **not** to have. If the person you are supporting repeatedly asks you for reassurance that something terrible is not going to happen, your job is to refuse to have that conversation and refuse to offer any reassurance. It's pre-agreed that if asked, you'll simply say "Sorry. We've agreed that topic is off the table." Or, make it fun. Build a little placard. "Nope!" Lift it when asked. Smile.

Remember that they have been provided with a method to self-soothe the anxious parts of themselves as an alternative to seeking reassurance from you or returning to the internal reassurance loop. They should be employing this, so don't worry, you're not being a horrible person. Only use the placard if you're both in on the joke!

Giving constant reassurance and endlessly discussing the details of the obsessive "problem" reinforces the problem. It keeps the focus on the intrusive content and **legitimises** it by giving it a platform. When you agree to have a conversation about the ins and outs of the worries, you are tacitly agreeing that those worries require attention in the real world. They don't. That's the core of the whole adjustment process. It seems cruel to say it but continued reassurance is enabling the problem, not solving it.

Your refusal to reassure can help them break the pattern. They will feel the urge to ask for your input or reassurance but hopefully, when you've perfected the art of loving refusal, they'll know it's futile, forcing an opportunity for greater self-reliance. They will stop asking you and start doing the necessary work.

This is the therapy doing its work. It's part of the plan. The end goal is reliable **self-support** with increased resilience that renders your supporting role eventually redundant. That's the position to hold. Your loved one knows that. You can remind them, kindly, that you agree to prompt them to: -

a) *Hold their nerve.*
b) *Accept your refusal to offer reassurance.*
c) *Tolerate the discomfort of doing/not doing their avoidances and compulsions.*
d) *Self-soothe.*
e) *Re-focus their mind and attention with an immersive activity.*

Stick to this format and keep it simple. Let them determine the details of their behavioural experiment and also the pace of the challenges. Communicate with each other after each behavioural experiment. Adjust your teamwork as required.

Hopefully, united, you'll be a great force and progress will be swift.

I wish you both all the very best!

CHAPTER TWENTY-SEVEN – A BRIGHT FUTURE

Thank you for allowing me to share what I know with you. I consider it a privilege. I hope this book leaves you feeling satisfied, well-informed, and inspired to take some action. If not now, then maybe later.

If you're not feeling up to the behavioural challenges or don't have adequate support at this moment in time, then please don't push yourself to do the challenges until you do. Take what you've learned and let it percolate within you. Perhaps read another book on the subject, join a forum, learn some basic CBT online, or work with a therapist. Immediate relief would be a wonderful thing but it may be that there are a few steps to take. This book may be only one of them.

Remember to work on reducing anxiety generally. Calming tools do help. Everyone can try relaxation recordings, or meditation. These practices underpin stress and anxiety reduction and they are a good place to begin. I'm including a custom-designed hypnotherapy recording with this book. I said I'd remind you about it at the end of the book, so if you didn't check it out yet, here's the link: -

You can grab your free hypnotherapy companion recording with no signup here: -

www.youcanfixyouranxiety.com/calming-thoughts

You should find it soothing and helpful, and if all goes well, the words and ideas presented will stay with you, supporting what you've learned in this book. Don't worry, it's not mind-control. Hypno-recordings offer helpful "suggestions" that can be used or ignored and it wraps them up in an invitation to relax deeply and take a mental break. Then, it aims to have that comfortable glow go with you for the rest of your day. When received in a relaxed state of mind, the usual whirlwind of thought distractions can abate enough to allow a deeper appreciation of the suggestions that you can use. Relaxation, meditation, or hypno-recordings will help you to cultivate a calmer baseline state from which to tackle your behavioural challenges.

Keep in mind too, that the exposure and response prevention challenges are **graded**. That gives **you** control. If you are picturing your behavioural challenges as ordeals, or feel overwhelmed by the formal structure in this book, then do know that you can just hold the principles in mind. Then, you might just see an opportunity to challenge an obsession, avoidance, or compulsion less formally while you are going about your business. A moment of bravery might seize you.

What if I didn't do this safety behaviour today? I could go and do something else.

The formality of the treatment structure here serves to contain and clarify the process. It helps with creating a picture in the mind of where we are, where we want to go, and then, to be able to watch that process as it unfolds, recording progress. That is a great deal of clarity on an otherwise murky and mysterious foe but it's not the only way to do things. An informal approach is to internalize what you've learned here and aim to apply it when you spot an opportunity. Over time, that will yield results too. The message is the right one still, just minus the formal structure.

If you go the formal route, remember that graded means that you **choose** which challenges to undertake and in which order. Start small. Gain a little confidence and step up slowly as you are ready to. This does not need to be an ordeal and it shouldn't be. Go gently at first. Be bolder when you're holding a few wins. Know that we are all different. Take what works for you. Leave the rest. Supplement your knowledge and tweak the plans to your needs, strengths, and limitations. I'm handing you the structure. How you implement it is your choice.

And, I saved this part for last because it's the single most important point I can leave you with.

Your attention is your most valuable asset.

Attention is like a flashlight in the dark. Wherever we point it, that's what we'll see. Attention creates reality. We must point it towards our aspirations. We can't do that if our attention is stolen by the demands of obsessions and compulsions.

Recognise that your attention is a form of currency: a precious resource. It has intrinsic and significant value. What we value, we care for. Don't undervalue, or under-care for your attention. It is worth fighting for. Reclaimed, your attention can take you not only away from the dark shadows of the world but it can light the path to a liberated future. It is yours. It does not belong to the whims of obsessions and compulsions. It never did.

It's funny what sticks, isn't it? The most helpful thing that I heard somebody say recently was, "How did I do it? Oh... I was too stubborn to fail."

I wish you well, Fellow Traveller. Be brave. Be brilliant. Be well. The world needs your light.

Over and out.

🖤

ONE LAST THING

If you have enjoyed this book and perhaps more importantly, if it has helped you, I'd be most grateful if you could leave a review on the site from which you received this book.

As an independent author, your reviews are hugely important to me. Customer reviews are considered in the algorithms of online book retailers and positive and numerous reviews help authors to become visible among the many millions of books available. Your reviews are the lifeblood of my work, so if you would like to help, you'll be doing me a massive favour. Thank you in advance.

I'd love to stay connected with you. Please do join me by signing up for my readers group at: -

www.youcanfixyouranxiety.com/stay-connected

You'll receive two (extra) free super-soothing, life-affirming hypnotherapeutic recordings to use and keep and I'll keep you updated with news of new releases with special offers for reader's group subscribers. No spam, guaranteed, and you can unsubscribe at any time.

Or come over and join me by liking my Facebook page at: -

https://www.facebook.com/johncrawfordauthor/

And finally, you can read the first two chapters of "Anxiety Relief" free with no sign up here: -

http://www.youcanfixyouranxiety.com/free-anxiety-book-chapters

This book is also available in Ebook format.

Thank you for supporting my work!

OTHER WORKS BY THIS AUTHOR

Please visit my website at www.youcanfixyouranxiety.com if you'd like to learn more about the books or contact me.

Books with heart for people in distress.

www.youcanfixyouranxiety.com

About John Crawford

John Crawford is truly qualified to share expertise on how to overcome anger, anxiety, OCD and depression. Not only was he a professional therapist for fifteen years, he was himself held hostage by severe anxiety and depression for many years in his twenties. His understanding of the field is therefore more than purely intellectual. It's deeply personal and committed.

John ran his own thriving business as a one-to-one hypnotherapist/psychotherapist specialising in the treatment of anxiety, depression, and OCD, from 2003-2016. He quickly gained a solid professional reputation in the Bristol and Bath area of the UK for anxiety-related difficulties. He has over seven thousand hours of clinical experience in helping people to overcome their emotional and mental health challenges.

He is a significant contributor of sections of the training materials used by Clifton Practice Hypnotherapy Training (CPHT), a now international Hypnotherapy Training Centre with twelve branches in the United Kingdom. CPHT is recognised for its outstanding Solution-Focused Brief Therapy training.

John has spoken professionally for the Association for Professional Hypnosis and Psychotherapy, Clifton Practice Hypnotherapy Training, OCD Action (the largest national OCD charity in the UK), as well as regularly at smaller supervisory events for local practitioners. He has also written for the highly respected online anxiety sufferers' resource, No More Panic. He was a registered and accredited member of three leading therapeutic organisations - Association for Professional Hypnosis & Psychotherapy, National Hypnotherapy Society and National Council of Psychotherapists, up until 2016 when he closed his main one-to-one practice to focus on writing and teaching.

His main qualifications include: -

Diploma in Hypnotherapy and Psychotherapy - Clifton Practice Training (formerly EICH)

Hypnotherapy Practitioner Diploma - National externally (NCFE) accredited to NVQ 4.

Diploma in Cognitive Behavioural Hypnotherapy - Externally (NCFE) accredited to NVQ4.

Anxiety Disorders Specialist Certification - The Minnesota Institute of Advanced Communication Skills.

He lives happily in Bristol (UK) with his wife and cat and produces music in his spare time.

Full Copyright Notice

The Anxiety And OCD Workbook

A CBT And Acceptance-Based Guide To Managing Intrusive Thoughts And Compulsive Behaviours

JOHN CRAWFORD

Copyright © 2023 by John Crawford

All rights reserved.

First Published: November 2023

www.youcanfixyouranxiety.com

No part of this book may be reproduced in any form or by any electronic or mechanical means including information storage and retrieval systems, without permission in writing from the author. Short quotes are permissible providing that credit is given to this author in the quoting work.

Every effort has been made in the writing of this book to give credit where it is due, including short quotes, and there is no intention to infringe upon any copyrights. If you believe that there is any part of this work that infringes your intellectual property in any way, please let me know and I will gladly remove it immediately.

Please visit: http://www.youcanfixyouranxiety.com for updates, offers, news, enquiries and events.

Printed in Great Britain
by Amazon